Developmental State in Practice

MW00682259

This book is the product of research undertaken at the African Development Bank (AfDB) on the lessons that the continent of Africa can draw from the role of the state in Asia's rapid economic development in the last 50 years. The book applies a cross-national comparative framework to analyse Africa's performance drawing broadly on the developmental states of Asia (i.e. Japan, China, India, Vietnam, etc.) with focus on South Korea. The book argues that for Africa to replicate Asia's developmental success, it may require more than just tweaking the public sector machinery. Dedicated institutions and a citizenry capable of demanding accountability from governments must become key ingredients of the development strategy.

The book also provides insight into the learning experiences of Asia, in addressing key national policy challenges i.e. land reform and quality of public administration at the federal and local levels, enhancing technical skills, boosting capabilities for sciences, engineering and mathematics, and industrialization.

Steve Kayizzi-Mugerwa was recently Economic Governance Advisor, Prime Minister's Office, Kingdom of Eswatini (2019) and Advisor at the Independent Evaluation Office, IMF (2018). At the African Development Bank, he was, successively, Lead Economist, Director (Strategy and Policy; Country Operations; Development Research) and Acting Chief Economist and Vice President. He holds a PhD from the University of Gothenburg, with a dissertation on economic adjustment in Zambia, and became an Associate Professor there in 1994. He has worked or undertaken research at the following universities: Makerere, Zambia, Nairobi, Cape Town (Adjunct Professor, 2015–2020), Stockholm, Lund, Helsinki, New York (Visiting Scholar at Africa House), and Cornell (Visiting Fellow at the Institute for African Development) and published widely. He was also Senior Economist at the IMF and Fellow and Project Director at the World Institute for Development Economics Research of the United Nations University, based in Helsinki.

Charles Leyeka Lufumpa is Acting Vice President and Chief Economist for Economic Governance and Knowledge and Director of Statistics at the African Development Bank Group. He has led several Bank initiatives, in collaboration with the UN and the African Union, for the collection, management, and use of social and economic statistics to enhance Africa's statistical agenda. Notably, an African Statistical Portal, hosted by the AfDB, was developed to which all African national statistical offices have real-time access. Following his BA in economics and statistics at the University of Zambia, he proceeded to Iowa State University, where he completed MSc (1989) and PhD degrees (1991) in agricultural economics and forest resource economics and statistics, respectively. His research interests are in statistics, poverty analysis, infrastructure development, agricultural innovation, and environmental economics. Dr. Lufumpa has co-edited (with Professor Mthuli Ncube) two volumes of research work in the recent past: *The Emerging Middle Class in Africa*, Routledge, 2014, and *Infrastructure in Africa: Lessons for Future Development*, Bristol Policy Press, 2017.

Routledge Studies in Development Economics

Edited by Osmel E. Manzano M, Fernando H. Navajas and Andrew Powell

For more information about this series, please visit: www.routledge.com/series/SE0266

Developmental State of Africa in Practice

Looking East with Focus on South Korea

Edited by
Steve Kayizzi-Mugerwa and
Charles Leyeka Lufumpa

A Synthesis of Country Case Studies Commissioned
by the African Development Bank

Routledge
Taylor & Francis Group

LONDON AND NEW YORK

First published 2021
by Routledge
2 Park Square, Milton Park, Abingdon, Oxon OX14 4RN

and by Routledge
52 Vanderbilt Avenue, New York, NY 10017

Routledge is an imprint of the Taylor & Francis Group, an informa business

British Library Cataloguing-in-Publication Data
A catalogue record for this book is available from the British Library

Library of Congress Cataloging-in-Publication Data
A catalog record has been requested for this book

ISBN: 978-0-367-61931-2 (hbk)
ISBN: 978-1-003-10714-9 (ebk)

Typeset in Galliard
by codeMantra

Contents

Figures

Tables

Preface

This book comprises a synthesis of findings from a larger volume of studies and a literature review commissioned by the African Development Bank (AfDB) from African research networks and universities and from a South Korean institution on the developmental state as a framework for economic development and transformation and how it can or is being applied in Africa. The research project, entitled "The African Economy: Development Policy in Practice—Lessons from South Korea's Development Experience," was launched in 2014, with financial support from the Korean Trust Fund hosted at the AfDB.

The main purpose of this book, and the research that preceded it, is to examine the plausibility of the developmental state model in Africa, where start conditions, while evincing similarities with those of East Asia in the 1950s and 1960s, such as colonial legacy, land alienation, steep inequalities, and rampant poverty, have in some ways been significantly different i.e. Japan's regional significance and deep, and almost classical, US interest in the region. The incongruity of the advice given to African countries by bilateral and international agencies over the past decades i.e. eschew state intervention as much as possible, on the one hand, and the lessons emanating from the Asian experience i.e. active state participation in all aspects of economic life as long as it is market conforming, on the other, provided the point of departure for the commissioned studies.

In terms of coverage, the AfDB's Chief Economist and Vice President commissioned a total of five book-length country studies from African research networks and/or universities and one from a South Korean research agency based in Seoul. The African countries were chosen to provide a broad coverage of African development experience as possible, without losing the thread of comparability: Cameroon, Côte d'Ivoire, Nigeria, South Africa, and Zambia. The South Korean team took as case studies Botswana, Ghana, Mauritius, and Rwanda, thereby increasing the overall African country evidence by another four countries. Although South Korea was the main object of comparison for African case studies, the broader East and South Asian experiences are, where relevant, drawn upon to provide additional insights.

The institutions and staff members that contributed to the six country case studies from which the synthesis volume is drawn are as follows:

- *Korea Institute for International Economic Policy (KIEP)*, Seoul, South Korea:

    Dr. Deok Ryong Yoon (Senior Fellow).
- *Université de Yaoundé II*, Yaoundé, Cameroon:

    Professor Henri Ngoa Tabi (Lecturer/Researcher, Team Leader), Professor Henri Atangana Ondoa (Lecturer/Researcher), Dr. Patrice Ongono (Lecturer/Researcher), Dr. Françoise Okah Effogo (Lecturer/Researcher), and Dr. Gérard-José Ebode (Lecturer/Researcher).
- *Le Centre Ivoirien de Recherches Economiques et Sociales (CIRES)*, Abidjan, Côte d'Ivoire:

    Professor Assi José-Carlos Kimou (Researcher and Team Leader), Dr. Namizata Binate (Researcher/Fellow, UNU-INRA), Dr. Yapo N'Dia Victor Bouaffon (Researcher), Dr. Nahoua Yeo (Researcher), Dr. Placide Zoungrana (Researcher), Tanoh Ruphin Doua (Research Associate), Kodjo Pierre Innocent Kelassa (Research Associate), and Beugré Jonathan N'Guessan (Research Associate).
- *Nigerian Economic Society (NES)*, Ibadan, Nigeria:

    The assignment was undertaken by NES as a collective. Professor Olu Ajakaiye was the Project Team Leader.
- *Development Policy Research Unit (DPRU)*, School of Economics, University of Cape Town, South Africa:

    Dr. Kenneth Creamer (Member, President's Economic Advisory Team, Pretoria), Ross Harvey (Former Associate, South African Institute for International Affairs), Ass. Professor, William Gumede (Wits University), Ebrahim-Khalil Hassen (Public Policy Analyst), Prof. Steven Friedman (Johannesburg University), Prof. Brian Levy (Johns Hopkins University), and Anthony Altbeker (Independent Researcher).
- *Southern African Institute for Policy and Research (SAIPAR)*, Lusaka, Zambia:

    Dr. Jessica Achberger (Senior Research Fellow), Alex Caramento (Research Affiliate), Dr. Frank Chansa (Lecturer, University of Zambia (UNZA)), Caesar Cheelo (Associate Executive Director, SAIPAR), Abson Chompolola (Lecturer, UNZA), Dr. Marja Hinfelaar (Director of Research and Programs, SAIPAR), Opa Kapijimpanga (Founder and Director of AFRO-DAD), Professor John Lungu (Copperbelt University, Graduate School), Dr. O'Brien Kaaba (Lecturer, UNZA), Edna Kabala-Litana (Lecturer, Copperbelt University), Dale Mudenda (Researcher, UNZA), Dr. Chrispin Mphuka (former Head of Dept. Economics, UNZA), Obrian Ndhlovu (Lecturer, UNZA), Dr. Mushiba Nyamazana (Researcher, UNZA), Prof. Manenga Ndulo (Executive Director, SAIPAR), and Venkatesh Sheshamani[+] (Formerly Professor, UNZA).

The request for the case studies on the developmental state came directly from country representatives sitting on AfDB's executive board, reflecting the broad interest that the developmental state debate has commanded among African policymakers. In the event, the start of the project coincided with the beginning of AfDB's staggered return of staff and equipment from Tunis, Tunisia, where it had spent a decade in institutional exile, back to its statutory headquarters in Abidjan, Cote d'Ivoire. Thus, individual country studies could only be commissioned in early 2015, and many did not commence until later in the year.

In using the material from the studies mentioned above for the synthesis book, the main goal of the editors was to ensure that arguments in the chapters flowed as seamlessly as possible, with an introductory flourish, a discussion of the evidence, comparative examples drawing on all studies, and a definitive policy conclusion. This meant, however, that the structures of the original studies could not be maintained. The text acknowledges by name or team reference (i.e. Nigeria Team, South Africa Team, etc.), specific arguments, tables, or illustrations drawn from the commissioned studies. Given the synthesis nature of the book, individual chapters have not been ascribed to specific authors or teams.

In Africa's policy circles, the term "developmental state" has become the watchword for a nuanced but still decidedly interventionist approach to economic management, including the revival of national development planning and the eradication of any residual reservations over the once-derided practice of picking winners i.e. state capitalism or, more pointedly, market socialism. "De ja vu" could be a fitting comment on what seems to be a return to the development thinking of the post-independent decades in Africa, but without the geopolitical undercurrents of that era, with the exception that developmental states in East Asia were decidedly capitalist projects and not socialist or command-economy type efforts that were common in Africa in the 1960s and 1970s.

The policy discussion in this volume focuses on ten areas of Africa's developmental state debate: economic management; national planning and results monitoring; human development, spatial inclusion, and shared growth; industrial policy, export orientation, infrastructure, and science and technology; financing development; peace and security; policy autonomy; governance and accountability; incentive structures and contestability; and reciprocity and partnerships with the private sector.

The five takeaways from this synthesis of findings are as follows:

First, although the developmental state model is far from a straitjacket for economic development, varying in detail of emphasis from country to country and region to region, it has only succeeded where there is evidence of (i) commitment at the highest levels of national leadership and (ii) shared benefits at the local level i.e. the process comprises a long-term social compact for development (i.e. shared growth) than a full-fledged theology of how countries can systematically emerge from poverty. Since national leadership is important and the processes that lead to political change are endogenous, African countries cannot presume that a mere adoption of the developmental state model will generate development success.

Second, it is indisputable that for the benefits of the developmental state to accrue will require the enhancement of technical capabilities within Africa's public sectors, in terms of policy formulation, planning, research and development, supervision and coordination, and implementation, monitoring, and follow-up. Ultimately, the developmental state cannot be sustained by political platitudes and high-sounding phrases and takes lots of work to get it right. As is well known, African governments had embarked on various forms of state-led development frameworks (dubbed African socialism) in the 1960s, which resembled much of what the developmental state portends today. Their singular failure was absence of technical, analytical, and bureaucratic capability to sustain government action and follow-up. Leaders mistakenly thought that in the absence of an integrated and consistent policy framework, good ideas could self-propagate.

Third, expanded state involvement in economic development should not mean private sector exclusion. The developmental state model is most impactful when the public and private sectors reach a bargain that ensures mutual benefit i.e. an efficient bureaucracy and productive sector economies. However, today, many African countries lack a well-rooted business class with which government can establish a coalition of the willing. Globalization and its impacts have disincentivized national attempts at rearing own local capitalists.

Fourth, a singular challenge for African leaders is how to coalesce around a long-term national development policy agenda that is impervious to derailment by regime change. Countries such as South Korea, Singapore, and Taiwan were literally catapulted from abject poverty to relative affluence in less than half a century by focused and determined governments pursuing a long-term development agenda supported by the population. While the countries of East Asia have shown that economic transformation, which is the sine qua non of the developmental state, can be gained within a relatively short time span, it requires policies that are coherent and institutions implementing them that are disciplined. For many reasons, policy coherence has been a major challenge among African countries, with the details of the development agenda shifting markedly with changes in leadership.

Fifth, while the developmental state must be grounded in what is politically and economically feasible, the development success of South Korea, a country which had been destroyed by the Korean War of the 1950s, partly lay in its leaders' ability to stake out an ambitious agenda which was shielded from partisan politics i.e. the leaders dared the country to dream big, but within national capacities to deliver. South Korea's circumstances were unique in many ways, not least the technical prowess that took root during Japanese rule of the country, but the message to African countries seems to be to take advantage of all opportunities available in the policy and marketplace to push the development agenda forward in a forceful but measured and, hence, sustainable manner.

The last editorial touches to this volume were appended in mid-June 2020, when the Covid19 pandemic, having inflicted immeasurable damage on the global economy, was showing the first, if tentative, signs of ebbing in several parts of the world, with governments taking staggered steps to reopen their economies. For reasons to be clarified by future research, the general consensus seems to be that African countries, in spite economic and health system weaknesses, did not comprise the epicenter of the affliction. Although the book does not attempt to assess the effects of the pandemic on the aspiring developmental states, the economic impact has, nevertheless, been considerable, with heightened fears of de-globalization. In most of Africa, the emerging atmosphere is not that of mourners at a wake but rather of somber reflection and determination, in light of the challenges ahead. What is not in dispute is that, in the last six months, African populations and their leaders have seen more powerful demonstrations of how their institutions work under pressure than perhaps ever before. Already, many governments are bent on adjusting their systems of governance in light of the lessons learnt during this unprecedented natural experiment.

Acknowledgments

The editors would like to thank the Korean Trust Fund, hosted by the African Development Bank, and the Government of South Korea for co-financing the six studies commissioned under the project. The editors would also like to thank, without implications, all the six contributing institutions and their staff for their collaboration in preparing the detailed country case studies, in all amounting to close to 1,800 pages, on which this synthesis draws.

In 2018, the Research Department of the Bank requested one of the editors, Steve Kayizzi-Mugerwa, as a consultant, to compile a draft synthesis report of findings from the above studies, while also consolidating the drafts received from the institutional collaborators listed above. Professor John Anyanwu was the task manager for this part of the project, and his guidance was much appreciated. The administrative support of Mrs. Abiana Nelson proved crucial during the completion of the draft.

The final preparation of this synthesis volume, together with an extensive update of the literature and the information coverage, began in early 2020. Charles Leyeka Lufumpa would like to thank staff in the Economic Complex of the Bank, notably the Department of Statistics, for the statistical and technical support received, including updates of data, graphs, and other illustrations, and for fact checking the manuscript. We thank Ms. Amah Koffi for her administrative support and Routledge staff for all the advice and assistance received during the preparation of the manuscript for publication.

Steve Kayizzi-Mugerwa, PhD
Lorton, Virginia, USA

Charles Leyeka Lufumpa, PhD
African Development Bank, Abidjan, Cote d'Ivoire

Acronyms

ADB	Asian Development Bank
AEO	African Economic Outlook
AER	Agency for Rural Electrification (Cameroon)
AfDB	African Development Bank
AGOA	African Growth Opportunity Act
AMCON	Asset Management Corporation of Nigeria
ANC	African National Congress (South Africa)
APC	All Progressives Congress (Nigeria)
APRM	African Peer Review Mechanism
ARVs	Antiretroviral drugs
ASGISA	Accelerated and Shared Growth Initiative for South Africa
AU	African Union
BCEAO	Banque Centrale des États de l'Afrique de l'Ouest
BEAC	Banque des États de l'Afrique Centrale
BEE	Black Economic Empowerment
BNDES	O banco nacional do desenvolvimento economico e social (Brazil)
BNETD	Bureau National d'Etudes Techniques et Développement (Côte d'Ivoire)
BPP	Bureau of Public Procurement (Nigeria)
BTL	Build, Transfer, and Lease
CAISTAB	Caisse de Stabilisation (Côte d'Ivoire)
CEMAC	Communauté économique et monétaire de l'Afrique centrale
CFA	Communauté française d'Afrique
CFC	Crédit Foncier de Cameroun
CIRES	Le Centre Ivorien de Recherches Economique et Sociales
CONSUPE	Contrôle Supérieur de l'Etat (Cameroun)
COSATU	Congress of South African Trade Unions
DBSA	Development Bank of South Africa
DPRU	Development Policy Research Unit (Cape Town)
ECCAS	Economic Community of Central African States
EEZs	Exclusive Economic Zones
EFCC	Economic and Financial Crimes Commission (Nigeria)

EITI	Extractive Industries Transparency Initiative
EMEP	Enlarged Meeting for Export Promotion (South Korea)
EPB	Economic Planning Board (South Korea)
EPZ	Export Promotion Zone
ETRI	Electronics and Telecommunications Research Institute (South Korea)
FDI	Foreign Direct Investment
GATT	General Agreement on Tariffs and Trade
GDP	Gross Domestic Product
GEAR	Growth, Employment, and Redistribution (South Africa)
GESP	Growth and Employment Strategy Paper (Cameroon)
HIPC	Highly Indebted Poor Countries
HIV/AIDS	Human immunodeficiency virus/acquired immunodeficiency syndrome
HRC	Human Rights Commission (Zambia)
ICPC	Independent Corrupt Practices and other Related Offences Commission
ICT	Information and Communications Technology
IDC	Industrial Development Corporation (South Africa)
IEO	Independent Evaluation Office (of the International Monetary Fund)
IMF	International Monetary Fund
INDECO	Industrial Development Corporation (Zambia)
KAIST	Korea Advanced Institute for Science and Technology
KEPCO	Korea Electric Power Corporation
KFEM	Korea Federation for Environmental Movement
KICAC	Korea Independent Commission Against Corruption
KIMM	Korean Institute of Metals and Materials
KIST	Korea Institute for Science and Technology
KOAFEC	South Korea-Africa Economic Cooperation Conference
KOGAS	Korea Gas
KOISRA	Federation of Korean Industries
MCC	Millennium Challenge Corporation
MDGs	Millennium Development Goals
MDRI	Multilateral Debt Relief Initiative
MITI	Ministry of International Trade and Industry (Japan)
MUZ	Mine Workers Union of Zambia
M-PESA	Mobile Money Platform (Kenya)
NACC	National Anti-Corruption Commission (Cameroon)
NACRDB	Nigerian Agricultural, Cooperative, and Rural Development Bank
NAFI	National Agency for Financial Investigation (Cameroon)
NAFRA	National Food Reserve Agency (Nigeria)
NAIP	National Agriculture Investment Plan (Nigeria)
NALDA	National Agricultural Land Development Agency (Nigeria)

NEPA	National Electric Power Authority (Nigeria)
NEPAD	New Partnership for Africa's Development
NES	Nigerian Economic Society
NGOs	Non-Governmental Organizations
NIPA	National Institute of Public Administration (Zambia)
NPLs	Non-Performing Loans
NVM	New Village Movement (South Korea)
OAU	Organization of African Unity
OECD	Organization for Economic Cooperation and Development
PHGN	Power Holding Company of Nigeria
PICC	Presidential Infrastructure Coordination Commission (South Africa)
PMCDR	People's Movement Coalition for Democracy and Reunification (South Korea)
PPP	Public Private Partnership
PPP	Purchasing Power Parity
PRSP	Poverty Reduction Strategy Paper
PTDF	Petroleum Technology Fund (Nigeria)
PWAS	Public Welfare Assistance Scheme (Zambia)
R&D	Research and Development
RDP	Reconstruction and Development Program
SAA	South African Airways
SACCORD	Southern African Center for the Constructive Resolution of Disputes (Zambia)
SAIPAR	Southern African Institute for Policy and Research
SANRAL	South African National Roads Agency
SAPs	Structural Adjustment Programs
SDGs	Sustainable Development Goals
SMEs	Small and Medium-size Enterprises
SODEPALM	Société pour le Développement du Palmier
SODESUCRE	Société pour le Développement du Sucre
SODERIZ	Société pour le Développement du Riz
SOEs	State-owned Enterprises
SONARA	Société Nationale de la Raffinage
STD	Sexually Transmitted Diseases
STEM	Science, Technology, Engineering, and Mathematics
TB	Tuberculosis
TDX	Time-Division Exchange
TICAD	Tokyo International Conference on African Development
TRC	Truth and Reconciliation Commission (South Africa)
TVET	Technical and Vocational Education and Training
UNCTAD	United Nations Conference for Trade and Development
UNECA	United National Economic Commission for Africa
UNICEF	United Nations Children's Fund
UNIP	United National Independence Party (Zambia)

UNKRA	United Nations Korea Reconstruction Agency
UNZA	University of Zambia
VPC	Village Productivity Committee (Zambia)
WAEMU	West African Economic and Monetary Union
WHO	World Health Organization
WIDER	World Institute for Development Economics Research (United Nations University)
WTO	World Trade Organization
ZASCA	Supreme Court of Appeal of South Africa
ZCCM	Zambia Consolidated Copper Mines

1 Africa looking East
An introduction

1.1 Background

African policymakers, while disavowing the dirigiste inclinations of the past and reaffirming their capitalist credentials to a globalized audience, still avidly argue that national development is too important to be left to the vagaries of markets and the dictates of strangers. Governments, they intone, must continue playing a "constructive role" and cannot be vague about their intentions. As pointers to the new thinking—and borrowing a leaf from countries like South Korea, Singapore, and India—many African governments have designed attractive vision statements that extend well into the mid-21st century, while at the continental level, a similarly outstretched development blueprint, **Africa 2063**, was devised by the African Union, based in Addis Ababa. Generally, the visions evince the goal of reaching middle income status within a generation, while Africa 2063 projects the continent becoming a key member of the international community.

This book is a synthesis of findings from six country case studies and a literature review commissioned by the African Development Bank on the relevance of the developmental state model in Africa. It is a contribution to Africa's search for transformative models for economic development, including reexamining the role of the state as both an enabler and direct participant in the economy. The analyses in the book are mainly based on comparisons of the development experiences of South Korea (South Korea Team, 2017), the archetypical example of East Asia's "rags to riches syndrome," with those from five African countries, Cameroon (Cameroon Team, 2017), Côte d'Ivoire (Côte d'Ivoire Team, 2017), Nigeria (Nigeria Team, 2017), South Africa (South Africa Team, 2015), and Zambia (Zambia Team, 2017), and with reference to a range of other East Asian and African experiences. In the five African case study countries, governments have been vociferous in their praise of the developmental state model, including in their planning documents, although the pace at which its central tenets are being adopted on the ground is grudging and far between.

Developmental states came to be known as such not because they were exceptional from the outset nor because they had discovered huge amounts of natural resource deposits to finance their development but because they were able to overcome poverty and socio-economic frailty by building effective i.e. accountable institutional structures and forming workable domestic alliances, including with the private sector, for growth and development (Johnson, 1982). Although the case study countries for the developmental state research project were chosen to demonstrate the breadth of development experience in Africa, the countries were, South Africa excepted, at roughly the same level of economic development in the early 1960s as South Korea, the future "Miracle on the Han River."

South Africa, the most industrialized country in Africa, is a special case in this regard. It achieved independence from Britain in 1934, although majority (black) rule was delayed until 1994. At the beginning of the 1960s (when South Africa was still steeped in the policy of Apartheid), its economy, in key aspects already part of the West, was much bigger than that of South Korea. In 2019, South African GDP was less than a quarter of the latter's US$1.7 trillion economy. Whether South Africa can claim to have garnered aspects of the developmental state today, or could indeed become one with time, has generated much debate in recent years (Thompson and Wissink, 2018; Ukwandu, 2019).

For African governments, the lure of East Asia's developmental state experience lies in how countries in the region were able to pursue sustained growth over several decades, in the absence of rich natural resource endowments, without compromising their institutional and policy autonomy. The main task of the exercise was, therefore, to assess whether African countries could derive useful lessons of experience from the developmental states of East Asia, notably South Korea, and to identify what practical features of that knowledge could be replicated or more succinctly adapted by them to suit their socio-economic structures in the pursuit of rapid economic growth and robust development.

It is sometimes argued that the factors behind East Asia's emergence in the 1950s and 1960s were too episodic and regional specific i.e. the Cold War, global trade liberalization, China's ascent, regional and global, access to Japanese and US investments and buoyant markets, for African countries to draw beneficial lessons of experience from them some two decades into the 21st century. It must be underlined, however, that from the point of view of feasibility, the most endearing feature of developmental states in East Asia was the enhancement of technical and bureaucratic capacities, including for planning, implementation, delivery, and accountability, at the national and local levels as a prerequisite for effective development policy i.e. it was largely endogenous.

Africa's increasing fascination with the East has not been a one-sided affair. Asia had become a key economic partner for Africa, epitomized by expanding investment and trade flows and, at least in the case of China, substantial tourism, and migration. The major Asian economies now hold regular meetings with African counterparts at the highest levels of government. For example, South Korea holds a regular Korea-Africa Economic Cooperation (KOAFEC) Ministerial Conference in Seoul, Japan now holds its Tokyo International Conference of Africa's Development (TICAD) series interchangeably between Africa and Japan, and China and India have similar vehicles that allow meetings to take place at the highest levels of government on a regular basis. In some ways, the

East has, in recent years, eclipsed the West in terms of high-level state to state contacts with Africa.

The first half of the 2000s showed a marked break from Africa's lethargic growth of the previous decades, thanks to above-average FDI inflows, low levels of external debt, rising commodity prices, and digital momentum.[1] Average growth reached double digits for some countries, especially in Sub-Saharan Africa, and for a while, the so-called Afro-pessimism was reversed in spectacular fashion. Among the expressions minted to capture the continent's unprecedented change of fortune, "African renaissance" became something of a staple in the discourse.

Improved growth and much more diversified sources of investment capital meant that African policymakers were much less constrained, than in previous decades, by the international lending agencies and their policies, and saw a rare chance to pursue homegrown policy initiatives of their own. Thus, countries ranging from Angola to Zambia, on own volition, issued a series of Eurobonds, many of them oversubscribed. While this raised confidence across the continent, compelling more countries to consider jumping onto the bandwagon, the short tenor, and high-coupon rates, often in double digits, meant that the Eurobonds were not a cheap or sustainable source of financing for Africa's long-term investment needs.

Many African countries continue to see these bond issues as morale boosters and an important form of market discovery—useful for gauging investor appetite and for own domestic benchmarking and yield-curve exigencies as governments look to deepening domestic financial markets. Effective capital mobilization, as East Asian examples show, requires a much broader strategy than merely accessing international financial markets. It calls for strong analytical capacities, immaculate planning, and, above all, policy coherence. All three require, in turn, effective bureaucracies that allow for rapid responses without losing sight of the goals set. This bureaucratic precision is not yet a common feature of African responses, although some countries are making more progress than others.[2]

1.2 Defining the developmental state

The developmental state literature has grown exponentially in recent years, taking on an ever-increasing number of cross-country examinations and extending the definition and implications of the model in ways not anticipated when East Asia embarked on its growth quest (Woo-Cumings, 1999).[3] This book follows the usual proposition that the developmental state is one that can engender a social compact for economic transformation, through industrialization, where the government (and its bureaucracy) is the principal agent/partner in the process. Moreover, such a state is driven by Weberian ideals, which include doing whatever is required, such as altering market incentives, reducing investment risks, proffering entrepreneurial visions, and managing the conflict inherent in the process of change, to safeguard the goals of economic development (Box 1.1).[4]

Box 1.1: Four operational characteristics/elements of a developmental state

The first element that is key for the operation of an effective developmental state is the *existence of an elite state bureaucracy staffed by the best managerial talent* available in the country. It is based on meritocratic recruitment and career advancement. This elite bureaucracy identifies and selects industries to be developed, decides on the best means to achieve industrial policy, and supervises competition between strategic sectors using market-conforming methods of state intervention.

The second element is that *this meritocratic bureaucracy is given adequate scope (bureaucratic autonomy) to take initiatives and operate efficiently within the political system.* The legal and judicial branches of the government are restricted to "safety valve" functions and do not interfere in the development process itself.

The third element comprises *the perfection of market-conforming methods of state intervention in the economy* to avoid putting the bureaucracy into a straitjacket. The first set of issues is related to policy plans and guidelines for the economy; forums for the exchange of ideas at the national level and within sectors; mechanisms for policy adjustment and revision, feedback, and resolution of differences; assignment of governmental functions to private and semiprivate associations; and reliance on public–private cooperation in high-risk areas. The second set refers to financing the state, including through the establishment of public financial institutions, targeting of tax incentives, and the creation of an investment budget that is separate from the general account budget; an antitrust policy geared toward international competitiveness goals; and government-conducted and sponsored research and development activities.

The fourth element is *existence of a development pilot agency that spearheads industrial policy and economic growth*, such as the role played in previous decades by the Ministry of International Trade and Industry (MITI) in Japan. Though small in terms of employees, MITI spearheaded Japanese industrial policy, funded research, and directed investment according to its assessment of the country's needs. It intervened at both the firm-level as well as the macrolevel. Despite the high level of autonomy, it was deeply embedded in society with close ties to private businesses, think-tanks, and vertical bureaus for the implementation of industrial policy at the micro level. MITI coordinated closely with the Bank of Japan and the Economic Planning Agency, especially in the matter of allocating foreign exchange to businesses.

Source: South Korea Team (2017) and Johnson (1999).

For the state to attract competent bureaucrats and motivated business partners, it must design effective incentive structures based on a credible process of reciprocity versus the private sector and implies a good understanding of social norms. Crucially, and controversially, because power and social standing are interlinked, the bureaucracy must be autonomous enough to be able to arbitrate between interest groups to avoid discontent and opposition. It can do this because it is assumed to enjoy "embedded autonomy" i.e. it interacts with interest groups effectively without in turn being adversely influenced by them (Chang, 1993, 1999; Evans, 1995).

In practice, social interactions are much more complex than this enabling analytical framework, shifting in time and space. Thus, even Japan and South Korea, the quintessential developmental states, have witnessed moments of policy contradiction, chaos, and even reversal during the past 60 years (Routley, 2014). In an insightful comparison of recent development experiences in Sub-Saharan Africa and Russia, Sindzingre and Dufy (2014) argue that the two regions, different in many ways, share the singular distinction of private sector capacity to resist or disregard national-level economic guidance, including the state's overtures to the private sector in attempts to boost export-oriented industrialization—this is probably because following decades of accumulated lack of trust in government, it has been harder to recoup popular confidence, even with the return of growth.

In recent analyses of the developmental state model, two operational concepts have emerged. The first relates to the structures required to make the developmental state function i.e. state capacity and the second to developmental roles i.e. the state's commitment to getting results. It can be argued that while the two concepts are separately attractive, they must operate in tandem for the essence of the developmental state to emerge. Thus, while Doner, Ritchie, and Slater (2005) define the developmental state as one possessing the ability to upgrade to higher-value activities i.e. economic transformation, some researchers argue that the disproportionate focus on growth, as opposed to changes in institutional structures, domestic alliances, and social inclusion, is a major source of ambiguity.[5]

Many researchers have argued that developmental states must also be judged by their commitment to an ambitious development ideology (Leftwich, 1995; Mkandawire, 2001; Vu, 2007). Others have noted though that too close a focus on the role of politics, which is ever shifting, can be misleading. In a study of Brazil, Schneider (2015) argues for a more disaggregated approach as it is possible to pursue developmental state policies in one sector (the auto industry) while failing to do so in others owing to external shocks and/or domestic political constraints.

1.3 Conceptual framework and key questions

The African Development Bank, as part of its support to Africa's policymaking and capacity building, and with financial support from the Government of South Korea, launched a project on the developmental state and its relevance to Africa's economic transformation in 2014. The project's concept note underlined that its value-addition was not so much in testing the validity of the developmental state model as in examining the plausibility of its propositions in two geographically and culturally distinct places i.e. South Korea, and East Asia more generally, and African countries, and with respect to the much-changed global environment since the 1950s and 1960s, when the first developmental states were launched. Some writers feel that so much has happened since the first developmental state experiments were undertaken in the 1950 and 1960s that today's African developmental state vintages can only be referred to as neo-developmental states i.e. indicating a different set of premises (Ansari, 2017, Cheeseman, 2018, Goodfellow, 2018).

The AfDB (2020) concurs with other continental organizations, such as the United Nations Economic Commission for Africa (UNECA), and the African Union (AU), that, among the multi-layered implications of globalization and expanding global value chains on Africa's political economy, growth, spatial development, and household inequality, the most important question of the day for the continent is what it will take for it to embark on a sustained process of economic transformation (African Union Commission, 2015).

As noted by the Zambia Team (2017), UNECA (2011) identifies the following five requirements for the construction of developmental states in Africa:

i. Capable and farsighted democratic leadership
ii. The creation of effective development coalitions
iii. The building of transformative institutions and primarily a competent and professional bureaucracy
iv. A focused industrial policy with a phasing-out process to protect local industries, which is necessary for their growth and consolidation
v. Heavy investments in skills, education, healthcare, and infrastructure (including economic infrastructure) for expanding human capabilities

For each case study country, the Bank commissioned an analytical report from a local university, think-tank, or similar institution.[6] The South Korea team was explicitly instructed to isolate the salient features of the developmental state model as applied to that country (i.e. initial conditions/ structural impediments, policy content, institutional resilience/rigor, and implementation and follow-up modalities) and to discuss their possible application to Africa, with concrete examples.[7] The five case study teams, using a similar approach, were urged to compare South Korea's experience with that of their countries with respect to the colonial background, the evolution of development policies and national development programs, the development and effectiveness of institutional structures, and policy implementation and outcomes. The case study teams followed each country's development policies from the late-1950s or early 1960s (the era of independence for African case study countries, except South Africa—where the bulk of the analysis is from the period after 1994).[8]

The case studies are rich in content and policy insights, with a variety of views on the relevance of the South Korean experience and that of the developmental state model more generally, for Africa. They also make suggestions on the policy adjustments required for countries to emulate South Korea and other East Asian countries. This book synthesizes these multi-layered views and outcomes of the case studies complemented by an extensive literature review (Kayizzi-Mugerwa, 2016) into a single volume, drawing on each country case study's arguments and suggestions for the way forward.

The following broad questions comprise the issues on which the analyses in the synthesis book are focused:

- To what extent is South Korea's experience, and that of its East Asian neighbors, relevant for African countries?
- Was the emergence of developmental states unique (and hence difficult to emulate) in terms of timing (i.e. global trade liberalization, Cold War, and before China's emergence) and space (i.e. social homogeneity, national language, and culture, access to Japanese and US investments and markets), or is it amenable to replication by newcomers, including in Africa?[9]
- In the latter regard, how did South Korea and other developmental states deal with key policy challenges, including those of political economy, and what lessons of strategy, institutional development, and implementation are there for Africa's late industrializers i.e. how should they best harness human and physical resources for economic transformation?

1.4 Developmental state in practice: lessons and implications for African countries

This section discusses ten lessons of practice that aspiring African countries, including those in the case studies, can draw from the developmental state experiences of South Korea and its neighbors. For concreteness, they are placed in two broad categories: (A) *economic management and social inclusion* (economic management; national planning and results monitoring; human development, spatial inclusion, and shared growth; industrialization, infrastructure, science, and technology; and financing development) and (B) *institutions and governance issues* (peace and security; governance and accountability; policy autonomy; and incentive structures and contestability; and reciprocity and partnership with the private sector).

A. Economic management and social inclusion

1. Economic management
   In pursuing its domestic and external objectives, South Korea, like its neighbors, demonstrated a great deal of discretion in defining taxation and regulatory frameworks, and subsidy and incentive regimes. Although a capitalist approach generally pervaded economic policy in

South Korea, with emphasis on savings and investment, hard ideological positions that threatened to derail the country from the chosen development path were avoided, hence policies were pragmatic. Above all, the government pursued a rigorous budgetary process with feedback loops from financing to results. Even when the thrust of development policy was disrupted by domestic politics or external shocks, which happened on several occasions, the process tended to return to the prescribed path within a relatively short time span. Using the language of fiscal policy, the social system of the country seems to have robust inbuilt stabilizers.

In recent years, African countries, among the case studies and more generally, have shown a remarkable capacity, thanks to better performance by their ministries of finance, central banks, and other agencies, to maintain economic stability and growth, mobilize resources, and reduce donor dependency. The improvements, notably lower debt burdens, have emboldened African policymakers in several countries, resulting in a range of policy innovations, including on issues of creating fiscal space, financing projects jointly with the private sector, and even bartering natural resources for infrastructure projects with China. Strong centralized bureaucratic systems for delegating economic management policies, that characterized developmental states in South Korea and the rest of East Asia in the formative years, are yet to take concrete shape in Africa's aspiring developmental states as discussed below.

2.   National planning and results monitoring

South Korea and other East Asian countries gave the highest priority to coordinated national planning and policy implementation; in fact, they were the artifacts of their approach. Specialized agencies—with dedicated units for gathering statistics, research, monitoring, review, and follow-up—were set up to complement the policy, supervisory, and analytical work of the government. In other words, the government saw the importance of accompanying aspirations for rapid development with a concretized process for delivery. The South Korean government set up a powerful Economic Planning Board very early on in the process and gave it the incentives, power, and prestige (it was headed by a Deputy Prime Minister) it needed to be effective in spearheading development—notably it had budget-setting functions. The Prime Minister attended many of the meetings of the Board, giving the body additional political clout.

Although African countries have formulated bold national development plans during the past 50–60 years, for many reasons, the sharp focus on delivery exhibited by the East Asian economies has been missing in Africa's efforts. Few plans were explicitly linked to national budget frameworks and other accountability mechanisms, and hence delivery was subject to the vagaries of national politics, which weakened policy implementation. The alternative approaches implied by the Poverty Reduction Strategy Papers (PRSPs), that were introduced by multilateral development institutions during the era of structural adjustment policies (SAPs) and rising external indebtedness, in the 1980s and 1990s, failed to enhance policy coherence.

In recent decades, African countries have reverted to national planning, the rehabilitation of development banks and related agencies, and the refurbishment of the cooperative unions. There is a real risk, however, that in the enthusiastic reclaiming of previous approaches, the reasons why a whole set of institutional structures was abandoned might be forgotten—they had failed to deliver. Hence, to meet the challenges of the day and avoid popular disappointment, the goals of these new or revisited approaches to national planning and more effective government must revolve around the cardinality of delivery (as opposed to mere political grandstanding or nostalgic revival of unviable institutions).

3. Human development, spatial inclusion, and shared growth

The notion of shared growth is a novel feature of development associated to South Korea and East Asia, more generally—with regimes seeing an egalitarian distribution of incomes and assets not only as a key pillar of their development strategy but also as a guarantor of its sustainability. Land reforms in the earlier phases of the development push in South Korea proved crucial in establishing a broadly egalitarian development ethos that has stood the test of time.

The land reform of 1950 lay the ground for rapid economic growth in subsequent decades, while the emphasis on education, skills development (with compulsory education at the primary level declared in the early 1950s), and health provision boosted social welfare and productivity. Training the youth for technical jobs of the future was also an important consideration as elaborated below.

African countries have been less successful than East Asia in undertaking land reforms and social reforms targeted at reducing poverty in both rural and urban areas. Moreover, owing to failure to share the benefits of recent high growth with the rural populations, Sub-Saharan Africa is recording rising levels of income inequality. Today, African inequality is globally only lower than that of Latin America, a more recent trend as its inequality was lower than that of Asia as recently as the 1990s.

From policy documents, it would seem that Africa is keenly aware of the importance of sharing the benefits of economic growth with the broader population, including with women, girl children, the youth, and rural dwellers—through, for example, the extension of social services and utilities such as electricity and creation of off-farm employment in the countryside. Policy platitudes can only go so far, and many governments and their supporters appreciate that implementation and follow-up are what matters in the long run.

4.   Industrial policy, export orientation, infrastructure, and science and technology

In the developmental state model, industrial policy is the essence of economic transformation. South Korea's example demonstrates that the industrialization that creates employment, promotes exports, and pushes the economy toward higher value chains is by no means spontaneous. It requires good analysis and research, planning and implementation, and, above all, reciprocity between government and business. In successful East Asian countries, science, technology, and research went hand in hand in conceiving development in key areas of the economy—from agriculture to nuclear energy to government administration.

Many African governments now routinely highlight industrialization, and associated technology development and innovation, in their policy statements—and some have developed research units to investigate the issues of the day. Additionally, science, engineering, and technology (STEM) are now given lots of emphasis in African education, although mostly at tertiary levels with little preparation at the basic levels of education, owing to paucity of resources and the large numbers of learners that have been unleashed at that level by universal primary school programs adopted across the continent.

In terms of creating an enabling environment for industrialization, governments are providing incentives in terms of infrastructure extension, land availability, and even support to R&D and have received good rankings in the World Bank's Ease of Doing Business indices. Thanks to new technologies, notably ICT, some African countries are leapfrogging to sophisticated economic niches, including financial and allied service sectors.[10] The question raised repeatedly in the case studies is whether there is sufficient interaction and coherence between policy and practice to generate the momentum needed to make a real difference on the ground i.e. to generate critical mass in terms of the technical, human, and financial resources required to power industrialization and economic transformation on a sustainable basis in the decades ahead.

5.   Financing development

Closing the savings and investment gap is a key plank of the developmental state model. African countries, notably in Sub-Saharan Africa, have not been able to raise savings and investments rates to anywhere near what East Asian countries accomplished in the earlier phases of their development. Exports were a major financier of development in East Asia, but Africa's trade faces a steep learning curve with respect to global value chain development, especially in manufactures.

South Korea grew its export capacity not through sporadic export promotion efforts but by devising integrated schemes that linked all key players, including export associations, and sought to touch as many bases as possible. For instance, South Korea used its development bank to strategically kickstart projects in the export- or import-substitution oriented manufacturing industry, with ripple effects in the rest of the economy.

At the macrolevel, the government introduced several credit and ownership restrictions to entry into the financial sector as means of ensuring that domestic firms were sufficiently protected from bigger and more experienced financial institutions and banks from the West. A guiding principal was to conduct the interventions in as market-conforming a manner as possible i.e. requiring a high level of supervisory discipline and autonomy within the civil service.

In recent years, new forms of banking and finance have emerged on the African scene[11] driven by the expanding use of ICT, such as mobile banking, and increases in unrequited resource inflows, notably remittances from the Diaspora. However, breakthroughs in the export of manufactures are taking place in unexpected places in Africa—notably Ethiopia and Rwanda.[12]

B.   Institutions and governance issues

6.   Peace and security
The distribution of affluence around the world today seems to prove the assertion that development is impossible without peace and security. The permanent cessation of hostilities in East Asia, enabling the anchor power at the time, the USA, to transfer its focus on economic reconstruction and development, had enabled South Korea and its neighbors to kickstart economic development from a low base. Some observers have seen the role of the US and Japan, as both investors and market destination for South Korean manufactures, as crucial factors for starting off the developmental states of the region.

Vietnam, a country very much in neo-developmental state mode, has demonstrated in recent years, that although opportunities could come knocking, they are only useful if seized i.e. few could have predicted that the country could turn the adversity of the Vietnam war into a platform on which to partly base its export-oriented industrial strategy as well as tourism.[13]

In recent decades, African countries have become more peaceful, and national and regional conflicts are at historical lows. However, efforts to reap the peace dividend are halting. The legacy of prolonged conflict continues to be felt through a high cost of doing business and an even higher risk premium on investing in Africa.

7.   Policy autonomy
African countries have always attached considerable importance to their right to exercise national policy autonomy, what Tanzania's Mwalimu Julius Nyerere called pointedly "self-reliance," and it is by far the most attractive feature of the developmental state to African aspirants. Since the independence years, there have been many African attempts at

defining "indigenous" strategies for development, borrowing, in some cases from aspects of traditional society i.e. Nyerere's Ujamaa. Indeed, the developmental state model is attractive partly because it responds to this long-craved need for African countries to be in control of their affairs. More recently, African governments have returned to the promotion of industrial policies as well as to the identification of national champions.

The recent revival of national airlines across Africa, despite the problems associated with the airline industry globally, is a case in point. Many African countries point to Ethiopian Airlines as an example of African success in a global industry that is worth emulating. However, few have attempted to understand the causes of Ethiopian's relative success—the company is run with a high degree of autonomy and as a precursor of the country's competitive potential in the global economy: providing transport services, enhancing the country's technical capabilities in aviation engineering and ICT, raising corporate competences across the economy, and enhancing the country's regional prestige as a global gateway. It is telling that many of the new African airlines have sought technical assistance from Ethiopian or have ceded shares to the company, which is government-owned back home, to benefit from its managerial expertise and global network.

As South Korea demonstrates, the developmental state model links policy autonomy to a high degree of bureaucratic discipline, driven by strong institutions with the capacity to set priorities and goals and to identify the policy actions, including budgeting, required to meet them. This distinguishes it from the approaches of African governments in the 1960s and later decades, which evinced ambitious goals but ultimately exhibited limited follow-through. The goal of the developmental state is to be able to implement policies that work and not just "home grown."

8.   Governance and accountability

Good governance and accountability are the backbone of the developmental state. South Korea's example indicates that the challenges of governance and accountability persist even in successful cases. But what matters, especially in the area of public finance management, is the system's ability to subject itself to public scrutiny and to adjust accordingly.

Moreover, there is an ongoing debate on whether autocratic rule is necessary in the earlier phases of development, to focus bureaucrats and the populations on the essentials, with countries only graduating to full-fledged democracy when they are richer. Proponents of this view contend that governance and accountability are closely correlated with a country's level of development, pointing to a "chicken and egg" issue.

It is easy to be sidetracked by such niceties when the message is otherwise quite clear i.e. that governance is still a major challenge to development in most parts of Africa. While developmental states in

East Asia experienced governance issues of their own in the past, a major difference with African countries is that corruption among some of them threatens to become systemic, and their development programs and strategies could well be derailed if remedies are not found.

9. Incentive structures and contestability

A major lesson to draw from the experience of South Korea and other "developmental states" is that governments there never kept their eyes off the disciplining device of economic competition—i.e. domestic actors and markets were exposed to competition as a means of enhancing economic efficiency. To ensure that markets were contestable required an efficient policy implementation and regulatory mechanism that could mediate credibly between the domestic business sectors, hence South Korea's emphasis on the creation of a meritocratic bureaucracy.

The incentive structures in South Korea's civil service pivoted on a competitive elitism where entry into most spheres of government service, SOEs, and pilot agencies required the passing of entrance examinations, while career advancement was also rigorous. On the other hand, during the 1960s and through the 1980s, private companies competed for foreign exchange allocations and credit subsidies. African governments acknowledge that discipline in the civil service is the key to success and are putting in place appropriate incentive structures. But they are invariably starting from a low base, and the notion of contestability is still novel. There is an inherent fear among African governments that, in the absence of modern sector jobs, have always used public-sector employment as a means of sharing the national cake, seeking after meritocracy might have a countervailing impact on social inclusion.

10. Reciprocity and partnership with the private sector

The system of reciprocity between the government and the private sector in South Korea succeeded because both sides stood to gain from the implementation of effective policies—including the insistence on competition between domestic business entities—with the government realizing its development targets and the business sector its portfolio implementation plans. It was a form of constrained maximization, with each side agreeing that the other had comparative advantage in its areas of specialization—governing versus doing business. The constraint was to operate within the priority areas suggested by the national development plan.

As observed above, such compromises were based on a level of mutual understanding that required a good knowledge of domestic social structures and good analytical capacities, especially on the part of the bureaucracy. While similar approaches were attempted in African countries, institutional indiscipline and cronyism nullified domestic contestation. Reciprocity never became a useful basis for enhancing government-business relations (Singh and Ovadia, 2018).

African leaders are not oblivious to the challenges, and recent years have seen the production of vision statements by many African governments, highlighting the crucial role of the private sector and the importance of involving civil society in the development process. Their usefulness and impact have not yet been tested.

1.5 Outline of the rest of the book

The rest of the volume is divided into two parts, with a concluding chapter:

1.5.1 Part I: Debate, relevance and context

Chapter 2 undertakes a selective review of the literature on the developmental state, including theoretical and empirical issues, with the latter drawing on experiences from South Korea, and East Asia more generally, Africa, and Latin America.

Chapter 3 provides the country context for the six case studies: South Korea, Cameroon, Côte d'Ivoire, Nigeria, South Africa, and Zambia. For each country, it undertakes a broad sweep of the development strategies, institutional frameworks, and implementation experiences. It also looks at the impacts of globalization on countries' development and way of doing business.

Chapter 4 discusses the challenges of governance, transparency, and elite capture, which are not insignificant in Africa's low-income and emerging economies. It discusses the anti-corruption strategies pursued by South Korea and African countries in recent decades and the roles of civil society organizations as agents of inclusion and restraint.

1.5.2 Part II: Implementation and impact

Chapter 5 examines national planning, and the closely interrelated issues of decentralization and rural development in South Korea and the African case study countries, and the lessons to draw on how to address policy incoherence and spatial exclusion in rapidly changing development environments.

Chapter 6 looks at the issue of social inclusion, comparing the responses of South Korea and those of the African cases to the challenges of inadequate social services (education and health), poverty reduction, and employment creation (including discussions of skills enhancement, job creation, and labor market flexibility).

Chapter 7 focuses on the lessons that Africa countries can learn from South Korea's push for industrialization, including how governments sequenced actions that led to the emergence of a competitive industrial sector that eventually graduated to higher industrial export niches. It also examines the concepts of contestability and reciprocity which were used effectively to raise domestic competitiveness in South Korea and discusses Africa's prospects for catchup.

Chapter 8 undertakes the policy discussion and concludes the book.

Notes

1 On the impact of ICT on Africa's recent and potential growth and the prospects for leapfrogging, see for example Chakravorti and Chaturvedi (2019), which argues that the "ease of creating digital jobs" will be pivotal to Africa's development. See also African Development Bank (2020).
2 The Republic of Rwanda is often given as a good example of rapidly rising public sector competences. However, in terms of breadth and sophistication, the South African civil service is unmatched on the continent.
3 For reviews on the implications for Africa, see for example Kayizzi-Mugerwa, 2016; Routley, 2014; Subira, 2011.
4 Some have argued, pointing at decades of dictatorship and military rule in East Asia and Brazil that in practice the developmental state model possesses an "autocratic streak" (Nigeria Team, 2017).
5 A recent set of articles on Brazil (*The Quarterly Review of Economics and Finance*, Vol. 62, No. 1, 2016) have argued that while Brazil has not generated breakneck growth rates in the past decades, it has evolved a development model which has been more responsive to the needs of the poor than other emerging economies. This has led Amann and Barrientos (2016) to wonder in the editorial of the above: "Is there a Brazilian development 'model'?"
6 See Appendix I for details on participating institutions and teams.
7 For comparison, the South Korea Team chose Botswana, Ghana, Mauritius, and Rwanda.
8 The Nigerian case study also took up state-level case studies of Kaduna, Lagos, and Rivers.
9 See for example the issues raised by Evans (1998, 2008), Kanyenze et al. (2017) and Ikpe (2018) on the transferability of development experiences as well as on the changing global context.
10 See for example, Behuria and Goodfellow (2019) for the case of Rwanda, which according to them is trying to leapfrog into higher value service sectors through use of ICT.
11 Kenya's M-PESA launched by the telecommunications giant, Safaricom as a provider of mobile banking, has exported its services to beyond the region, now operating in Afghanistan, Albania, India, and Romania.
12 See for example Goodfellow (2018) and Cheeseman (2018).
13 See for example Masina (2012) and his view on the drivers of industrial policy in recent decades in Vietnam.

References

African Development Bank (2020) *African Economic Outlook. Developing Africa's Workforce for the Future*, AfDB: Abidjan.
African Union Commission (2015) *Agenda 2063. The Africa We Want*, African Union Headquarters: Addis Ababa.
Amann, E. and Barrientos, A. (2016) 'Introduction—Is There a Brazilian Development 'Model'?' *The Quarterly Review of Economics and Finance* 62(1):7–11
Ansari, S. (2017) 'The Neo-Liberal Incentive Structure and the Absence of the Developmental State in Post-Apartheid South Africa,' *African Affairs* 116(463):206–232.
Behuria, P. and Goodfellow, T. (2019) 'Leapfrogging Manufacturing? Rwanda's Attempt to Build a Services-Led 'Development State',' *The European Journal of Development Research* 31:581–603.
Cameroon Team (2017) «Etude Sur L'Economie du Cameroun. La Politique de Développement dans la Pratique Enseignements Tires de L'Expérience de Développement

de la Corée du Sud» Report to the African Development Bank on the *Developmental State in Africa, Lessons from South Korea Project*, Université de Yaoundé II: Yaoundé.

Chakravorti, B. and Chaturvedi, R. (2019) 'Research: How Technology Could Promote Growth in 6 African Countries,' *Harvard Business Review*, December 4.

Chang, H. (1999) 'The Economic Theory of the Developmental State,' in M. Woo-Cumings (ed.), *The Developmental State*,182–199, Cornell University Press: Ithaca

Chang, H. (1993) 'The Political Economy of Industrial Policy in Korea,' *Cambridge Journal of Economics* 17(2):131–157.

Cheeseman, N. (2018) 'Why Rwanda's Development Model Wouldn't Work Elsewhere in Africa,' *The Conversation*, January 8.

Côte d'Ivoire Team (2017) « Etude Sur L'Economie Ivorienne. La Politique de Développement dans la Pratique Enseignements Tires de L'Expérience de Développement de la Corée du Sud » Report to the African Development Bank on the *Developmental State in Africa, Lessons from South Korea Project,* Le Centre Ivoirien de Recherches Economiques et Sociales (CIRES): Abidjan.

Doner, R., Ritchie, B. and Slater, D. (2005) 'Systemic Vulnerability and the Origins of Developmental States: Northeast and Southeast Asia in Comparative Perspective,' *International Organisation* 59:327–361.

Evans, P. (2008) 'Is an Alternative Globalisation Possible?' *Politics and Society* 36(2):272–305.

Evans, P. (1998) 'Transferable Lessons? Re-Examining the Institutional Prerequisites of East Asian Economic Policies,' *Journal of Development Studies* 34(6):66–86.

Evans, P. (1995) *Embedded Autonomy: States and Industrial Transformation*, Princeton University Press: Princeton.

Goodfellow, T. (2018) 'Taxing Property in a Neo-Developmental State, the Politics of Urban Land Value Capture in Rwanda and Ethiopia,' *African Affairs* 116(465):545–572.

Ikpe, E. (2018) 'The Enduring Relevance of the Developmental State Paradigm across Space and Time: Lessons for Africa on Structural Transformation and Agriculture in Oil-Rich Contexts,' *Journal of Asian and African Studies* 53(5):764–781.

Johnson, C. (1999) 'The Developmental State: Odyssey of a Concept,' in M. Woo-Cumings (ed.), *The Developmental State,* Cornell University Press: Ithaca.

Johnson, C. (1982) *MITI and the Japanese Miracle: The Growth of Industrial Policy 1925–75,* Stanford University Press: Stanford.

Kanyenze, G., Jauch, H., Kanengoni, A., Madzwamuse, M. and Muchena, D. (eds.) (2017) *Towards Democratic Developmental States in Southern Africa*, Weaver Press: Harare

Kayizzi-Mugerwa, S. (2016) 'Developmental State in Africa: The Quest for Inclusive Growth and Economic Transformation,' *Annual Public Lecture 2015*, Nigerian Economic Society: Ibadan.

Leftwich, A. (1995) 'Bringing Politics Back In: Towards a Model of the Developmental State,' *Journal of Developments Studies* 31(3):400–427.

Masina, P. (2012) 'Vietnam between Developmental State and Neoliberalism: The Case of the Industrial Sector,' in C. Kyung-Sup, Fine, B. and Weiss, L. (eds.), *Developmental Politics in Transition*, 188–210, Palgrave Macmillan: Basingstoke and New York.

Mkandawire, T. (2001) 'Thinking about Developmental States in Africa,' *Cambridge Journal of Economics* 25(3):289–313.

Nigeria Team (2017) 'Towards Developmental State in Nigeria: Lessons from Korea,' Report to the African Development Bank on the *Developmental State in Africa, Lessons from South Korea Project*, Nigerian Economic Society: Ibadan.

Routley, L. (2014) 'Developmental States in Africa? A Review of On-going Debates and Buzzwords,' *Development Policy Review* 32(2):159–177.

Schneider, B. (2015) 'The Developmental State in Brazil: Comparative and Historical Perspectives,' *Revista de Economica Politica* 35(1):114–132.

Sindzingre, A. and Dufy, C. (2014) '"Developmental' Policies and Rent: Comparing Russia and Sub-Saharan Africa,' *Post Print*, Centre National de la Recherche Scientifique, Université Paris: Nanterre.

Singh, J.N. and Ovadia, J.S. (2018) 'The Theory and Practice of Building Developmental States in the Global South,' *Third World Quarterly* 39(6):1033–1055.

South Africa Team (2015) 'The Role of Institutions in Underpinning Inclusive Economic Growth in South Africa. Country Development Policy in Practice: Lessons from the South Korea Development Experience,' Report to the African Development Bank on the *Developmental State in Africa, Lessons from South Korea Project*, Development Policy Research Unit, School of Economics, University of Cape Town: Cape Town.

South Korea Team (2017) 'KOAFEC—Development Policy in Practice Project,' Report to the African Development Bank on the *Developmental State in Africa, Lessons from South Korea Project*, Korea Institute for International Economic Policy (KIEP): Seoul.

Subira, L. (2011) *A Developmental State in Africa. What Can Policy Makers in Africa Learn from the Ideas of Developmental State?* Published MA Thesis, University of Witwatersrand: Johannesburg.

Thompson, P. and Wissink, H. (2018) 'Recalibrating South Africa's Political Economy: Challenges in Building a Developmental and Competition State,' *African Studies* 18(2):31–48.

Ukwandu, D.C. (2019) 'South Africa as a Developmental State. Is It a Viable Idea?' *African Journal of Public Affairs* 11(2):41–62.

United Nations Economic Commission for Africa (UNECA) (2011) *Economic Report on Africa 2011. Governing Development in Africa: The Role of the State in Economic Transformation*, UNECA: Addis Ababa.

Vu, T. (2007) 'State Formation and the Origins of Developmental States in South Korea and Indonesia,' *Studies in Comparative International Development* 41(4):27–56.

Woo-Cumings, M. (ed.) (1999) *The Developmental State*, Cornell University Press: Ithaca.

Zambia Team (2017) 'The Zambian Society and Economy: Development Policy in Practice in Comparison with South Korea,' Report to the African Development Bank on the *Developmental State in Africa, Lessons from South Korea Project*, Southern African Institute for Policy and Research (SAIPAR): Lusaka.

Part I

Debate, relevance, and context

2 Developmental state and relevance for Africa

An overview

2.1 Introduction

This chapter looks at the relevance of the developmental state model in Africa, including a discussion of the importance of initial conditions, institutional structures, and implementation processes for outcomes. Drawing on South African experience, the South Africa Team (2015) argues that a successful transfer of development lessons demands more than simply adopting policy frameworks. For late (late) industrializers in Africa, copying, reinventing, and adding value to proven ideas for development from East Asia might be a faster path to economic transformation than adherence to development blueprints from the region.[1]

While South Korea is by no means a big Asian player in Africa, a role currently assumed by China and India, its population of about 51 million is close to that of many African countries, while levels of development in the late-1950s and early 1960s were also similar i.e. characterized by capital scarcity, malnutrition, and deep poverty. During the initial phases of South Korea's transformation, it demonstrated a policy and institutional autonomy and an aptitude for mobilizing the population which endeared it to policymakers in many African countries. Equally impressive, South Korea evolved from a war-ravaged, aid-dependent, country to a full-fledged member of the Organization of Economic Cooperation and Development (OECD), with one of the highest per capita incomes in the world, in a matter of decades. It showed that start conditions, while important, are not destiny.

The rest of the chapter proceeds as follows: Section 2.2 looks at the issue of replication, and whether it is worthwhile to seek out the original blueprint of the developmental state models to be successful. Section 2.3 looks at the intriguing question of whether the type of rapid development witnessed in South Korea, and other East Asian countries could be initiated under a democratic dispensation. Sections 2.4–2.7 discuss more pointedly the relevance of the developmental state framework for African countries.

2.2 The replication question

In recent decades, East Asian economies, and more recently China, have become important reference points for African countries (Box 2.1). They pursued

heterodox policies for decades, notably "governing" the market (or giving domestic firms a "helping hand"), which did not curtail their growth rates—they
remained among the fastest growing areas in the world. The focus on self-
determination and ability to shape the political institutions according to the
needs of the country have also been important attractions. Whether the rapid
development witnessed in East Asian can be replicated by other regions of the
world is one of the more intriguing questions of the post-WWII years (Cheng,
Haggard and Kang, 1998; Kohli, 1994; Levi-Faur, 1998).

There are a tripartite set of factors that have come to influence the evolution
of the developmental state experience and the chances of replication. First, initial conditions and structural enablers or impediments to development for the
country in question matter a great deal. The South Africa Team (2015) argues,
for example, that if South Korea had had to contend with entrenched mineral
(and land) rights issues, such as those of South Africa, during its epoch-making
land reform of the 1950s, its eventual development path could have been quite
different from what we know today.

Second, and closely related to the first, is the global environment in which
countries operate, which could be supportive or adverse. The opening up of the
global markets and expansion of trade (under the General Agreement on Tariffs
and Trade (GATT)), during the parallel and formative years of South Korea's
economic development, is sometimes referred to as being (and feeling) lucky.[2]
This is because most developing countries are "small" and cannot individually
influence the global environment.[3]

Third, while countries take their initial conditions and geography as given,
they have much more influence and control on domestic policy factors, such as
the quality of economic policies and institutional capacities for strategy formulation, implementation, and follow-up. This also refers to the quality of national
leadership, including the "malleability" of institutions and the extent to which
social and political action can be expressed (Chang, 2002; Evans, 1989, 1998).
The importance of a robust institutional framework for an aspiring developmental state cannot be overstated.

However, the path to a developmental state is not cast in stone. It is noteworthy that economic transformation started happening in South Korea in the
1960s while it was under military dictatorship (as was the case in Brazil, another example of a developmental state, at the time)[4]. In China, on the other
hand, the Communist Party spearheaded the country's growth miracle, which
spanned several generations of break-neck growth. India, another growth miracle in its own right, was also undergoing rapid transformation despite its vast
and non-converging and even confrontational array of political parties, administrations, and social segments.

Also important to highlight is the fact that geo-political adversity helped focus
the minds of policymakers in East Asia (notably, the military standoff between
South Korea and North Korea).[5] The challenges of delivering payoffs to key constituencies under conditions of extreme regional insecurity and severe resource
constraints partly explain the impressive policy focus and performance of South

Korea and Taiwan, for example. On the other hand, "systemic vulnerability" was less severe in Indonesia, Malaysia, The Philippines, and Thailand and the behavior of the ruling elites more relaxed. They faced no great pressure to build domestic political coalitions that would deliver prosperity under peaceful conditions to retain power. In retrospect, they, like some African countries, had much less ambition in investing in state-building efforts and the pursuit of the developmental state model discussed above (Booth, 1999; Kim, 2005; Vu, 2007).

In a rapidly expanding literature, there have been dissenting views with respect to the applicability of the developmental state model outside of East Asia (Box 2.1).[6] Moreover, Mollaer (2016) has pointed out that the model portrays a state which is quite sanitized from interest group influence i.e. domestic politics. Economic development is conflict–ridden, and emerging state structures can only be a "bargain" deriving from a societal process of give and take.

The extent to which African countries could emulate the developmental states of East Asia, especially their focus on the long term and ability to mobilize the populations, remains an open question. Meyns and Musamba (2010) have argued that while the examples from East Asia are attractive, many aspects of their experience cannot be replicated in Africa not only for reasons of time and space but also because in the absence of state capacity and commitment, the transfer of institutions is problematic. Still, the fact that East Asia's development has excited a comparative debate on Africa's development prospects is not at all a bad thing.

Box 2.1: Not as incredible as they sound? Dissenting views on the East Asian developmental states

Several researchers have criticized the "overdrive" that often accompanies discussions of how development happened in East Asia, as it focuses almost exclusively on the perceptibly impressive results and much less on the process—including the political economy of development. This Box is a rendition of some of those critical arguments, drawing on the country case studies.

The incredibility of "imbedded but autonomous." The first criticism, also voiced in the main text, is that the model treats the state bureaucracy as a neutral arbitrator. The model posits that the Weberian bureaucracy that manages the developmental state is socially embedded but apolitical in its construct. This allows it to pursue "a self-evident national interest." In practical terms, how can taxpayer money be expended for the creation of such an aloof institution? What are its social-economic underpinnings and those of the state it represents? Can the state realistically operate independently of the social structures of the country and the implied conflicts between interest groups?

Importance of including the external sphere. While the developmental state model focuses on institutional arrangements at the domestic level, especially the importance of disciplined leadership and how the pilot agency shepherds the process, ignoring the specific international conditions that facilitated the East Asian "miracle" leads to erroneous conclusions. The injection of sizeable amounts of American money into Japan, Taiwan, and South Korea was crucial in setting up the region for growth. It helped the economies to recover from the effects of WWII and those of the Korean war and to form the all-important flying gees phenomenon that differentiated the region from others (Kasahara, 2013). For example, during 1946–1978, South Korea received US$6 billion in US aid compared to US$6.89 billion for all of Africa and US$14.8 billion for Latin America during a period of 32 years.

A case for recognizing failed attempts. The developmental state model is based almost exclusively on successful cases, disregarding those where genuine efforts and commitments had been derailed by exogenous factors (i.e. "failed" developmental states). In the 1960s and 1970s, many African states belonged to this group. They had embarked on strategies that could be classified as developmental i.e. enthused a developmentalist ideology (e.g. Kenneth Kaunda's "Humanism") and tried to create the requisite technical and administrative state capacity. External shocks in the form of rising oil prices, falling prices for domestic exports, and rising indebtedness in efforts to offset economic downturns eventually disrupted their developmental projects. They then embarked on structural adjustment policies financed by the IMF and World Bank—putting paid to any hopes of emulating East Asia for more than two decades. It can be argued that overcoming economic adversity is the essence of the designation "developmental state."

Source: Zambia Team (2017), Arrighi (2002, 2008), Mkandawire (2001), Pempel (1999), and Wade (1992).

2.3 Democracy in the developmental state

Democracy in the Developmental State. Although the character of political leadership in East Asia varied a great deal among countries, few were outright democracies in the 1960s and 1970s. For several of them, the formative stages of the developmental state took shape under the iron fist of military dictatorship, with severe constraints on human rights and freedom of speech and association. Free labor unions and related activities were not encouraged in much of the region at the time. For much of that period, South Korea was a repressive military dictatorship, while in Singapore, political freedoms were restricted (Haggard, 1990; Wade, 1990).

This association of the initial phases of the developmental state with authoritarian political tendencies has made African researchers and policymakers wonder whether an African state can be developmental and democratic (in the Western sense) at the same time or whether it must, of necessity, follow East Asia's examples, where economic development and affluence preceded democracy. Mkandawire (2001) points out, however, that Mauritius and Botswana, the two African countries most often included among developmental states, are democracies and that it is possible to attain the main results of a developmental state without necessarily carrying the authoritarian baggage (Hillbom, 2012; Kanyenze et al., 2017; Nigeria Team, 2017).

Still, the idea of a "democratic developmental state," which enthused Meles Zenawi (2006), Ethiopia's late Prime Minister, left many researchers wondering whether it was applicable, especially when championed by an autocratic leader (Clapham, 2018; Woldegiyorgis, 2014). While Ethiopia's above-average economic performance over the past 25 years is widely acknowledged, its record on civil rights and the promotion of democracy has been criticized in the past decade, not least by the African Peer Review Mechanism (APRM, 2011).

It is noteworthy that South Africa, perhaps the continent's most advanced economy today, has explicitly committed to becoming a democratic developmental state, driven by the understanding that economic transformation must mean something for the people (South Africa Team, 2015)[7] i.e. "to build the capabilities of people to improve their incomes, while intervening to correct historical inequalities." Accordingly, the South African state will seek to "unite the country around a common program" and enable "citizens to be active in their own development." Above all, it will discourage the "sit back and the state will deliver" mentality (Republic of South Africa, 2012).

In discussing the plausibility of the developmental state in South Africa, Kuye and Ajam (2012) note that while the developmentalist language has permeated government statements and those of the ruling party, the ANC, the South African state lacks the institutional structures and bureaucratic discipline to go beyond an impressionistic rendering of what is required to implement the model. Sibiya (2019) has expressed the view, common among the country's intelligentsia, that South Africa's developmental state is a "dream deferred."

2.4 Relevance of the developmental state model for Africa

From the point of view of African governments, the most attractive features of the developmental state model are the absence of ex ante policy prescription and the flexibility inherent in drawing from a menu of indeterminate approaches. This strategic ambivalence allows countries to borrow from what has worked in other places, adjusting accordingly to suit their political and resource constraints. Thus, Ezema and Ogujiuba (2012) have argued that the economic development of late starters such as Nigeria will critically depend on how successful they are in choosing and assimilating key lessons and innovations from the experiences of others.

The South Africa Team (2015) notes that the ideas behind the developmental state have had an appeal that extends beyond East Asia and Latin America. Post-WWII Europe produced several successful developmental states, with the US's Marshall Plan for rebuilding Europe providing an early blueprint of the thinking that pervades the developmental state model today. For example, Loriaux (1999) argues that 1950s France had a striking resemblance to Japan when it came to the bricks and mortar of the developmental state: "It was characterized by the preponderance of a certain kind of actor, pursuing a certain kind of ambition, and employing a certain kind of power." The Nordic model, based on a tripartite agreement between the state, employees, and labor unions (also known as the solidarity model), drove development in the Nordic states of Denmark, Sweden, and Norway (Bigsten, 2003). The idea of a social compact for development is as much a Nordic model concept as that of the developmental state.

According to Lazonick (2011), even the US demonstrates developmental state features. Technical breakthroughs of the last century and a half derived from targeted public investment in physical infrastructure and human capital: railroads, mainly through the government giving land concessions to rail companies; creation of land grant universities across the US (Cornell, MIT, Purdue etc.) and encouraging them to embark on mechanical, as opposed to liberal arts, education; agricultural stations that undertook seed multiplication and related research activities, helping to raise agricultural productivity across the nation's grain belt; the growth of the aviation industry as part of the military-industrial complex; jet engines; the GI bill that created a large college-educated labor force post-WWII; the building of the interstate highway in the 1950s and 1960s that connected the country, raised labor mobility, and reduced the cost of doing business; support to computer and ICT technologies; and support to research in life sciences. What was also significant, and something that South Korea mimicked decades later, the US government pointedly allowed the private sector to exploit the various platforms for profit without surcharge.

Other examples that exhibited the making of the developmental state included smaller economies like Finland, at Europe's periphery, where government support helped to herald the growth of ICT, which would emerge in the form of the globally renowned brand of Nokia, and Austria, at Europe's center, where the role of the state was instrumental in mobilizing society behind reconstruction and development after WWII (Vartiainen, 1999). More recently, Brazil cobbled together a remarkable developmental state under democratic conditions during the rule of the Workers' Party (PT). The experience of China adds yet another dimension to the state's role in development (Mabasa and Mqolombo, 2016). In Africa, Botswana and Mauritius were able to effectively use the state to stimulate high-growth rates, boost trade, and reduce poverty (Carroll and Carroll, 1997). More recently, Rwanda has used developmental state techniques to enhance the reputation of its bureaucracy and boost its capacity to set and meet development deadlines, though from a noticeably low physical and human capital point of departure (South Korea Team, 2017).

Although the East Asian developmental states developed under more favorable international trade conditions than available now for African countries, their example is instructive because they were proactive in seeking opportunities from the beginning (Bagchi, 2000; Beeson, 2009; Pempel, 1999). It is clear, in retrospect, that the East Asian countries not only pursued a pragmatic approach to industrialization and hence benefitted from an expanding global economy, but also leveraged their US links better than many other countries, including Latin America and even Europe. In the end, South Korea, and its neighbors, built market-based economies, pursuing what has been characterized by Wade (1990) as "governing the market," while resisting policy impositions from international lending agencies.

Researchers like to refer to developmental state "potentiality" or to "de facto" developmental states to describe efforts (albeit in early stages) by African countries to pursue the developmental state path of the East Asian economies more systematically (Dadzie, 2013; Mbabazi and Taylor, 2005). They argue that while some African countries display developmental state features, the factors that will influence 21st century developmental states will be quite different from those that confronted the first generation, 65 years ago (Zambia Team, 2017).[8] Mkandawire (2001) has argued that assessments of developmental states should include the content and quality of their policies and strategic efforts and not just the outcomes. In this reasoning, states could be acknowledged as developmental (i.e. are developmentalist in intent) even if they fail to deliver in practice, owing to exogeneous factors (Box 2.1). This more inclusive approach, i.e. which acknowledges African efforts, would eliminate the sense of determinism (and regional bias) that pervades the current discourse on developmental states (Shaw, 2004).

As for any other model of economic development, the concept of developmental state has encountered considerable criticism. Moreover, since developing the country is the principal role of the state, researchers see a tautology in the term "developmental state" (Amsden, 1994). The use of the word "development" has been taken to task as it is context-specific and sometimes fails to account for some of the factors that are key to human progress (Ake, 1981).[9]

2.5 Africa's search for sustained development

During the 1960s, African policymakers everywhere pushed for the ownership of the "commanding heights" and the promotion of national champions, such as national airlines, railways, development banks, and insurance companies (Hydén, 1983; Mkandawire, 1999, 2010; Republic of Kenya, 1965). A key argument at the time was that public sector support and direct involvement were vital for the promotion of capital accumulation and technological change in early phases of economic development. Leaders that sought a more capitalist-oriented approach, favoring the private sector, such as Félix Houphouët-Boigny of Côte d'Ivoire and Jomo Kenyatta of Kenya, were derided in the politically charged atmosphere of the time as sellouts.[10]

Uniquely for a region often ridiculed for lacking strategic coherence, Africa's development challenges and search for transformation have attracted frequent intervention at the continental level. In 1980, the Organization of African Unity (OAU)[11] launched the Lagos Plan of Action, a policy blueprint for Africa's economic self-sufficiency and an alternative to aid dependence and economic reform measures dictated by institutions outside Africa. The Plan of Action had many elements that would fit directly into the developmental state model, including a framework for state-supported industrialization and emphasis on domestic resource mobilization and on developing managerial and technical capacities at the national level. Owing to lack of resources and weak implementation, however, the ambitious program had little real impact on African development in subsequent decades.

While South Korea and its neighbors were undergoing rapid growth and improvements in social welfare, many African countries, following a brief post-independence boom in the 1960s, were experiencing slow and halting growth. Researchers referred to Africa's long period of negative per capita growth from the late-1970s to the 1990s as its "growth tragedy" and the period as "lost decades." Although the poor performance was blamed variously on geography, the disease burden, paucity of social capital, ethnic fractionalization, and conflict, policy-related shortcomings such as too low saving, ineffective planning, corruption and cronyism, and a rampant skills deficit were also significant (Collier and Gunning, 1999; Dixit, 2006; Easterly and Levine, 1997; Kayizzi-Mugerwa, 2003). However, the adverse international political economy of the period, including odious foreign debts and a sharply increasing illicit flow of funds out of Africa, aggravated the economic adversity (Kasekende, Ndikumana and Brixiova, 2010).

During the era of external shocks and structural adjustment policies in the 1980s and 1990s, African governments ceded economic analyses and policy design to the international agencies, such as the IMF and the World Bank, and bilateral donors (Eurodad, 2006; Ezema and Ogujiuba, 2012). The latter assumed the policy waterfront, so to speak—policy analysis, solution prescription, project financing, and monitoring and assessing of progress (Kayizzi-Mugerwa, 1998, 2019). Often, the lenders' medium to long-term strategies for countries had more policy impact than national development plans. Since, in contrast to Africa, many other developing regions, notably East Asia, were doing much better at identifying and implementing policies for their economic transformation, a lively debate flourished in the 1990s, onward, on Africa's "exceptionalism" a reference to the continent's (especially Sub-Saharan Africa's) institutional and socio-economic weakness.[12]

In October 2001, the New Partnership for Africa's Development (NEPAD) was launched, with active South African involvement, in response to changing global conditions and Africa's growth surge. In contrast to the Lagos Plan of Action, NEPAD did not seek to pursue economic self-sufficiency nor policy autonomy for the continent. Instead, the emphasis was on establishing beneficial partnerships for the implementation of an African-designed and owned framework for economic development—to attract investment for infrastructure development and industrialization.

The strategy document "Africa 2063—the Africa We Want"[13] (African Union Commission, 2014), presented to African leaders in Addis Ababa in 2014, best encapsulates the developmental state vision of African countries. First, it appealed to a reversion to the Pan African vision of "an integrated, prosperous and peaceful Africa, driven by its own citizens and representing a dynamic force in the global arena." Second, it presented a set of critical enablers for Africa's transformation: Africa must own its reforms as well as mobilize populations around them; generate its own resources to finance development, as opposed to depending on donors; and insist on accountable leadership and responsive institutions. Aware that these themes were not new and had been underlined in previous continental policy initiatives, Africa 2063 underlined the importance of "changed attitudes and mindset" of both the leaders and the population.

2.6 Africa's brightening visions

In recent years, some African countries have responded to the policy overtures mentioned above, as well as the UN-led development goals,[14] by setting up ambitious national visions and development plans of their own. For example, Kenya's Vision 2030 (Republic of Kenya, 2007) projects a country that will be able to provide a high quality of life for all its citizens by 2030, while Uganda's Vision 2040 (Republic of Uganda, 2013) sees the country transforming from a peasant into a modern economy, with a high level of technological sophistication, within a generation. Nigeria's Vision 2020 (Federal Republic of Nigeria, 2006) seeks to attain the number one position in Africa in attracting FDI, tourists, and business travelers. Malawi's Vision statement (Republic of Malawi, 1998) mentions the importance of establishing a "technologically-driven" economy, as opposed to dependence on peasant-driven agriculture, and that of food security and nutrition and a fair and equitable distribution of income. Cameroon's Vision 2035 (Cameroon Team, 2017; Republic of Cameroon, 2009) projects a newly industrializing country powered by its natural resources and prospering in national diversity, while Zambia's Vision 2030 (Republic of Zambia, 2006; Zambia Team, 2017) expects the country to reach middle-income status by 2025. On the other hand, Mozambique saw Agenda 2025, at its launch in 2003 (Republic of Mozambique, 2003), following decades of civil strife, as the principal means for forging national unity and building an "enterprising and continuously successful" country.

From the beginning of 2000s and onward, African economies began to show improvements in economic performance, thanks to commodity booms, improvements in policy management, and expanding domestic aggregate demand. Consequently, the rate of domestic and foreign investment rose sharply, targeting areas key to preserving the growth momentum, such as manufacturing, transport and energy infrastructure, mining, oil and other natural resources, and modern agriculture. This raised optimism all around, mostly among leaders and technocrats, but increasingly amongst the population.

In an overview of regional performance, the African Development Bank (2015) estimated that during this period, half of the ten fastest growing economies in the world, averaging growth rates of above 7%, were African. Analysts argued, pointing at the well-distributed growth numbers covering the various regions of the continent, that Africa was well on its way to becoming a global growth pole in its own right.[15]

Despite the turnaround, there were variances in performance at the national level, in cases owing to prolonged inclement weather and civil conflict. Table 2.1 provides a broad-brush picture of recent African economic performance, with GDP per capita for each country in 2014[16] correlated with its average growth rate during 2006–2014. The results show that Africa's relatively rich countries i.e. with "very high" or "high" GDP per capita levels were confined to the northern and southern tips of the continent i.e. Algeria, Botswana, Egypt, Morocco, South Africa, and Namibia or were oil exporters i.e. Angola, Equatorial Guinea, Gabon, and Nigeria. None of the countries was performing extraordinarily well in terms of growth to provide the "flying gees" impact mentioned earlier in the case of East Asian countries on their region.

The poorer African countries (in terms of GDP) grew faster than their richer neighbors during 2006–2014, enabling some catchup, thanks to good economic policies, new resource discoveries, and the end of civil wars. Table 2.1 shows that growth was on average above 5% for countries with "low" to "very low" GDP per capita levels in 2014 (Burkina Faso, Democratic Republic of the Congo, Kenya, Liberia, Tanzania, Uganda). It is significant that the "very high" growth rates were achieved by two groups of countries: those with limited natural resource endowments such as Ethiopia, Mozambique (i.e. before gas exploitation), Rwanda, and Sierra-Leone (whose mineral wealth is unexploited) and those with large oil and mineral endowments: Angola, Ghana, and Zambia. What Table 2.1 illustrates above all is that high and sustained levels of growth were possible, even for Africa's low-income countries, through improvements in government policies and the business environment.

Table 2.1 Correlating African Countries' GDP per Capita (2014) to Average Growth Rates (2006–2014)[a]

GDP per Capita			Average Growth (%)		
Very high	–	Equatorial Guinea, Libya, Algeria, **South Africa**, Tunisia	Gabon, Mauritius, Botswana, Egypt, Namibia	Seychelles	–

GDP per Capita			Average Growth (%)		
High	–	Swaziland	Morocco, Cabo Verde, Congo Republic, Sudan	**Nigeria**	Angola, Ghana, **Zambia**
Medium	–	Senegal	**Côte d'Ivoire**, Mauritania, Djibouti, **Cameroon**, Lesotho, Chad	Sao Tome and Principe, Kenya	–
Low	Eritrea	Zimbabwe, Gambia, Comoros, Guinea Bissau, Madagascar, Guinea	Benin, Mali, Togo	Tanzania, Burkina Faso, Uganda	Rwanda, Ethiopia, Sierra-Leone, Mozambique
Very low	Central African Republic	–	Burundi	Niger, Liberia, Malawi, Democratic Republic of Congo	–
	Very low	Low	Medium	High	Very high

GDP per Capita (in PPP, US$ 2014)		Average Growth (2006–2014 in %)	
Very high	Above $10,000	Very high	Above 7.0%
High	$4,000–$10,000	High	5–7%
Medium	$2,000–$4,000	Medium	4–5%
Low	$1,000–$2,000	Low	2–4%
Very low	Below $1000	Very low	Below 2%

[a]Note: African case study countries are in bold. Note that the designations in the legend are only applicable to information in the table.

Source: African Development Bank (2015).

2.7 Conclusion

The developmental state experience, as depicted by South Korea, and its East Asian counterparts, is relevant for Africa because it does not portray flawless states, with uncontested mandates and enamored populations from the outset—such accoutrements would have made it seem like a special case and difficult to learn from (Kim, 1997). Instead, South Korea and its neighbors confronted critical development issues during their formative years and development trajectories that are well known to African countries, including serious economic policy weakness, external dependence, corruption, autocratic rule, and even organizational chaos in the public sector (Myrdal, 1968).[17] In some cases, the political and structural challenges were so deep-seated as to threaten progress altogether.

In recent years, African countries have responded to the development challenges by developing their own vision statements, most of them targeted at raising economic growth and reaching middle income status within a generation, while others have underlined the importance of achieving full-fledged democracy as a prelude to sustainable development. Moreover, in many African countries, a social compact for development between the government, the private sector, and civil society, that was a pillar for the developmental states of East Asia, is beginning to coalesce—no longer driven by donor conditionality but as part of the new development realities on the continent.

A lesson from the South Korean experience that seems relevant for many African countries today is that paucity of resources, imperfect institutional structures, social strife, and economic adversity are not excuses for policy diffidence and inaction. A political leadership, supported by a dedicated bureaucratic structure and an animated population, that is able to articulate a credible development vision has a good chance of turning around economic performance and sustaining the country's growth and transformation. In other words, entrenched economic hardship is not destiny. South Korea's example also shows that despite sometimes dramatic changes in the country's leadership, the sense of institutional continuity and focus on the essentials of economic development never dissipated i.e. national development had become the country's political ethos, and regimes were measured accordingly.

Notes

1 This is the same admonition as asking countries to play catchup. However, for low-income countries, the resources required to undertake such technological adjustments can be prohibitive, and "clever" resource mobilization strategies are required. See also Timmer (1998) on Taiwan and the review by Castel-Branco (1996).
2 However, luck is reputedly evenly distributed in the population: some take advantage of it, while others do not.
3 Recent big developing country exceptions being China and India.
4 The Zambia Team (2017) has noted for example that during the 1960s, the general assessment of South Korea was that it was a "hopeless case" (Adelman, 2000, 2007). Poverty was widespread and over 60% of the population lived below the absolute poverty level. Per capita income in 1962 was only US$105 (about US$800 today, allowing for inflation).
5 For instance, with respect to land reform and rural development.
6 The Confucian ethic is a running theme throughout the economic and social relations of the region (Weiming, 2000).
7 It is probably the only African country that has defined itself explicitly as such and one of the few that could harness the resources to implement it if the politics were right. This is laid out in the National Development Plan 2030 (Republic of South Africa,

2012), which also underlines decentralization and fiscal federalism as key strategies. See also South Africa Team (2015).
8 More recently, Ethiopia and Rwanda (Booth and Golooba-Mutebi, 2012; Kelsall, 2011; Kelsall and Booth, 2010) have been identified as patrimonial developmental states, where the dynamics revolve around a strong leader. Ovadia (2016) has discussed development challenges and options in a set of African countries that he calls "petro-developmental states."
9 See, for example, the essays edited by Monga and Lin (2015) where Africa's economic development and its implications for the economics discipline are discussed.
10 Referred to in leftist and radical circles of the time as neocolonialists and imperialist lackeys (Côte d'Ivoire Team, 2017).
11 The OAU, established in 1963, became the African Union (AU) in 2002.
12 The Economist Magazine (2000) referred to the Africa of the 1990s as the "hopeless continent."
13 The title "Africa 2063" is a play on the fact that the OAU was launched in 1963. It projects where Africa would be 100 years later.
14 The Millennium Development Goals (MDGs) and Sustainable Development Goals (SDGs) have greatly influenced the positions taken by African governments on African development. SGDs contain a considerable amount of developmentalist language.
15 Mckinsey, the global consultancy was categorical in its enthusiasm (see its report from 2010), referring to the leading African economies as "lions on the move." Ultimately, African growth declined, in tandem with that of the global economy. However, an important point was made by the growth boom experience: Africa would no longer be the growth laggard of the world.
16 Expressed in US$ purchasing power parity.
17 South Korean leaders escaped path dependence because, in contrast to Myrdal's Asian Drama, they were able to foresee the consequences of their predicament and created ideas to forestall them.

References

Adelman, I. (2000) 'Fifty Years of Economic Development: What Have We Learned?' Paper presented at the *Annual World Bank Conference on Economic Development*, Paris, June.
Adelman, I. (2007) 'Moving Out of Aid Dependence: Lessons from the South Korean Experience,' *Lecture Notes*, University of California: Berkeley.
African Development Bank (2015) *African Economic Outlook, 2015. Regional and Spatial Inclusion*, AfDB: Abidjan.
African Peer Review Mechanism (APRM) (2011) *Country Review Report. Federal Democratic Republic of Ethiopia*, African Union Commission: Addis Ababa.
African Union Commission (2014) *Agenda 2063. The Africa We Want*, African Union Commission: Addis Ababa.
Ake, C. (1981) *A Political Economy of Africa*, Longman: New York.
Amsden, A. (1994) 'Why Isn't the Whole World Experimenting with the East Asian Model to Develop?' *World Development* 22(4):627–633.
Arrighi, G. (2002) 'The African Crisis: World Systemic and Regional Aspects,' *New Left Review* 15(May–June):5–38.
Arrighi, G. (2008) 'Historical Perspectives on States, Markets and Capitalism, East and West,' *The Asian-Pacific Journal* 6(1):1–25.
Bagchi, A. (2000) 'The Past and Future of the Developmental State,' *Journal of World Systems Research* 11(2):398–442.

Beeson, M. (2009) 'Developmental States in East Asia: A Comparison of the Japanese and Chinese Experiences,' *Asian Perspective* 33(2):5–39.

Bigsten, A. (2003) 'Relevance of the Nordic Model for African Development,' in S. Kayizzi-Mugerwa (ed.), *Reforming Africa's Institutions. Ownership, Incentives and Capabilities*, 322–341, United Nations University Press: Tokyo and New York.

Booth, A. (1999) 'Initial Conditions and Miraculous Growth: Why Is South East Asia Different from Taiwan and South Korea?' *World Development* 27(2):301–321.

Booth, D. and Golooba-Mutebi, F. (2012) 'Development Patrimonialism? The Case of Rwanda,' *African Affairs* 111(444):379–403.

Cameroon Team (2017) «Etude Sur L'Economie du Cameroun. La Politique de Développement dans la Pratique Enseignements Tires de L'Expérience de Développement de la Corée du Sud» Report to the African Development Bank on the *Developmental State in Africa, Lessons from South Korea Project*, Université de Yaoundé II : Yaoundé.

Carroll, B. and Carroll, T. (1997) 'State and Ethnicity in Botswana and Mauritius: A Democratic Route to Development?' *Journal of Development Studies* 33(4):464–486.

Castel-Branco, C. (1996) 'What Are the Major Lessons from East Asian Development Experience?': www.iese.ac.mz.

Chang, H. (2002) 'Breaking the Mould: An Institutional Political Economy Alternative to the Neo-liberal Theory of the Market and the State,' *Cambridge Journal of Economics* 26(5):539–559.

Cheng, T., Haggard, S. and Kang, D. (1998) 'Institutions and Growth in Korea and Taiwan: Bureaucracy,' *Journal of Development Studies* 35(6):87–111.

Clapham, C. (2018) 'The Ethiopian Developmental State,' *Third World Quarterly* 39(6):1151–1165.

Collier, P. and Gunning, W. (1999) 'Explaining Africa's Economic Performance,' *Journal of Economic Literature* 37(1):64–111.

Côte d'Ivoire Team (2017) «Etude Sur L'Economie Ivorienne. La Politique de Développement dans la Pratique Enseignements Tires de L'Expérience de Développement de la Corée du Sud» Report to the African Development Bank on the *Developmental State in Africa, Lessons from South Korea Project*, Le Centre Ivoirien de Recherches Economiques et Sociales (CIRES): Abidjan.

Daddi, T. (2013) 'The Emergence of Democratic Developmental States in Africa: The Ethiopian Experience,' *SSRN Electronic Journal* 1(1):1–31.

Dadzie, R. (2013) 'Economic Development and the Developmental State,' *Journal of Developing Societies* 29(2):123–154.

Dixit, A. (2006) *Predatory States and Failing States: An Agency Perspective*, Center for Economic Policy Studies, Princeton University: Princeton.

Easterly, W. and Levine, R. (1997) 'Africa's Growth Tragedy: Policies and Ethnic Divisions,' *Quarterly Journal of Economics* 112(4):1203–1250.

Eurodad (2006) World Bank and IMF Conditionality: A Development Injustice,' *Eurodad Report* Eurodad: Brussels.

Evans, P. (1989) 'Predatory, Developmental, and Other Apparatuses: A Comparative Political Economy Perspective on the Third World State,' *Sociological Forum* 4(4):561–587.

Evans, P. (1998) 'Transferable Lessons? Re-Examining the Institutional Prerequisites of East Asian Economic Policies,' *Journal of Development Studies* 34(6):66–86.

Ezema, B. and Ogujiuba, K. (2012) 'The Developmental State Debate: Where Is Nigeria?' *Journal of Sustainable Development* 5(1):100–113.

Federal Republic of Nigeria (2006) *Vision 2020*, Abuja.

Haggard, S. (1990) *Pathways from the Periphery: The Politics of Growth in the Newly Industrialised Countries*, Cornell University Press: Ithaca.

Hillbom, E. (2012) 'Botswana: A Development-Oriented Gate Keeping State,' *African Affairs* 111(442):67–89.

Hydén (1983) *Beyond Ujamaa in Tanzania. Underdevelopment and an Uncaptured Peasantry*, University of California: Los Angeles and Heinemann: London.

Kanyenze, G., Jauch, H., Kanengoni, A., Madzwamuse, M. and Muchena, D. (eds.) (2017) *Towards Democratic Developmental States in Southern Africa*, Weaver Press: Harare.

Kasahara, S. (2013) 'The Asian Developmental State and the Flying Geese Paradigm,' *Discussion Papers*, 213, United Nations Conference on Trade and Development: Geneva.

Kasekende, L., Ndikumana, L. and Brixiova, Z. (2010) 'Africa's Counter-cyclical Responses to the Crisis,' *Journal of Globalization and Development* 1(1): Article 16, January.

Kayizzi-Mugerwa, S. (1998) 'Africa and the Donor Community: From Conditionality to Partnership,' *Journal of International Development* 10(2):219–225.

Kayizzi-Mugerwa, S. (ed.) (2003) *Reforming Africa's Institutions. Ownership, Incentives and Capabilities*, United Nations University Press: Tokyo and New York.

Kayizzi-Mugerwa, S. (2019) 'On the Hazards of an Externally Driven Research Agenda: How Structural Adjustment Policy Concerns Overshadowed Africa's Academic Discourse for a Generation,' Paper Presented at a Cornell/SAIPAR Summer Conference on *Africa's Grand Challenges: The Role of Research and Education Systems*, Institute for African Development, Cornell University: Ithaca, and Southern African Institute for Policy Analysis and Research: Lusaka.

Kelsall, T. (2011) 'Developmental Patrimonialism? Rethinking Business and Politics in Africa,' *ODI Policy Brief* (2): June.

Kelsall, T. and Booth, D. (2010) Developmental Patrimonialism? Questioning the Orthodoxy on Political Governance and Economic Progress in Africa,' *ODI Working Paper* (9): July.

Kim, C. (2005) 'An Industrial Development Strategy for Indonesia: Lessons from the South Korean Experience,' *Journal of the Asia Pacific Economy* 10(3):312–338.

Kim, E. (1997) *Big Business, Strong State: Collusion and Conflict in South Korea Development, 1960–1990*, State University of New York Press: Albany.

Kohli, A. (1994) 'Where Do High Growth Political Economies Come From? The Japanese Lineage of Korea's 'Developmental State',' *World Development* 22(9):1269–1293.

Kuye, J. and Ajam, T. (2012) 'The South African Developmental State Debate. Leadership, Governance and a Dialogue in Public Sector Finance,' *African Journal of Public Affairs* 5(2):48–67.

Lazonick, W. (2011) 'Nine Government Investments that Made US an Industrial Economic Leader,' *Huffington Post*, November 08, New York.

Levi-Faur, D. (1998) 'The Developmental State: Israel, South Korea, and Taiwan Compared,' *Studies in Comparative International Development* 33(1):65–93.

Loriaux, M. (1999) 'The French Developmental State as Myth and Moral Ambition,' in M. Woo-Cumings (ed.), *The Developmental State*, 235–275, Cornell University Press: Ithaca.

Mabasa, K. and Mqolomba, Z. (2016) 'Revisiting China's Developmental State: Lessons from Africa,' *Strategic Review for Southern Africa* 38(1):69–84.

Mbabazi, P. and Taylor, I. (2005) *The Potentiality of 'Developmental States' in Africa: Botswana and Uganda Compared*, Council for the Development of Social Science Research in Africa (CODESRIA): Dakar.

McKinsey (2010) *Lions on the Move: The Progress and Potential of African Economies*, McKinsey and Company: London and New York.

Meyns, P. and Musamba, C. (2010) 'The Developmental State in Africa: Problems and Prospects,' *INEF Report 101*, Institute for Development and Peace, University of Duisburg: Essen.

Mkandawire, T. (1999) 'The Political Economy of Financial Reform in Africa,' *Journal of International Development* 11(3):321–342.

Mkandawire, T. (2001) 'Thinking about Developmental States in Africa,' *Cambridge Journal of Economics* 25(3):289–313.

Mkandawire, T. (2010) 'On Tax Efforts and Colonial Heritage in Africa,' *Journal of Development Studies* 46(10):1647–1669.

Mollaer, Ö. (2016) 'Developmental State: A Theoretical and Methodological Critique,' *Bulletin of Economic Theory and Analysis* 1(1):1–12.

Monga, C. and Lin, J. (2015) *The Oxford Handbook of Africa and Economics*, Volumes 1&2, Oxford University Press: Oxford.

Myrdal, G. (1968) *Asian Drama*, Allen Lane and The Penguin Press: London.

Nigeria Team (2017) 'Towards Developmental State in Nigeria: Lessons from Korea,' Report to the African Development Bank on the *Developmental State in Africa, Lessons from South Korea Project*, Nigerian Economic Society: Ibadan.

Ovadia, J., (2016) *The Petro-Developmental State in Africa. Making Oil Work in Angola, Nigeria, and the Gulf of Guinea*, Hurst Publishers: London.

Pempel, T. (1999) 'The Developmental Regime in a Changing World Economy", in M. Woo-Cumings (ed.), *The Developmental State*, 137–181, Cornell University Press: Ithaca.

Republic of Cameroon (2009) *Vision 2035*, Yaoundé.

Republic of Kenya (1965) *African Socialism and its Application to Planning in Kenya*, Ministry of Finance and Economic Planning: Nairobi.

Republic of Kenya (2007) *Vision 2030*, Nairobi.

Republic of Malawi (1998) *Vision 2020*, Lilongwe.

Republic of Mozambique (2003) *Agenda 2025—The Nation's Vision and Strategy*, Maputo.

Republic of South Africa (2012) *National Development Plan, 2030*, National Planning Commission: Pretoria.

Republic of Uganda (2013) *Vision 2040*, Kampala.

Republic of Zambia (2006) *Vision 2030*, Lusaka.

Shaw, T. (2004) 'Two Africas? Two Ugandas? An African "Democratic Developmental State"? Or Another "Failed State?"' *Working Paper* 125, Research Center on Development and International Relations, Aalborg University: Aalborg.

Sibiya, A.T. (2019) 'A Development State in South Africa is a Dream Deferred?' *Daily Maverick*, January 7.

South Africa Team (2015) 'The Role of Institutions in Underpinning Inclusive Economic Growth in South Africa.' Report to the African Development Bank on the *Developmental State in Africa, Lessons from South Korea Project*, Development Policy Research Unit, School of Economics, University of Cape Town: Cape Town.

South Korea Team (2017) 'KOAFEC—Development Policy in Practice Project,' Report to the African Development Bank on the *Developmental State in Africa, Lessons from South Korea Project*, Korea Institute for International Economic Policy (KIEP): Seoul.

The Economist Magazine (2000) 'Africa—Hopeless Continent,' May 11.

Timmer, P. (1998) 'Catch Up Patterns in Newly Industrializing Countries. An International Comparison of Manufacturing Productivity in Taiwan 1961–1993,' *Research*

Memorandum GD-40, Department of Technology and Development Studies, Eindhoven University of Technology: Eindhoven.

United States Agency for International Development (2012) *Case Study. South Korea: From Aid Recipient to Donor*, USAID: Washington, DC.

Vartiainen, J. (1999) 'The Economics of Successful State Intervention in Industrial Transformation' in M. Woo-Cumings (ed.), *The Developmental State*, 200–234, Cornell University Press: Ithaca.

Vu, T. (2007) 'State Formation and the Origins of Developmental States in South Korea and Indonesia,' *Studies in Comparative International Development* 4(4):27–56

Wade, R. (1990) *Governing the Market: Economic Theory and the Role of Government in East Asian Industrialisation*, Princeton University Press: Princeton.

Wade, R. (1992) 'East Asia's Economic Success: Conflicting Paradigms, Partial Insights, Shaky Evidence,' *World Politics* 44(2):270–320.

Woldegiyorgis, A. (2014) 'The Ethiopian Development State and its Challenges,' Paper, Tempere University, Finland, available at *Social Science Research Network*: https://papers.ssrn.com.

Woo-Cumings, M. (ed.) (1999) *The Developmental State*, Cornell University Press: Ithaca.

Weiming, T. (2000) 'Implications of the Rise of "Confucian" East Asia,' *Daedulus* 129(1):195–218.

Zambia Team (2017) 'The Zambian Society and Economy: Development Policy in Practice in Comparison with South Korea.' Report to the African Development Bank on the *Developmental State in Africa, Lessons from South Korea Project*, Southern African Institute for Policy and Research (SAIPAR): Lusaka.

Zenawi, M. (2006) 'African Development: Dead Ends and New Beginnings (Preliminary Draft)': https:/mestawot.wordpress/2008/04/14/.

3 Country case study context

South Korea, Cameroon, Côte d'Ivoire, Nigeria, South Africa, and Zambia

3.1 Introduction

This chapter provides a contextual background for this comparative study of the developmental state in Africa by drawing on the development experiences of South Korea and five African countries—Cameroon, Côte d'Ivoire, Nigeria, South Africa, and Zambia—in the past several decades, focusing on issues of institutional capabilities, macroeconomic frameworks, and global context. The five African economies discussed here are individually important in their sub-regions, are well-endowed in natural resources, unlike South Korea, and are, with the exception of South Africa, which is an upper middle-income country, lower middle-income economies.[1] For governments in all five countries, the rapid development of East Asia in the past five to six decades has attracted much interest, with leaders seeking to fashion their policies on those of the developmental states—notably forward planning, implementation discipline, shared benefits, and resolute structural problem solving.

For African policymakers, the notion of self-determination is probably the most attractive aspect of the developmental state model as it suggests that the arc of economic development, including managing the market, can be bent by the purposes of the state. However, the economic foundations of the East Asian developmental states were laid principally in the 1960s and 1970s, when the world was a more parochial place, before the advent of globalization, and governments had a greater sway on domestic economies than is the case today (Rey, 2013). Hence, some researchers have argued that Africa's developmental state quest should have begun at least a half century earlier (Hayashi, 2010). The depth of the Asian Financial Crisis of the late-1990s, in the face of globalization, showed that the developmental states cannot rest on the laurels of past conquests and that some of their earlier achievements had brought with them baggage, as suggested ahead, that needed to be expunged (Fischer, 2004).

The chapter argues that while there is no formula for aspiring countries to graduate into developmental states, there are three issues worth bearing in mind: (i) developing bureaucratic capacity for managing institutional and policy change is paramount; (ii) pursuing a flexible, but market-based, approach to economic development that allows for meaningful private sector participation is an important basis for sustainability; and (iii) a national leadership that has the capacity and foresight to stake out an ambitious long-term development agenda, sustain its implementation, and maintain popular support for the chosen policy path or, more correctly, not lose direction in the face of political headwinds is the key to success.

3.2 South Korea

Class Act in the Periphery. In retrospect, there was no reason to believe that the South Korea of the 1950s would emerge to become the de facto example of how to do development in the latter half of the 20th century and beyond. The South Korean story and that of many Asian economies today is of interest to African countries because there was, in spite of the culturally tinged reconstructions of recent years, nothing at all predestined about their success. On the face of it, what the change agenda in South Korea required was far from extraordinary: institutional rigor, broad social and political commitment, and a focus on the long term. These seem both sensible and doable for many countries, even today (South Korea Team, 2017).

The difference was of course that already in the 1960s, South Korea had put these prerequisites at the center of its developmental strategy and was fully committed to them—while other aspirants, notably in Africa, were often half-hearted implementers. The geo-political factors that worked in the country's favor during the Cold War, often cited as responsible for tipping the scales in South Korea's direction, could have gone either way and, in any case, were merely the icing on the cake, not the defining movers of progress.

South Korea's forward march post-WWII began appropriately with land and associated reforms in 1950, whose goal was to raise agricultural productivity and achieve socio-economic equality, including in rural areas. Though interrupted by the Korean war (1950–1953), the agrarian reform was crucial in later years for underpinning the government's strategy of self-sufficiency in food production, as the ultimate social safety net. It also subsequently provided a basis for the country to pursue sustained industrialization efforts via basic agroindustry. The land redistribution created an egalitarian ethos that still characterizes the country's broader policy thrust today.

From the outset, the South Korean government identified an educated labor force and physical infrastructure as crucial ingredients of its development strategy to be combined in later years with the imperative of information technology. Crucially, the state used the financial aid from the United States to boost education, including erecting institutions for technical training. Moreover, primary education became compulsory in the 1950s, boosting literacy and numeracy in the 1960s and beyond. Above all, South Korea and East Asian nations bucked the trend of the late-1950s and early 1960s by relentlessly pursuing outward-looking development frameworks, characterized by an emphasis on exporting manufactures, when many other developing countries promoted inward-looking policies and self-reliance.

Making of a Developmental State. In 1961, South Korea entered the, per-haps, defining phase of its modern history when General Park Chung Hee over-threw a civilian government and embarked on far-ranging structural reforms. He became the face of government for the next two decades (he was assassinated in 1979), taking the country through crucial steps i.e. compressed economic transformation[2] on the way to becoming the developmental state that we know today. A key feature of the Park years was the keen focus on national planning. Unlike in many African countries, during this time, plans in South Korea were meticulously designed and focused on the key issues of the day. Their execution and follow up mattered for national welfare and for the prestige of the govern-ment i.e. plans were not proforma statements (Table 3.1).

Table 3.1 South Korea: Emphases of the First to Seventh Five-Year National Development Plans 1962–1996

Plan and Period	Policy Emphasis
First Five-Year Economic Development Plan (1962–1966)	• Balancing components of industrial sector: electronics for export given high priority; of secondary priority were energy, electricity production, domestic consumer goods, and fertilizers and cement (the latter as inputs for other sectors of the economy).
Second Five-Year Economic Development Plan (1967–1971)	• Rapid catch-up via import-substitution, with focus on large-scale industries: steel, machinery, and chemical.
Third Five-Year Economic Development Plan (1972–1976)	• Continued emphasis on heavy industry and chemicals, and export-orientation, ensuring self-sufficiency in industrial inputs, and generating employment outside the vicinity of the capital, Seoul.
Fourth Five-Year Economic Development Plan (1977–1981)	• Focus on raising competitiveness of the industrial sector, taking advantage of the country's low-cost, high-skill work force to produce machinery, electronics, and ships for export. Enhanced investment in power generation, including nuclear energy.
Fifth Five-Year Economic and Social Development Plan (1982–1986)	• Shift from heavy industry to technology-intensive sectors: precision machinery, electronics, and information-related. More attention devoted to building high-technology products, with high demand on the world market (precursor of cell-phone global leadership).
Sixth Five-Year Economic and Social Development Plan (1987–1991)	• Focus on industries that could compete in a liberalized regime. Systematic phasing out of targeted financial support to sectors and shifting focus to skills development and support to R&D to benefit all industries, especially small and medium-sized firms, that had been neglected thus far.
Seventh Five-Year Economic and Social Development Plan (1992–1996)	• Focus on high-technology fields: microelectronics, new materials, fine chemicals, bioengineering, optics, and aerospace. Government and industry would work together to build high-technology facilities in seven provincial cities to balance the geographical distribution of industry throughout South Korea.

Source: South Korea Team (2017), Republic of Korea (various years) and Matles and Shaw (1990).

Two issues emerged quite early in South Korea's industrial policy push of the 1960s: the need for a vast number of skilled industrial workers and the importance of putting in place a conducive environment for the development of a competitive private sector-led economy. It is also important to point out that at no time did the government lack ambition, which was, however, based on informed analyses of available alternatives and their challenges and opportunities. The first national development program (1962–1966) chose, for example, the nascent electronics sector as the target for investment and technology flows from Japan and the US and not the fertilizer, textile, cement, energy, and other consumer goods sectors, which were treated as second-order priorities.

In terms of executing the first development plan, the Korean Electronic Industries Association emerged as a powerful lobby group and protector of South Korean interests in the industry—focusing on technological mastery and sophistication. The tripartite collaboration between the private sector (i.e. the Samsung Group), the government (i.e. its creation of the Korean Telecommunications Corporation), and the research community (i.e. Korean Institute of Science and Technology) created a veritable backbone for the electronics industry in South Korea, bringing it to the global frontier within a generation and, crucially, with important spinoffs that proved beneficial to other parts of the economy i.e. the transport and logistics sectors. The construction of the machinery industry was given greater emphasis and higher priority during the second and third national development plans, 1967–1971 and 1972–1976, respectively. The building of the heavy industry area of Changwon, with 104 factories scheduled for construction, was embarked on at this time.

The fourth national development plan (1977–1981) prioritized petrochemicals, nuclear power, and shipbuilding—a typical move toward heavy engineering industry development. It also portrayed the government's first attempts at encouraging strategic partnerships between domestic and foreign firms, as had earlier been demonstrated in the case of the automobile industry, where Kia collaborated with Japanese Mazda, in a bid to garner both financing and technical knowhow (Green, 1992). Notably, the state set up joint ventures between its two energy and chemical focused SOEs, Korean Oil Corporation and Korea Pacific Chemical Corporation, and foreign companies, such as Gulf Oil. In the event, South Korea, in the absence of own oil resource endowments, was able to create extensive oil-refining capacity and to establish a full-fledged export industry in oil products.

On the other hand, the nuclear power development program was piloted by the Korean Electric Corporation, together with research institutes in the country, as well as the Korean Nuclear Engineering Services company that had been created as a special purpose vehicle for nuclear power development already in 1962. On the other hand, shipbuilding received a boost when, following the oil crises of the 1970s, the global cost structure for ship construction turned decidedly into South Korea's favor, against the Nordic countries, such as Sweden and Finland. South Korea did not shy away from seizing latecomer advantage.[3]

Deliberate and Consequential. It should be noted, at least in retrospect and in contrast with African country experience, that each step toward the

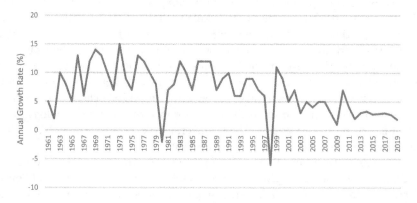

Figure 3.1 South Korea: GDP Growth, 1961–2019 (%)
Source: World Bank (various issues).

developmental state in South Korea was quite deliberate, entailing the creation of laws and statutes targeted at attaining socio-economic and rapid growth objectives i.e. nothing was left to chance. There is a whole list of laws that were promulgated during the last 60 years to create specialized agencies or to launch initiatives deemed crucial to promoting state interests. Early examples included the Law on Land Improvement (1961), Shipbuilding Encouragement Law (1962), Machinery Act (1967), Law on Rural Modernization (1970), and Law for Promotion of Overseas Resources Development (1979). Thus, where African countries formulated detailed development strategies, which they often abandoned in the face of economic adversity or regime change, South Korea crafted laws, which became part of the country's legal framework, to drive the reform process. They remained on the books until proscribed by other legislation. However, there is a school of thought that argues that such an overload of laws and regulations had regional, political, and cultural antecedents and might not be replicable or necessarily for development success (Hayashi, 2010; Wade, 2018).

In the 1990s, the government of South Korea was well aware that the new GATT measures and its OECD membership would change its way of doing business, while the breakneck growth rate of the past could not be sustained (Figure 3.1). It, thus, embarked on a deliberate but sequenced liberalization of the economy. Its first actions were targeted at boosting contestability in the banking sector by removing the incentive and subsidy superstructure that had characterized the formative years of the developmental state. The liberalization of the financial sector in the early 1990s had brought in many new players, but the reform of the regulatory oversight was incomplete. Moreover, in the more free-wheeling atmosphere that had emerged, with increased direct lending to conglomerates, banking institutions had accumulated non-performing loans. Additionally, the government had loosened some of its industrial policy tools i.e. disbandment of the EPB and was not able to effectively monitor "over investment," notably among the chaebols in the heavy industry sectors. Debt accumulation was poorly monitored as a result, contributing to the subsequent bankruptcies of several leading conglomerates, including the Kia Group, Sammi Steel, the Jinro Group, and the Hanbo Group, with economy-wide implications (Shina and Parkb, 1999).

South Korea and Asian Financial Crisis 1997–1998. The Asian Financial Crisis dealt a big blow to the South Korean economy, depleting its reserves, down to only about US$9 billion at the end of 1997,[4] while economic growth fell to –5.5% in 1998 (Figure 3.1). Given the break-neck growth of the previous decades, some people compared the impact of the financial crisis on South Korean livelihoods to that of the Korean War of the 1950s (Coe and Kim, 2002; Kwon, 1998; Lee and Rhee, 1999). The government was forced to approach the IMF (and several other lenders) for financial support, which in the end totaled some US$57 billion—the largest rescue package led by the IMF in history at the time. As in the well-known cases of African countries, it came with a list of conditionalities (Box 3.1).[5]

Box 3.1: South Korea: post-crisis structural reforms

Structural Conditionality Comes to South Korea. The IMF and the international community had offered its multi-billion support to South Korea on condition that it undertook structural reforms, notably adjusting its approach to the SOEs—quite insightful as most aspiring developmental states see state ownership of businesses as pivotal to their development ambitions. In 1998, the South Korean government embarked on the restructuring and privatization of the electricity parastatal, KEPCO, the steel giant, POSCO, and the telecom conglomerate, Korea Telecom (Lim, 2003). In early 1999, a council to regulate and monitor SOEs, headed by the Minister of Planning and Budget and comprising vice-ministers from all relevant sector ministries, experts from civil society, and academics, was created (OECD, 2000).

Reforming the Electricity Sector. In 1999, the government adopted a plan for restructuring the electricity sector to ensure reliable power supply, raise delivery efficiency, and enhance service and customer choice (Kim and Kim, 2006). In 2001, KEPCO's generation division was vertically split from its transmission and distribution divisions. The hydro-electrical and nuclear power companies were to remain state-owed, while the generation subsidiaries would be privatized (Lim, 2003). KEPCO's evidently rapid turnaround and the much-discussed power crisis in California, in 2000, where privatized power utilities had failed to take up the slack in the delivery of power to homes and businesses, restrained what had initially been an aggressive push for further privatization by the new government (Lim, 2003).

Eradicating Blind Spots. In 2007, the government introduced an Act targeted at the management of public institutions, whose goal was to enhance transparency, accountability, and participation. The goal of the government was to detect "blind spots" that could have gone undetected in the past in the aura of self-congratulation that had pervaded the years of rapid growth and high export volumes. The government uncharacteristically made a request to each SOE to draft a debt reduction strategy. Notably, KEPCO sought to lower its debt-to-equity ratio from 200% to 150% in the medium term by selling assets, lowering operational costs, and undertaking other efficiencies.

ICT Sector Reforms. The ICT industry played a major role in South Korea's recovery from the Asian Financial Crisis, contributing to between 30 and 40% of recent growth of the economy. Although the ICT Promotion Fund was set up before the Asian Financial Crisis to finance new ventures and products, skills training, and R&D (Kim, 2009), it proved useful after the crisis. Between 2000 and 2002, the government rolled out internet training and computer literacy programs to more than 10 million people, including the unemployed, pensioners, and stay-at-home-mothers (Kim, 2009). It expanded the use of e-Government projects—using locally designed and funded networks—hence boosting the country's ICT industry. The government wholly privatized Korea Telecom in 2002, which introduced an independent management model for the company, with the CEO appointed at a shareholders meeting, following the recommendation of an independent committee.

South Africa Team (2015), Kim (2009), Lim (2003), OECD (2000)

For many researchers, the Asian Financial Crisis of 1997–1998 provided something of a natural experiment—the behavior of the developmental state before and after the cataclysmic event—hence, helping to test the veracity of the developmental state model (Dittmer, 2007; Fung, 2013; Woo, 2000). The questions revolved especially around how the East Asian economies would seek to preserve their policy autonomy—especially the elite bargain that they had struck between the state and the business sector which had made rapid industrialization possible. Given that Thailand, Indonesia, and, to a lesser extent, Malaysia and Singapore were also affected, some scholars have noted that the events of the late-1990s were proof that globalization was unforgiving of nationalist foibles, industrial cherry picking, and attempts to tame the market (Ahn, 2001; Bagchi, 2000; Krugman, 1994; Makin, 1999).

The Asian Financial Crisis, critics argued, had exposed the double-edged sword of state intervention i.e. the directed loans that the government provided to targeted companies and other similarly cozy relationships made it difficult for the state to intervene effectively or to take the decisions required for the country to regain economic momentum. Thus, where there had been praise in the past for the innovation of targeted financing, critics now questioned the whole concept of socializing financial risk, which had formed the bedrock of the developmental state model in South Korea since the formative years of the 1960s. They argued that the public sector's financial support to the private sector not only had implied a soft budget constraint for the leading companies but had also imbued "a too big to fail" mentality among a sizeable number of the firms (chaebols), with attendant moral hazard, and absence of accountability and responsibility (Woo-Cumings, 1999).

Critics also expressed the view that the high rate of investment, which had reached 40% of GDP in the 1990s, notably when financial markets were demonstrating high levels of inefficiency was neither sustainable nor necessary (Fischer, 2004).[6] Given that banks had borrowed heavily internationally to finance the conglomerates, there was considerable concern among international banks about the country's financial health. Data gaps, meanwhile, had prevented timely analysis and mitigation of financial sector stresses (Independent Evaluation Office, 2003).

By August 2001, South Korea had repaid the last of its loans to IMF and other international lenders. The reforms adopted at the end of the 1990s and beginning of 2000s had helped to boost the country's resilience, including response to further global crises in the years ahead (IMF, 2004, various years). Some researchers have wondered whether the lessons of the Asian Financial Crisis i.e. the importance of stronger capital buffers and eliminating the moral hazard and contingent liabilities linked to financial and other strategic support to SOEs had been learnt by South Korea and its neighbors, given the depth of previous government interference in the economic sphere (Kawai, Newfarmer, and Schmukler, 2005; Rhee and Lee, 2012).

Still, it is notable that South Korea, and other East Asian economies, were back to growth in just a couple of years, while it took decade-long structural adjustment measures, supported by the international development community, notably the African Development Bank, Bilateral donors, IMF and the World Bank, before African economies could recover from the global commodity shocks that had hit the continent. Although South Korea's quick recovery reflected, to some degree, the seriousness of its adjustment measures, the receipt of an unprecedently large volume of financing, from multilateral and bilateral lenders, was an important factor—providing a soft landing and shifting market sentiment. Regionally, there were important geopolitical dynamics at play as well. Hence, while Africa's shock-driven economic predicament was at most a national-cum-regional challenge, that of East Asia had systemic implications for the global economy, and lenders had acted accordingly.

On structural reforms, an important lesson from South Korea, as proud a country as any in Africa, is that sometimes, it is necessary to take bitter medicine to return the economy to stability and growth. However, the conditionalities attached must be politically tenable i.e. undertaken from own premises and with full involvement of domestic institutions and agencies. Further, that there must be a clear-exist strategy from such externally funded programs and the conditionalities that they impose on domestic policy discretion.

Emerging Lessons from South Korea's Country Study. First, an important aspect of South Korea's economic management, on which all country study teams agreed, seeing it as a quintessential element of the developmental state, was that the government there walked the talk even in periods of economic adversity, such as the Asian Financial Crisis. During the 1990s (Figure 3.1), with the country's labor cost advantage steadily eroded by the emergence of low-cost producers such as China, Malaysia, and Vietnam, South Korea sought to augment the competitiveness of its private sector through dedicated measures to boost technical skills and competences and to encourage, in cases directly involving government agencies, R&D efforts that benefitted all domestic producers. Thus, the authorities had a good feel for when to undertake strategic changes in direction. When South Korea's growth leveled off at the end of the 1990s, following 15 years of exceptional performance, and with evidence of rising unemployment and inequality, it resisted the temptation of curbing the outward orientation of the economy, while actively seeking multilateral assistance. South Korea drew little pleasure from undergoing an IMF-supported program at the end of the 1990s and beginning of the 2000s, but it well recognized the dangers of moral hazard that hovered over the economy and which threatened to escalate if radical structural reforms were not taken (Cherry, 2005).

Second, South Korea's planning processes were both technical and formalized i.e. they were well linked to budgets, time bound in terms of deliverables and monitored and evaluated i.e. laissez faire was not part of the vocabulary. Crucially, there were implications when the process fell short of expectations i.e. accountability was expected for the resources expended because policymakers were not simply going through the motions. Above all, initiatives that did not fit into the overall concept were pushed aside, and quick amendments were suggested. As export promotion was the real policy push behind the national planning process in South Korea, the government had an up-to-date knowledge of the nature of the constraints to be addressed as well as the opportunities to be sought in the market place—this derived from its insistence on clear-eyed research initiatives undertaken by its agencies and universities. It also did not shy away from providing financial support to sections of the economy that it deemed to be strategic i.e. it was ready to pick winners if the circumstances called for it. Attempts to master the market by the government were not always on the mark, and there would be rude awakenings in the future.[7]

Third, the mobilization of resources to finance the rapid catch-up efforts critical to launching the future developmental state in South Korea was a major policy consideration (South Korea Team, 2017): (i) the government ensured that credit was affordable. It thus controlled or had direct influence on the bulk of the financial sector, linking credit provision tightly to its industrial policy; (ii) the government raised capital, on the international markets, through the financial system, which it largely controlled, and distributed it among "private firms, contingent on their performance in the global market" (South Korea

Team, 2017); and (iii) the role of the Korean Development Bank, founded already in 1954 as a financier and domestic risk taker in the implementation of South Korea's industrial policy, was vastly expanded and was, like Brazil's Development Bank (BNDES), able to finance infant industries in many sectors (Steinberg, 2016; Torres and Zeidan, 2016).

Fourth, nurturing effective state-business relations was central to the formulation of a credible development strategy in South Korea and is worth emulating by other aspiring developmental states (Sen and Te Velde, 2009). As a result of this approach, "industrial capitalists became agents of the state in carrying out its economic development plans, engaging in a government-monitored contest to secure loans guaranteed by the state" (Lim, 2003). This ultimately created *chaebols*, companies which, though privately owned, behaved, and were treated as quasi-SOEs—a good example of the socialization of private risk for which the country became renowned. By the end of the 1980s, total sales of the top four *chaebols*, Samsung, Hyundai, Daewoo, and Lucky-Goldstar, accounted for half of the country's gross income (Kearney, 1991; Lim, 2012). This of course subsequently raised issues of crony capitalism and moral hazard, which, however, were easier to manage than no industrial base at all.

3.3 Cameroon

Development Quest in a Natural Resource-Rich Country. Cameroon achieved its independence from France in 1960, becoming a federation a year later when territory adjacent to Nigeria, and previously colonized by the UK, was added to it. The country is strategically placed in Central Africa, sharing borders with six countries, and is an important gateway to landlocked neighbors such as Chad—it hosts the pipeline that transports the latter's oil to the sea—and the Central African Republic. It has a population of some 26 million (2019), the bulk of which depends on agriculture for livelihood. Cameroon adopted the motto of "peace, work and fatherland."

Cameroon is well-endowed in natural resources, including arable land, forests, vast crude oil and natural gas deposits, a range of minerals, including aluminum, and wind and geothermal resources (Muh, Amara and Tabet, 2018). Relative to other African countries, the industrial sector, based on agro-processing, is reasonably large, comprising a fifth of GDP for most of the 2000s. The country, a diversified producer of agricultural commodities and oil and gas, is also the de facto motor of the Economic Community of Central African States (ECCAS) (Bamou-Tankoua, 2002; Cameroon Team, 2017).[8]

However, the merger of the country's francophone and anglophone political traditions into a unitary state in the 1960s has led to perennial frictions ever since (Wautelet, 1990). Several constitutional amendments have been undertaken in the last 50 years in a bid to improve the economic and political relations between the two communities (Mbome, 1992; Olinga, 1996).

The discovery of oil in the late-1970s boosted GDP (Figure 3.2) and alleviated the country's foreign exchange constraints, at least for a while. In macroeconomic

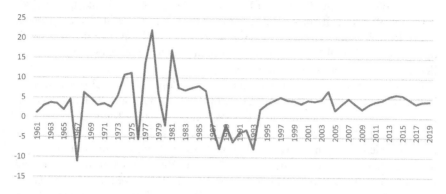

Figure 3.2 Cameroon: GDP Growth, 1961–2019 (%)
Source: World Bank (various issues).

terms, the expanding oil sector raised relative wages in the economy, while lowering profitability in manufacturing and agriculture i.e. there was a real appreciation of the exchange rate.[9] During the years of plenty, the government departed from the national development plans and embarked on additional projects in the belief that the resource inflows were permanent. Moreover, over the following decades, oil booms and busts distorted the planning and investment horizons of the government and the private sector (Assiga-Ateba, 1998, 2006; Gauthier and Zeufack, 2010)

In 1982, the country became a unified republic and, for a period, "one-party democracy." Although Cameroon has since moved toward pluralism and the first multiparty elections were held in 1992 and won by the incumbent, Paul Biya, a definitive political accommodation is yet to be reached. The political turbulence of the past decades, mainly concentrated among English-speaking regions of the country to the west, and the spillover from Nigeria's Boko Haram insurgency in the far north, have had serious economic impacts—disrupting the production of export crops, including bananas, palm oil, and rubber. The number of internally displaced persons and refugees has grown in recent years, while development partners and NGOs have charged the belligerent parties of human rights abuses.

The President's push in September 2019 for a "great national dialogue" has not yielded much enthusiasm outside his political circles. In January 2020, the US removed Cameroon from the economically significant AGOA program for "persistent human rights violations" (Office of the United States Trade Representative, 2019). The resulting economic, political, and security pressures as well as external shocks arising from oil exports have meant that the country's elaborate development strategies have not been implemented as planned (Fonjong, 2019).

Responding to External Shocks. During the second half of the 1980s, and the first half of the 1990s, Cameroon dealt with a succession of external shocks that reversed its growth trajectory, heightened the budget deficits, and raised the incidence of poverty in the country (Sikod and Teke, 2012). First, during 1986 and 1993, with the decline of coffee, cocoa, and oil prices, the country's terms of trade declined by some 60%. The second shock was the decline in oil output as investment there fell sharply, while the third was the real exchange appreciation of the CFA franc—the regional currency which was pegged to the French franc (and in later years to the Euro). A decade of negative growth in the late-1980s and early 1990s, following one of ebullient optimism (1977–1986), raised economic and political pressure in the country. In barely four years, between 1990 and 1994, external debt rose fourfold from 28 to 131% of GDP, pushing growth to a lower plateau from which the economy is yet to emerge (Figure 3.2).

In the circumstances, Cameroon had no choice but to embark on structural adjustment policies (SAPs) supported by the IMF and World Bank and bilateral donors, notably France. Among African countries, Cameroon became a prime example of the impacts of the Dutch Disease phenomenon caused by a sudden explosion of natural resource wealth and its impacts on public sector efficiency through the expansion of off-budget current and capital expenditures by the government and then a sharp reversal as commodity prices fell.

Cameroon subsequently benefitted from the Highly Indebted Poor Country (HIPC) program and the Multilateral Debt Relief Initiative (MIDRI), reaching HIPC completion point in 2006, with total debt relief of some US$4.5 billion. In lieu of the debt forgiveness, the government committed to undertaking poverty reduction measures based on donor-supported poverty reduction strategy papers (PRSPs) (Republic of Cameroon, 2010). During the following decade, PRSPs became the de facto national development plans, also incorporating Cameroon's commitment to the Millennium Development Goals (MDGs). Aside from maintaining macroeconomic stability and promoting growth, the PRSPs sought to create a conducive environment for human capital development, with emphasis on education and health, and private sector, infrastructure, and natural resource development. They also underlined the importance of improving governance to fight off official corruption (Ngoa et al., 2017).

Although the PRSPs were reputedly the product of a participatory process, there was no coherent approach to implementation. They required in one case the simultaneous implementation of some 200 measures in 14 policy action areas. There was simply not enough capacity or interest within government to undertake the mapping and budget follow through required to meet program requirements and assess whether the new approach was meeting targets. Policymakers did not feel that they were in the driver's seat and saw the exercises as largely proforma.

Despite the external shocks and internal strife, including the global financial crisis of 2008/09 and the deterioration of security in the region, Cameroon showed considerable resilience (Figure 3.2). Still growth, at about 4% on average since the 1990s, was below the double-digit "tiger levels" once targeted by the government. Looking ahead, continued political and structural tenacity will be crucial as Cameroon seeks to return to the rapid development on which it had embarked in earlier decades (Cameroon Team, 2017; Ntaryike, 2015).

Financial Repression versus Financial Liberalization. Cameroon has sought to leverage its enormous natural resources and strategic position in the region to boost its role as a gateway to the landlocked countries in the region and harness its own development. However, the region is turbulent, limiting the potential for investment and engaging in new trade opportunities.

Like many of its Francophone neighbors, Cameroon belongs to the CFA zone, which has proved to be an important agency of restraint, protecting countries from the inflationary excesses seen in other regions of Africa. But also imposes constraints on its policy discretion, even though it is by far the most important economy in the CEMAC regional grouping. Still, the monetary and economic arrangements in the region have been blamed for financial repression and absence of financial inclusion. During the period 1965–1990, for example, the regional central bank, BEAC, adjusted its discount rate only five times compared to annual adjustments of policy rates in African countries outside the CFA zone. On the other hand, as a shareholder in the commercial banks, the government did little to encourage savings, with market forces playing almost no role in the allocation of domestic credit. Available credit was steered to the SOEs, while the private sector, notably small and medium-sized enterprises, were neglected (IMF, 2009).

Thus, while the South Korea government saw its role as including efforts to amplify private sector access to credit, including from international markets, in Cameroon, the government perceived private firms as competitors in business. The government's control of the financial sector and unadulterated support to the parastatal sector contributed to the crisis of the banking system in the decades ahead. Indeed, for some SOEs, including the state-owned oil company, Société Nationale de la Raffinage (SONARA), arrears to the state-dominated banking system had become chronic at the end of the 1990s (IMF, 2018; Nachega, 2001; Tybout et al., 1996).[10]

During the 1980s and 1990s, under SAPs, financial liberalization became a major reform pillar : including the liberalization of interest rates, elimination of administrative credit allocation; strengthening the regulatory and supervisory role of the Central Bank (the BEAC); the restructuring of the state-owned commercial banks and other financial institutions; and allowing entry of new institutions (foreign and domestic) into the financial sector (Ayuk, 2012). The government retained stakes (35–85%) in at least four large commercial banks to ensure that it would remain a major player in the financial sector.

An IMF (2009) report on Cameroon's financial sector sustainability indicated substantial improvement during the 2000s, with no systemic risks. It noted, however, that low levels of bank profitability, with the return on assets as low as 1%, was a serious challenge and also noted that indigenous banks were more vulnerable to credit shocks than subsidiaries of foreign banks. The government was in a bind, wishing to encourage greater Cameroonian participation in the financial sector, while aware that the capitalization of local banks was low and their non-performing loans (NPLs) high, at above 10%. Moreover, Crédit

Foncier de Cameroun, CFC, the national housing bank, which had potential for expansion, given the backlog of housing in the country, was seriously under-capitalized and, in effect, bankrupt. If not restructured, it had the potential to unravel the progress achieved thus far in reforming the financial sector.

A decade later, in the 2010s, the banking system remains quite cautious in extending credit to the private sector, as the structural impediments mentioned above have persisted. Total credit to the private sector, as a percent of GDP, has gone up by a few notches from about 13% in 2013 to just above 15.5% in 2018. Despite the stated ambition to grow indigenous private businesses by improving access to long-term financing, short-term credit dominates, accounting to over 90% of the loans. National savings had declined to 15% of GDP compared to an average of 24% during 1980–1989.

Vision 2035: In Search of Coherence. As many other Francophone countries in West Africa, Cameroon has in place an elaborate national planning structure, based in the Ministry of the Economy and Planning. Although the latter

---

Box 3.2: Cameroon—Vision 2035

The theme of Cameroon's Vision 2035 is "An emerging, democratic and united country in diversity." It enounced four objectives: the reduction of poverty and raising of social welfare; transforming Cameroon into a middle-income economy; taking the country to the level of a newly in-dustrialized country; and maintaining national unity and promoting democracy. Its strategic approach was sevenfold, with close linkages to the developmental state model discussed earlier:

(i) with respect to growth, emphasis on increased investments in infra-structure, rapid modernization of production, a better business climate and governance, as well as incentives for employment creation.

(ii) achieving the Millennium Development Goals "no matter how late" and to ensure that the population is entirely mobilized in the fight against climate change.

(iii) an improved financial system to mobilize domestic and foreign investment.

(iv) the pursuit of an ambitious industrialization strategy.

(v) devising a strategy for national integration and the advancement of democracy.

(vi) a private-sector promotion strategy, and

(vii) a good governance and management strategy with a blueprint for a resource allocation strategy.

Source: Cameroon Team (2017) and Republic of Cameroon (2009)

has produced regular five-year development plans since the early 1960s, owing to lack of finances, politically instigated mid-stream changes in priorities, and absence of strong links to the national budget, they have largely fallen short in terms of implementation. The latter has meant that many plan interventions are not budgeted for and, hence, have little relevance.

In 2009, Cameroon launched its Vision 2035 document, with the ambition of projecting a homegrown approach to development, using language that is familiar from the developmental state discourse, with becoming a middle-income country as a major goal (Kasahara, 2013). It outlined strategies for effective industrial development, domestic resource mobilization, and private sector promotion policies and how a more coherent implementation process would ensure good results (Box 3.2).

In pursuit of Vision 2035, Cameroon has embarked on a range of infrastructure projects, including the deep seaport at Kribi and the Lom Pangar Hydropower project. Also, significant, it has established a gas-fired electricity generation plant (also at Kribi), which has diversified the country's energy sources. The expanding supply of cheap power augurs well for Cameroon's industrialization effort and creation of a conducive environment for private sector development and regional competitiveness. It could also help entrench Cameroon's position as the anchor economy of Central Africa and supplier of energy to its less diversified neighbors.

Diversifying Development Financing. Cameroon has relied on four main sources of external financing in the past decade: remittances from the Diaspora, bilateral loans (mainly France and China), multilateral projects and programs (African Development Bank, IMF and World Bank), and borrowing from international markets (Eurobond). External debt (as % of GDP) has risen steadily since the completion of the HIPC and MDRI operations some 20 years ago. Thus, while external debt was only about 10% of GDP in 2010, it had risen to 35.7% in 2017, with only about 40% of it acquired on concessional terms. In the late-2010s, total external debt totaled US$10 billion, with Chinese loans accounting for a third. The latter have been crucial for financing the country's ambitious infrastructure investment program.

As in other African countries, the increase of remittances from the Cameroonian Diaspora has had notable economic impacts i.e. they currently (pre-Covid19) comprise the principal inflow of foreign resources and have helped improve the balance of payments, while boosting recipient livelihoods. It is estimated that 80% of the money is used by recipients for consumption, notably health and education, and the rest for investment in small and medium-sized enterprises. Thanks to multiplier effects, there have been quite positive impacts on the economy (Gayi, Nkurunziza, and Kasahara, 2007).

Cameroon launched its first Eurobond issue for US$750 million in November 2015, with a 10-year tenor and coupon rate of 9.75%. Its reception was subdued, however, with the country requiring a partial guarantee from the AfDB to proceed. While previous African issues had been oversubscribed, that for

Cameroon was slow to reach full subscription, while its coupon rate was several hundred basis points higher than for Cote d'Ivoire and Senegal. Thus, from the point of view of the investors, the Eurobond's assessment of Cameroon's medium-term prospects, including economic performance and fiscal capacity, was grudging at best.

3.4 Côte d'Ivoire

Rise of the African Elephant. In terms of start conditions, Côte d'Ivoire was at independence in 1960 better positioned than many other countries in West Africa to pursue the precepts of a developmental state. Powered by cocoa and coffee exports, its economy was easily the largest within the West African Economic and Monetary Union (WAEMU).[11] As a first step, the government adopted a ten-year development plan, 1960–1970, which, unlike others in Africa, emphasized agriculture and rural infrastructure development. This was followed by three five-year development plans covering the period up to 1985. They underlined rapid growth, socio-economic and spatial inclusion, and poverty reduction and improved access to economic and social services. Within the international development community, the economic growth and social progress achieved by Côte d'Ivoire in the first two decades of independence (Figure 3.3) was referred to with the same level of praise as that of the East Asian economies.

Like its East Asian counterparts, Côte d'Ivoire had posted an average annual growth rate of above 7% between 1960 and 1979 (Figures 3.3), accompanied by balanced budgets, balance of payments surpluses, low levels of external debt, and an inflation rate of some 3.9%. The country became the regional magnate for foreign investment as well as migrant labor from neighboring countries—from immediate neighbors Burkina Faso, Ghana, Guinea, and Mali but also from further afield. The World Bank (den Tuinder, 1978) praised the government's liberal investment code and incentives to farmers and saw it as one of the few African countries likely to "take-off" in the medium term.[12] The country's progress was roundly referred to as the "Ivorian miracle." Its bulwark included the long and politically stable leadership of President Houphouët-Boigny, who believed in a mixed economy or state capitalism, and the country's good access to foreign capital, from international lending institutions and French investors. Gross capital formation rose from 14% in 1962 to 30% in 1978 (Côte d'Ivoire Team, 2017).

Up to 1990, some 30% of total domestic credit was targeted at the private sector, compared to 12.5% for Nigeria, 5% for Zambia, and 49% for South Korea. Besides, Côte d'Ivoire was undergoing rapid urbanization from 14% of the population in 1960 to 45% in 1978. After only 18 years of independence, the Ivorian miracle seemed to be based on solid achievements, but in retrospect, the conclusion was hurried. Ultimately, as the path to economic prosperity, agricultural commodity production, much like Zambia's hope that copper would pave its development path, proved infeasible.

During its formative years, Côte d'Ivoire had a relatively efficient bureaucracy, thanks to a good supply of well-trained Ivorians and French experts in the civil service as well as in education, health, and SOEs. Moreover, in 1978, the government created a special unit for managing large public projects, *Bureau National d'Etudes Technique et Développement (BNETD)*, which had many operational similarities to South Korea's Economic Planning Board, including direct support from the President (Diabi, 2000). Unlike South Korea where the developmental state process had achieved a self-sustaining dynamic by the early 1970s, the fate of the economy in Côte d'Ivoire was still closely tied to that of the political leadership i.e. to the person of the President. The country became an early example of a patrimonial state where the development impetus revolved around an able and charismatic leadership but with the momentum doomed to dissipate when the incumbent exited the scene.

As part of its national planning process, the government of Côte d'Ivoire started issuing vision documents regularly from the early 1970s. Vision 2000 was launched during the 1973–1974 fiscal year, while Vision 2010 and Vision 2025 were drafted during the 1983–1984 and 1993–1994 fiscal years, respectively. The latter Vision was issued at the beginning of a difficult economic and political period for the country and had been derailed by the end of the 1990s, when the military deposed the civilian government. However, partly owing to the solid ground laid in the first two decades of independence, the Elephant was destined to make a return in a decade or so.

Côte d'Ivoire, much like South Korea, was buoyed by the expanding global economy of 1960s. Unlike other African countries during this formative period, Côte d'Ivoire emphasized agriculture and the boosting of rural incomes and welfare, making it the darling of the multilateral agencies. In the early 1960s, the government created an agency (CAISTAB) to stabilize the prices of coffee and cocoa and hence farmers' incomes, while also protecting exports. Additionally, specialized SOEs were created for the production of sugar (SODESUCRE), rice (SODERIZ), and palm oil (SODEPALM). GDP grew by more than 10% per year during 1974–1978 (Figure 3.3), reaching a GDP per capita of US$2,237 i.e. Côte d'Ivoire had become a middle-income country already in the 1970s. The government and other stakeholders were convinced that the economy was on the verge of industrialization and takeoff (Kayizzi-Mugerwa, 1997).

While commodity exports provided a solid foundation for growth for almost two decades i.e. engendering the Ivorian miracle, cocoa and coffee production attracted immigrants and their families from neighboring countries, with political consequences of its own in the years ahead. The government also allowed the clearing of forests and the expansion of acreage to accommodate coffee and cocoa production, again with environmental consequences that were not fathomable at the time. The CAISTAB system was rattled by the unprecedented increase in cocoa prices (tripled) and those of coffee[13] (quadrupled) during 1975–1977. Although the state passed on some of the boom to farmers, it kept the bulk of the price increase, arguing that it was best placed to spend the windfall.

Figure 3.3 Cote d'Ivoire: GDP Growth, 1961–2019 (%)
Source: World Bank (various issues).

Henceforth, the incomes from the commodity exports were seen by the government in macro-fiscal terms. CAISTAB's reserves became a budgetary cushion, increasingly funneled to infrastructure development i.e. investments in urban infrastructure, including roads and the expansion of the port of Abidjan (Cogneau and Mesplé-Somps, 1999). In real terms, public investment grew by an unprecedented 36% per annum between 1975 and 1978, raising expectations to levels that were not sustainable, caused by an unprecedented commodity boom, which was soon reversed.

Although d'Ivoire's national development plans made several references to rural development during the 1970s and 1980s, it became clear with time that big projects meant mostly large urban infrastructure projects, while rural infrastructure projects were afterthoughts. Given regional power differentials, areas with limited significance to the urban areas in terms of commodity production saw little development of markets and modern services, with incomes much lower than in regions linked to the coffee and cocoa production chain. Hence, during the boom years of the 1960s and 1970s, rural–urban cleavages and even rural–rural ones were entrenched further instead of the reverse (Assiga-Baulin, 1974; Devarajan, 1991; Hecht, 1983).

Years of Economic Retrenchment. As the era of rapid development came to the end in the late-1980s on the back of external shocks, Côte d'Ivoire abandoned its national development plans, adopting instead SAPs with support from the World Bank, the IMF, and other donors. Following the death of President Houphouët-Boigny (in late-1993) and the devaluation of the FCFA (in early 1994), it became clear to policymakers that returning to the growth rates of the past would require a system overhaul. Even then, for fear of exacerbating political disaffection, the authorities were reluctant to officially admit that poverty incidence and spatial inequality had increased sharply. An explicit poverty reduction strategy was delayed until the late-1990s, even then under some pressure from the donor community (Cogneau, 2002; Kayizzi-Mugerwa, 1997).

There would be no quick respite as the economic decline played its full course. Starting with the late-1999s, Côte d'Ivoire witnessed a coup d'etat, contested elections, a civil war, and human rights abuses (Bastart, 2014). Under the pressures of external shocks and the imperatives of political succession, the political edifice, which the late president had so craftily overseen in his 33 years in power, started to crack. The coffee and cocoa-dependent economy was seriously affected by the breakdown of the rural infrastructure and payment systems as armed insurrection hived off parts of the country. Farmer access to fertilizer and related services became quite politicized and rural incomes collapsed forcing many farmers to revert to subsistence production (Gockel, R. et al., 2009). The impact on national welfare, urban and rural, was large. By 2008, national poverty incidence in Côte d'Ivoire was estimated at close to 50% compared to 36.8% in 1995 and 10% in 1985.

The Elephant's Return. In 2011, the new government led by Alassane Ouattara put together a team of technocrats in 2014–2015, to deliberate on Côte d'Ivoire's Vision 2040, the fourth in the series. It introduced an ambitious planning process that focused on "emergence." Its new vision statement read: "an industrial power, united in cultural diversity, democratic and open to the world" (Republic of Côte d'Ivoire, 2015). The levels of growth achieved by Côte d'Ivoire from 2011 onward, at above 7% per year, were only comparable to those of the first independence decade (Figure 3.3). During 2012–2015, Ivorian GDP increased by 25%, while it is expected to grow faster still during the 2016–2020 plan period (Ballo and Kimou, 2015; Jeuneafrique, 2015; Republic of Côte d'Ivoire, 2012, 2016).

In support of the country's emergence into a middle-income economy, Vision 2040 had adopted the confident theme "The Triumph of Côte d'Ivoire" (Box 3.3), which revolved around three pillars: sustainable development, responding to the call of globalization, and educating the nation for the future, notably how best to eradicate the serious shortcomings in the Ivorian education system. It marked the revival of the tradition of long-term planning for the country, which had served it well in the past, but had been abandoned in the 1990s. Reminiscent of South Korea's EPB, the work on Vision 2040 (*Etude Nationale Prospective Côte d'Ivoire*) was coordinated by the National Office for Vision and Strategic Intelligence of the Ministry of Planning and Development.

The new government underlined that to achieve the goals of Vision 2040 would require an attitude change in Côte d'Ivoire, including over issues of democracy, access to justice, and education and health services. It also highlighted that there was a strong correlation between economic development and how the authorities addressed issues related to the protection of human and property rights, gender disparities, youth violence and unemployment, the ease of doing business and private sector development, public sector transparency and accountability, and, not least, the protection of the environment.

Emulating the East Asian developmental states, Côte d'Ivoire is putting a lot of emphasis on human capital development, notably technical education and skills training, targeted at households and the business sector, as a gateway to industrialization (Republic of Côte d'Ivoire, 2009, 2015). The Vision 2040 statement also underlines good governance, bureaucratic competences, institutional coherence, and social cohesion as important additional vehicles through which its goals will be pursued, and as bases for assessing the progress being made. Miran-Guyon (2017) has argued that there is both a sense of rupture and continuity at the center of Côte d'Ivoire's desire for economic transformation i.e. wishing to break away from the old ways of doing things, while cherishing the legacy of rapid agriculture-led prosperity from a bygone era.

Box 3.3: Vision 2040: the triumph of Côte d'Ivoire

Vision 2040 evolved from the analysis of three competing scenarios relating to Côte d'Ivoire's response to emerging domestic and global challenges and opportunities:

i. *Côte d'Ivoire's Continued Decline:* This scenario assumes that owing to geopolitical and regional instability, continued domestic strife and institutional frailty, and an ill-performing economy, the country would not be able to emerge as planned. Moreover, the government would fail to address inter-ethnic strife, petty criminality, terrorism, and drug peddling. Under this scenario, regional bodies would not be able to help the country address the deteriorating situation.

ii. *Elephant with Feet of Clay:* This halfway house scenario sees some policy and structural advances in the country, including reductions in regional tensions, allowing the return of foreign investment, but with limited impact on regional integration and economic and monetary convergence. The implication is that, under this scenario, Côte d'Ivoire would not be able to capture the full benefits of globalization. Even given the modest progress made under this scenario, the costs of doing business would remain high, as would unemployment and inequality. Moreover, the quality of institutions as well as governance would not be strengthened, leaving a question mark over the democratic dispensation of the country. The conclusion is that the Ivorian elephant would have feet of clay in this scenario, unable to exit the vicious circle of fragile emergence.

iii. *The Radiation of the Elephant*: This is the preferred scenario. It assumes that the country would be able to achieve the desired domestic targets, given favorable regional and global developments and responses. By 2040, the scenario portrays Côte d'Ivoire as the economic engine of West Africa, having grown its industrial power thanks to a much-changed education infrastructure, with approaches that draw on the success stories of East Asia i.e. relentless focus on scientific research, technological innovation, and technical skills development. To achieve this, the country will need to base the production of its elites on technical competence and not on political influence and associated networks. The economy will be open and much more efficient, able to export high value-added products, including those intensive in scientific and technical knowledge. With respect to governance, the third scenario projects a country where the culture of democracy and the rule of law are well entrenched, social cohesion is assured and consensus is achieved in the political context over issues that are key to economic development.

Source: Republic of Côte d'Ivoire (2012, 2015, 2016).

The World Bank's Ease of Doing Business Report for 2019 included Côte d'Ivoire among the 10 countries that had made the most progress in improving the business environment, while its overall ranking (among 190 countries) was 110 in 2019, an improvement from 158 of 190 in 2014. Still, that progress is qualified with the UNDP's Human Development Index for 2018 ranking the country at 170 out 189 countries, partly because of its stagnated level of human capital development. In an introduction to a volume on Côte d'Ivoire's "emergence," Miran-Guyon (2017) argues pointedly that the country's overemphasis on infrastructure has diverted the focus from social sector development as "people cannot eat bridges and tar." Although the poverty rate in Côte d'Ivoire was estimated to be declining for the first time in decades, the poverty incidence of 46% (in 2015) was still high.

The Lure of International Financial Markets. The Elephant's return has led to excursions into the Eurobond market (Sanogo and Moussa, 2017). In 2014, Côte d'Ivoire issued a US$750 million Eurobond issue priced at 5.625% and tenor of 10 years. This was just the beginning, it returned to the Eurobond market in 2015 for an issue of US$1 billion, with a coupon rate of 6.625% and a three-year amortization plan (2026, 2027, 2028), which helped reduce redemption pressure. In 2017, the country returned to the markets once again, issuing a US$1.25 billion Eurobond with a 16-year tenor and coupon rate of 6.125% and a euro tranche of 625 million at coupon rate of 5.125% to be redeemed in eight years.

When borrowing for infrastructure development, Côte d'Ivoire's policy in the recent past decade seems to have been to "go for broke" (Independent Evaluation Office, 2018). Although external indebtedness has risen and the ratio between it and available foreign exchange reserves declined to about 20% in 2019, compared to 60% for South Africa, the Ivorian government, unlike its Zambian counterpart, whose Eurobonds have come under considerable market pressure in recent months, is not as worried about its external debt, as its export capacity is larger and better distributed among commodities. Côte d'Ivoire is also looking at expanding its electricity exports to neighbors, which would defray some of the fiscal and debt pressure. Moreover, despite the governance issues discussed ahead, rating agencies consider its economic management and growth numbers to have performed well in recent years.

Conclusions on Côte d'Ivoire. Like many of its neighbors, Côte d'Ivoire experienced a post-independence economic boom, which raised popular expectations as modern employment and services expanded, and manufacturing took root. Although the Ivorian miracle was sustained for close to two decades, it had ended by the mid-1980s without much evidence of economic transformation. Moreover, commodity dependence had eroded state institutions and heightened the urban bias of policies, while the price shocks had made the conduct of economic policy extremely difficult, given the CFA arrangements. The initial policy thrust and ideas for economic development had derived from President Félix Houphouët-Boigny, a forceful and charismatic leader but, who, like many others in the region, had paid succession issues limited attention. With his passing in 1993, his institutional and political legacy proved both frail and fractious. The country entered a period of internecine conflict that reversed many of the previous gains.

With the coming to power of President Alassane Outtrara in the early 2010s, the Ivorian government returned to the ambitious development stance of the era of Houphouët-Boigny, with an expansive infrastructure program financed by loans from the multilateral institutions and the donor community. A key difference from previous approaches is the recognition that much more needs to be done to strengthen bureaucratic structures, the business environment, and the technical capacities and skills of the population, especially the youth. There are some signs that progress is being made (Côte d'Ivoire Team, 2017), if at a slower pace than the government would have wished.

3.5 Nigeria

Africa's Giant in More Ways than One. During the last six decades, Nigeria has come to epitomize Africa's development challenges as well as promise. It achieved independence in 1960, following close to a century of British rule. In 2019, its population was estimated at some 200 million, 13% of Africa's total, while its GDP of some US$400 billion[14] in 2019, accounted for about a fifth of continental GDP. With over 250 ethnic groups and some 500 languages, the country is Africa's giant in more ways than one. Since independence, political governance in Nigeria has, so far (2020), been split, almost evenly, between democratic (31 years) and military (29 years) regimes. While domestic political instability, including civil war in the second half of the 1960s, derailed many of the development strategies devised by the governments at the federal and local levels, at no time did Nigeria cease to see itself as a regional and continental leader. It has played a leading role in conciliating regional conflicts and opposing colonial and racial domination, notably in Southern Africa (Nigeria Team, 2017).

For over half a century, oil has interchangeably been a source of optimism as well as pessimism in Nigeria—a misfiring engine for the country's anticipated economic transformation. Under the Petroleum Act of 1969, all rights pertaining to oil and gas exploration in the country were vested in the Nigerian state. The 1999 Constitution stipulates that when allocating oil revenue to the states, the following criteria should be followed i.e. population size, equality of states, internal revenue generation, land mass, as well as population density. Given the difficulty of measurement and lack of statistics, these provisions have not made it easier to address the controversies and acrimony related to sharing oil revenue (Gboyega et al. 2011).

The maximization of local content and the creation of local businesses and jobs downstream have received policy emphasis in Nigeria. Among policy measures have been regular adjustments to royalties and taxes and downstream monitoring and regulation. Besides, many institutions and agencies have been created in the last several decades to manage oil and gas at the federal and state levels—with some of them dedicated to collaboration with neighbors and the region and others acting as "eyes and ears on the ground" for the government (Adeolu and Oyejide, 2012; Oyewunmi and Olujobi, 2016). Not unexpectedly, institutional proliferation has bred confusion at the federal and state levels, with agencies striving to protect policy niches and income streams.[15]

In Search of Diversification. In spite of the structural and revenue diversification efforts of recent decades, oil remains the main source of revenue for the Federal Government and hence continues to be a major source of external shocks and disruptions in public spending (Khemani, 2001). For example, oil had generated over 70% of government revenue since the early 1980s, increasing above 75% for 20 years between 1991 and 2010, and falling only slightly thereafter. Such a high level of dependence on one source has left the government, and by extension the states (they receive a constitutionally determined share of the oil), little discretion. Fiscal policy has thus been procyclical, resulting in what has been termed a "deficit bias."[16] Extraordinary measures, including arbitrary cuts in key expenditures items, are often used to reduce the deficits.

The Nigeria Team (2017) argued that there have been a number of innovations at the state level to diversify revenue sources. Notably, Lagos State has improved its collection of rents from the many private properties in Lagos City. However, at the federal level the danger of debt escalation is not negligible. Nigeria's Paris Club debt cancellation exercise of 2005 wrote off some US$30 billion in external debt, with immensely positive impact on the country's ratings and capacity to borrow from international markets. While the debt burden remains largely sustainable i.e. still below 35% of GDP (2019), the fiscal deficit has been growing rapidly in recent decades—in the absence of a fiscal rule at the federal level. It will require astute macroeconomic management and coordination by the authorities to ensure that in closing the deficit, the debt overhang that bedeviled the economy in past decades, cutting off FDI flows, does not recur.

Nigeria is home to a large, youthful, and increasingly well-educated population that is looking beyond oil for opportunities. Its expanding middle class, including returnees from the Diaspora, is having an unmistakable impact on domestic expenditure patterns, service delivery, and technical innovations (Kayizzi-Mugerwa and Anyanwu, 2015). The latter has been demonstrated by the unqualified success of its film industry (Nollywood) and the rapid expansion of its transnational corporations in banking, insurance, and manufacturing. While having a homogeneous population is sometimes considered an asset in development, Nigeria and many African countries have shown that ethnic differentiation is not necessarily the same as ethnic fractionalization. Above all, despite hiccups, Nigeria has been relatively successful in constructing a multiethnic and multicultural society. Its entrepreneurs are, for example, building tourism niches on the basis of its rich cultural diversity.

From Vision to Action. Nigeria's Vision 2020 was launched in 2006 by President Obasanjo, while its blueprint, Vision 20:2020, was only presented in 2009 by his successor, President Yar'Adua. The involvement of the two presidents in setting a long-term vision for the country, during a decade of relatively good performance, seemed to augur for success. Looking back, the bulk of African visions launched in the 2000s had stretched into the 2030s and beyond. However, evincing confidence in its speed of implementation, Nigeria's Vision coverage only went up to 2020 i.e. the ambitious targets were expected to be met in a mere decade and a half. This made it the only the country in Africa where, writing in 2020, the results achieved can be measured against targets set 15 years previously.

In terms of messaging, Nigeria's Vision 2020 was brazenly ambitious (Box 3.4). A key target for the country was to become one of the world's 20 leading economies by 2020. It would also be the number one attraction in Africa for FDI, tourism and foreigners seeking residence for business purposes. Nigeria's GDP would rise to US$900 billion by 2020, with per capita income exceeding US$4000.

Power supply, a perennial policy challenge, was paid special attention in Vision 2020. Electricity production was expected to increase fivefold in a decade i.e. from 6,000 MW in 2009 to 35,000 MW in 2020—reducing the cost of doing business and spurring business startups as well as additional investment in already established firms. This mega scaling up would be achieved by creating financial incentives for the exploitation of new energy sources i.e. solar, thermal, wind, and gas. While Nigeria's natural gas was for decades treated as an annoying byproduct of oil production, to be flared off at source, the plan going forward was to establish an elaborate natural gas distribution infrastructure to take full advantage of its abundance, competitive pricing, and lighter environmental impact. Besides, the government committed to boosting manpower development within the power sector, notably technical capacity enhancement across the energy value chain.

In the event, Vision 2020 fell well short of its ambitious targets. During the 15 years of implementation, new leadership teams sought to profile themselves

Box 3.4: Nigeria's Vision 20:2020: ambitious but unimplemented

Nigeria's Vision 2020 had the following themes:

Infrastructure development, especially transport—aviation, road, rail, and marine—and energy, notably electricity generation has been highlighted in all Nigeria's post-independence plans. Increasingly, the emphasis has been on commercialization and undertaking joint projects with the private sector. The slow pace at which the unbundling of electricity has happened has given policymakers reason to rethink the approach—including how to craft incentives for private sector involvement. The macro-fiscal impacts of infrastructure should comprise a central element of the debate as well.

Job creation, in the millions, to address a backlog of poor employment numbers by promoting industrialization, based on intersectoral linkages, including within the oil and gas value chain.

Export diversification to help reduce the stranglehold that oil has on foreign exchange generation, while helping to make Nigerian manufacturing regionally competitive.

Investment in human capital was underlined by Vision 2020 as essential for raising competitiveness and the country's ability to enter more profitable niches of the global economy. The latter also required a healthy and productive population as shown by the examples of East Asia.

Private sector development has become the de facto strategy for most African countries. However, many businesspeople in Nigeria feel that the government only pays the private-sector lip service—say in the crucial matter of access to regular and cheap power.

Effective public governance and enhanced transparency requires a more rigorous commitment technology for both politicians and civil servants. Given Nigeria's federal system, it is not clear what incentive structure will be required to raise efficiency in the provision of services across government levels—federal, state, and local. Like in South Korea, monetary incentives on their own might not be enough to raise compliance and improve public policy implementation. A broad "coalition of the willing" for raising the country's standards and boosting its development will be required i.e. the concept of national as opposed to personal interest must be engendered among the rest of the population.

Other themes included food security, national security, land tenure reform, and wealth creation.

Source: Republic of Nigeria (2009).

by cherry picking from the long list of interventions and projects proposed by Vision 2020, while external shocks and political changes forced abrupt shifts in direction. Unemployment was some 23% in 2019 compared to 13.6% in 2008, poverty incidence at 70% in 2019 had risen markedly compared to 52% in 1999, while external debt had shot up to US$27 billion in 2019 compared to US$3.6 billion in 2009 (although in terms of GDP still well within debt sustainability thresholds). Crucially, and in spite of the policy efforts, Nigeria has not been able to halt the pace of deindustrialization. The share of manufacturing in GDP was about 10% in 2020, compared to double that 35 years earlier, in the mid-1980s.

With respect to the energy sector, the reforms there had less impact than expected, with the sector continuing to be the weakest link in the economic setup of the country. Only less than a quarter of the country's 12,000 MW production capacity has been available on a regular basis in recent years. The type of expansion envisaged by Vision 2020 has been out of the question. Recent policies have focused on opening the sector to more competition across the board i.e. generation, transmission, and distribution. The latter is seen as the main culprit, and the government has sought financial assistance from, among others, the World Bank to help address it, including boosting technical capacities for maintenance and repair of the distribution network. Several independent power producers have been licensed in the last few years, while many public–private partnerships in electricity production have been embarked on at state levels. There has been a steady improvement in institutional capacities, scientific research, and innovation in the power sector, with potentially positive outcomes. If power supply in Nigeria continues to be lethargic, the public sector's power reforms will be dismissed by the population as mere grandstanding.

Vision 2020 had appealed to the imagination of the ordinary Nigerian because it had been preceded by a bold consultation exercise that had sought views from states, local governments, and local and foreign development partners. But broad consultation without progress on the ground only led to popular frustration and cynicism. In light of the relative failure of Vision 2020 to deliver, there have been discussions within government circles about the possibility of launching a successor vision, possibly designated "Vision 2030" to help recoup some of the ground lost to Vision 2020's lack of traction. Commentators have argued that another proforma planning exercise is not what is needed to move the process forward i.e. that strategies embarked on for purposes of winning political points other than long-term benefits for the country will not lead to the structural transformation desired by Nigeria.[17]

Nigeria is immensely proud of its private sector ingenuity and can-do-spirit, demonstrated, as noted earlier, by the purposefulness and goal-orientation of its pan-African companies and other business ventures.[18] Still, it cannot be content with its lowly ranking on the World Bank's Ease of Doing Business index, at 131 of 190 economies, in 2019 (from 170 of 190 in 2014), which is behind many other African countries. It has shown most improvement in the so-called "stroke

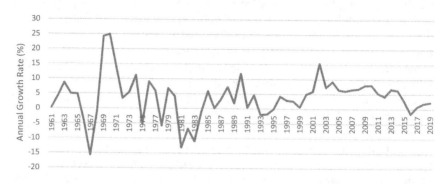

Figure 3.4 Nigeria: GDP Growth, 1961–2019 (%)
Source: World Bank (various issues).

of the pen" items of the index i.e. which only require policy pronouncements or related legislation, such as access to credit, acquiring construction permits, enforcing contracts, and protecting minority investors.

Sustaining Growth in the Democratic Era. Since the launch of the Fourth Republic in 1999, Nigeria has achieved political stability, as evidenced by the smooth transfer of power between regimes (Sanusi, 2012). Economic reforms at various levels, including power supply, have unraveled the control regime and refocused the use of oil rents from expanding the reach of government to supporting the diversification of the economy and improvements in governance and accountability. Thus, while democratic maturation has been slow and recalcitrant, few Nigerians would wish to return to military rule, as a viable means for bringing about further reforms (Nigeria Team, 2017). The country is today an aspiring developmental state, with all the policy challenges discussed earlier, but also the promise of rapid development, thanks to its vast physical and human resources and the government's determination to eradicate obstructions to reform.

While the powerful Federal Government has been the main instrument for maintaining economic coherence, peace, and security and advocating for economic transformation, economic management remains a work in progress (Adejumbi, 2011; Colman and Okorie, 1993; Ohiorhenuan, 1989).[19] Although the economy demonstrated more than a decade and a half of above average growth in 2000s (about 5% per annum), the impact of the oil sector remains pervasive, with growth still strongly correlated with oil prices (Figure 3.4).

Given the official policy of allowing for only limited adjustment of the naira to macroeconomic shocks, oil dependence and its spending effects have implied a real appreciation of the exchange rate and contraction of agriculture and manufacturing. Recent analyses have put Nigeria in a special category of oil-rich countries in Africa i.e. petro-developmental states, whose long exposure to the vagaries and international political economy of oil has led to a certain policy reticence at home that verges on fatalism i.e. "there is not much we can do" (Amuwo, 2008; Ovadia, 2016).

In terms of monetary policy, maintaining stability of the naira, and hence that of domestic prices, has been a key policy tool for the government. However, over the years, political considerations have tended to derail formal arrangements in favor of emergency measures by the Central Bank (including the introduction of multi-window forex operations), which often have resulted in rent-seeking activities. This has made it difficult for the government to adopt the business-inclined credit policy that South Korea used to support industrialization.

Financial Sector Development. Before 1986, the Nigerian financial sector was under full government control, but was then liberalized as part of the structural adjustment programs supported by multilateral institutions. With the deregulation, the number of banks increased from 45 in 1986 to 129 in 1991. Their numerical increase was not matched by monitoring and supervisory capacities at the Central Bank. The anticipated increase in competition among banks did not happen, and lending rates were rising, possibly because of the generally low return on bank assets.

In 1991, an Act was introduced to address the weaknesses listed above, notably the cost of finance. Ten years later, in 2001, a universal banking model allowed banks to diversify into non-banking financial businesses to enhance their profitability and allow for diversification in the financial sector. The issue of coherence arose once again, with the new approach to banking blamed for creating disarray in the financial sector. Banks were urged to refocus on their core banking activities. Mergers and acquisitions followed in efforts to deepen and stabilize bank operations and consolidate the financial sector (Central Bank of Nigeria, various issues; Okonjo-Iweala and Osafo-Kwaako, 2007).

In subsequent years, the issue of corporate governance in the banking sector was given specific attention, with the government revisiting and updating all laws related to corporate governance and transparency. In July 2010, the asset management corporation of Nigeria (AMCON) was established to address the issue of non-performing assets, which had accumulated during the aforementioned bank sector expansion, reaching 37% of total gross loans in 2009 and 20% in 2010, respectively.[20] In 2012, a cashless banking policy was introduced by the Central Bank to enhance electronic transactions.

The Eurobond Market. During the 2010s, Nigeria went to the Eurobond market, emerging with a full basket of bond issues of several vintages from 5 to 30 years, which have given the authorities the flexibility needed to manage sovereign debt and domestic expenditure, including through bond repurchases. Nigerian then issued Eurobonds in 2011, 2013, two in 2017, and another in 2018. The latter issue was notable for its packaging: it included a seven-year bond US$1.18 billion at a coupon rate of 7.625%, a 12-year bond of US$1 billion at 8.75%, and a 30-year US$750 million bond at 9.25%.

Moreover, the authorities also launched a Global Medium-Term Note program in London in 2017 with a ten-year bond of US$1.5 billion at 6.5% and a 30-year US$1.5 billion at 7.625%. Although the loan amounts were quite modest for an economy of Nigeria's size, they helped reduce the cost of domestic borrowing while paving the way for future operations, through learning by doing. The 30-year Eurobond has also been used as a benchmark by local banks in arranging their own long-term loan instruments. Since the bulk of the loans are for infrastructure construction, Nigeria's cost of borrowing is quite high. For example, its 30-year Eurobond has a coupon rate of 9.25%, which is high by regional and global comparison. It is an indicator that Nigeria is still considered a risky borrower (it is rated B+ by both S&P and Fitch). Authorities must devise ways to lower the country's risk profile and, hence, its cost of borrowing. This will not be easy, but the fact that the country is able to borrow from international markets on own account is an important first step. In spite of the anxiety regarding debt sustainability that has arisen during the Covid19 crisis, it is difficult to envisage Nigeria not returning to markets to mobilize resources in the medium term.

Conclusion. While the Nigerian Government has not used the term "developmental state" explicitly in describing its development ambitions, many of its recent policy declarations point in that direction. President Muhammadu Buhari first won power as a civilian leader in 2015 on the promise of economic modernization and transformation of Nigeria, a policy thrust that he reiterated during his reelection in 2019. At the state level, governors belonging to his All Progressives Congress (APC) have agreed a mutual policy pact targeted at ensuring that a minimum of "developmental strides" is achieved in the areas of health, education, infrastructure, security, and welfare during the second and last term of the Buhari regime. Nigeria will need to do more in areas that require concerted institutional effort and drawn-out structural reforms, such as improving energy supply and timely infrastructure construction and maintenance, that comprise the foundations of the developmental state to which the country is aspiring (Ai-yede, 2009; Ikpe, 2017).

3.6 South Africa

Dualistic Legacy. In the 1960s, the South African economy depicted both modern and informal and rural components.[21] While this economic dualism was also common among other African countries to the north, the sharp dichotomy under which it operated in South Africa set it apart. The modern economy comprised a large industrial sector powered by mining and allied activities, with significant links to banks, financial institutions, modern utilities, and social services. This part of the economy generated exports and modern employment and was linked to the international economy through FDI and listings on foreign stock exchanges. The more rudimentary parts of the economy, which sustained the majority of the population, comprised informal markets for goods and services in urban areas and peasant agriculture and related activities in the rural areas. The barrage of domestic regulations and attitudes that sustained the policy of Apartheid, notably its constraints on non-white labor and other discriminatory policies pursued by South Africa pre-1994, were an effective tax on the poorer parts of the economy and condemned the rest of the country to limited diversification and a low-level growth equilibrium (Lundahl, 1982; South Africa Team, 2015).[22]

Low Expectations. In 1994, South Africa's growth was above 3% i.e. as the country enjoyed something of a peace dividend (Figure 3.5, Panel 1). Real investment (both domestic and FDI) increased sharply, but so did domestic consumption. The buoyancy did not last. The economy was soon hit by the flight to safety second-round effects of the Asian Financial Crisis of the late-1990s which hit emerging economies. However, South Africa was then able to sustain close to a decade of robust growth in the 2000s, before another international financial crisis emerged during 2008/2009. Since then, South Africa has not been able to attract foreign investment at anywhere near the targets in its plan documents (South African Reserve Bank, various issues).

Since 2010, growth in South Africa has averaged less than 2% per year (Figure 3.5, Panel 1) i.e. a few notches above population growth of 1.6%, against plan projection of above 3%. This decade of low growth has been depicted as the "new normal" (Fedderke and Mengisteab, 2016; South African Team, 2015). On the other hand, since 1994, the rate of unemployment has risen by an additional 7–10% to 6.2 million and hovers above a quarter of the labor force, the majority youth (Figure 3.5, Panel 2). A World Bank report by Haddad et al. (2019) noted that in the 12 years since 2008, some 3.5 million people have entered the South African labor market, while only 1.6 million jobs have been created during the period.

In a dualistic economy, with a non-expanding modern sector, much innovation will be required to bring growth and employment to the levels projected by the National Development Plan (average unemployment was projected to fall to as low as 6% by 2020). The economy has underperformed, with job losses occurring mostly in the retail trade sector, manufacturing, and construction, where the most fragile households in the urban centers derive a livelihood. Paucity of employment has had notable knock-on effects on urban crime and rural despondency (Republic of South Africa, 2014). By these measures, the democratic dividend is yet to cascade to the lower echelons of society.

Addressing the Legacy of Inequality. On achieving majority rule in 1994, the new government had staked its agenda of economic transformation on the ANC's election manifesto, which drew inspiration from the *Freedom Charter* of the 1950s, emphasizing social housing, labor-intensive public works programs to provide employment, land redistribution, and other poverty fighting measures as well as expansion of the role of the state in the economy. In power, the ANC chose to roll out its programs in piecemeal fashion fearing negative investor reaction and constrained by a lack of resources (ANC, 1994; Congress of the People, 1955).[23] As Leubolt (2014) notes, the new leaders' dilemma lay in how to design a credible package of universal benefits targeted at its supporters, in a stagnant economy with declining revenues, without hurting future growth prospects.

On attaining power, the new government drafted a presciently named Reconstruction and Development Programme (RDP) to address the legacies of Apartheid. It aimed to pursue an integrated and sustainable development program, which was people-driven, ensured peace and security for all, and focused on

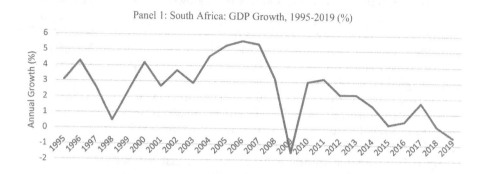

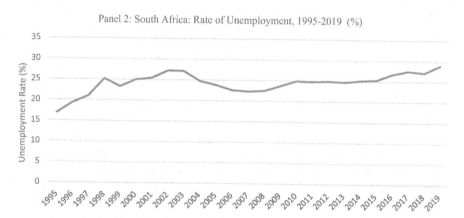

Figure 3.5 South Africa: Growth (Panel 1) and Unemployment (Panel 2), 1995–2019 (%)
Source: World Bank (various issues) and Reserve Bank of South Africa.

nation building i.e. linking reconstruction to development, meeting households' basic needs, developing human resources, and ensuring that the democratization of South Africa would influence all future development efforts in the country. The success of RDP was premised on the availability of resources, through taxation or expenditure reallocation. Fiscal exigencies, evolving political agendas and distractions of incumbency, took the punch out of this much-lauded program (notably, with respect to social housing), leaving behind only token pointers to what could have been, as well as popular resentment. Above all, RDP failed to generate the levels of economic growth commensurate with rising standards of living and poverty reduction.

The government introduced the Growth, Employment and Redistribution (GEAR) program in 1996, which sought to provide a macroeconomic rationale for the RDP's more socially oriented focus. It aimed to stimulate growth, while ensuring macroeconomic stability through fiscal consolidation, low inflation, and moderate public sector wage bill growth and exchange rate stability. Although the points of departure for GEAR's macroeconomic framework were quite different from those of the SAPs implemented in other African countries, the labor unions (notably COSATU) and other segments of civil society attacked the program for being neo-liberal.[24] In retrospect, the era of GEAR, which covered a good part of the 2000s, recorded higher growth than any period before or after (Figure 3.5).

Still, the ANC was of the view that an average growth rate of 3% was not enough to address South Africa's high levels of unemployment and spatial and income inequality (a Gini of over 60). GEAR was, thus, replaced by the Accelerated and Shared Growth Initiative for South Africa (ASGISA) which, with a nod to the developmental state model, focused on doubling the rate of growth (up to 6% in the medium to long term), poverty reduction, and employment creation (reducing unemployment from 28% in 2004 to 14% by 2014). When President Thabo Mbeki left power in 2008, replaced by Jacob Zuma, ASGISA was quietly abandoned.

Elite Bargain in a Time of Anxiety. With respect to South Africa's ambition to become a developmental state, as per its National Development Plan, the South Africa Team (2015) has argued that a decade-long elite bargain between the state and the mining industry, the motor of the economy for centuries, is a potentially critical impediment to achieving development goals.[25] Despite the transfer of political power in 1994 to the black majority, the elite bargain between the state, business, and traditional authorities continues in much the same way as before. In recent years, elites have ensured that mineral rents accrued to politically connected businesses, through Black Economic Empowerment (BEE) compliance and traditional authorities (Manson, 2013; Van Kessel and Oomen, 1997). Playing the BEE game became a survival strategy for established business elites and a stick employed by politicians to maintain the ruling coalition. In other words, and curiously, despite the intentions of the new government, and the monumental shift in political power, path-dependence has ensured that the elite bargain remains intact 25 years after majority rule was ushered in (Beresford, 2015).

South Africa's experience shows that harnessing natural resource wealth for inclusive development requires a state that is capable of designing policies focused on stopping rent-seeking activities and fostering inclusion. Despite a radical transfer of power to the black majority in 1994, South Africa has not implemented meaningful land reform nor reduced its dependence on mineral rents both economically and politically. While mining had clearly contributed to South Africa's development, it also laid the foundations for racial suppression which became difficult to reverse (Cawood and Minnitt, 1998; Plagerson et al., 2019). But while it is tempting to argue that South Africa should simply focus on harnessing its mineral wealth for downstream beneficiation to promote industrialization and modern employment, the NDP warns that, on its own, "beneficiation is not a panacea because it is also usually capital intensive, contributing little to overall job creation" (Republic of South Africa, 2012).

Looking ahead, a key challenge for South Africa will be how to manage the inevitable fiscal consolidation, the so-called "internal devaluation," especially when it comes to reducing the public sector wage bill. A major test will lie in how wage negotiations in the public sector and the broader economy are handled in the medium term. The government showed some determination to contain wage spending between 2009 and 2014 by letting its employee headcount decline by 1.3%, a small but important pointer, as previous years had shown increases. In 2014, the government announced a freeze on personnel headcounts for 2015/2016 and 2016/2017, with any additional departmental hires to be paid for from existing resource allocations.[26] Without a steady expansion in modern sector job creation outside government, it will be difficult for the public sector to withstand the pressure to increase employment within its ranks. The litmus test will be how well the government is able to deploy its fiscal arsenal to meet these challenges, including incentives to the private sector to increase hiring, while preserving its social obligations.[27]

Shaping the Future: Vision 2030. In 2012, the government introduced Vision 2030 to drive its developmental state ambitions. While it evokes the solidarity and mutual quest for success that has characterized South Africa's post-1994 policies, it also highlights some of the dilemmas inherent in attempting to close the opportunity gaps too quickly, in a country where the private sector controls 80% of the economy.[28] The Vision 2030 document is both eloquent and lyrical,[29] relating to the Constitution's core values of a united, democratic, non-sexist, and non-racial society, and a single integrated economy, while underlining the imperatives of poverty and inequality reduction; encouraging citizen and communal initiatives in the pursuit of development; strengthening democracy and holding government accountable; enhancing the capabilities of the people and the country through: skills development, boosting infrastructure, strengthening institutions, including those providing social services; and nurturing domestic and external partnerships (Box 3.5).

Box 3.5: South Africa's Vision 2030 through the developmental state prism

Defining a Capable and Developmental State. A state is capable when it has the capacity to formulate and implement policies that serve the national interest. It is developmental when those policies focus on overcoming the root causes of poverty and inequality and building the state's capacity to fulfill its role. The document is adamant that "building state capacity is the most important" function of the developmental state. It argues further that not all capable states are developmental; therefore, a vibrant democratic system is required for success.

Eight Objectives and Priorities of Vision 2030. Uniting all South Africans around a common program to achieve prosperity and equity; promoting active citizenry to strengthen development, democracy and accountability; bringing about faster economic growth, higher investment, and greater labor absorption; focusing on key capabilities of people and the state;

building a capable and developmental state; encouraging strong leadership throughout society to work together to solve problems.

Building a Capable and Developmental State. Stabilizing the political-administrative interface; making the civil service a career of choice, even among the most gifted youth; developing technical and specialist skills for core functions; strengthening the delegation, accountability, and oversight responsibilities; improving interdepartmental responsibilities and national, provincial, and local government coordination; buttressing local government functions and ability to deliver services; and clarifying governance of state-owned enterprises (SOEs).

Source: Republic of South Africa (2012).

The National Development Plan/Vision 2030 projected an increase in investment from 20%, the average that South Africa had posted since the early 1990s, to 30% by the end of the plan period. Since the government was clearly counting on increased FDI to achieve this, it was necessary to reduce the perceived risk of investing in the country. The 2010s witnessed fractious politics of succession, which eroded implementation capacity within government. The irony was that even as the government sought to strike a liberal tone versus foreign investors and the rating agencies, it was forced to adopt, in a bid to maintain its radical credentials at home, the moniker of "radical economic transformation" in formulating Vision 2030's Medium-Term Strategic Framework (MTSF) for the period 2014–2019. In 2015, charges of "state capture," targeted at the highest levels of state power, drowned out the messages of the MTSF and paralyzed the apparatus of national government.

So far, the morale boosting rhetoric of Vision 2030 has not delivered. In South Korea and other East Asian countries, the national development plan was the main policy driver, with its implementation carefully monitored by a dedicated pilot agency. Although the commissioners for South Africa's Vision 2030/NDP were drawn from the country's power elite, the less glamorous aspects of implementation were relegated to lower cadre officials. Moreover, the Vision's link to the budget seems to have been coincidental and not explicit. A perennial lack of resources made it almost impossible to move in any major way on the key initiatives of Vision 2030, notably SOE reform.

The Need for Structural Flexibility. The rating agencies have been unforgiving of South Africa's poor performance in recent years. In 2017, both S&P and Fitch downgraded South Africa's sovereign debt rating to junk status, citing structurally weak growth and a politically difficult reform agenda ahead—indicating that they would reconsider if they saw real movement on issues of major concern to investors i.e. the pace of structural reforms, especially within the parastatal sector. Moody's, on the other hand, kept its rating at Baa3 i.e. a few notches above junk status, but with a negative outlook.

The slow pace of the government's reform plans for its parastatals, notably Eskom and South African Airways, and the political difficulties associated with resolving the public sector wage bill, led Moody's to downgrade the country's rating to junk status in early 2020.[30] There will be implications for South Africa's ability to attract FDI and borrow on international markets as well as on the rand. Investors, domestic and foreign, have chosen to sit on the fence in recent years as they wait for South Africa's domestic politics to play themselves out. The country's Finance Minister was of the view that this last downgrade would finally nudge the reform process forward and eradicate the latent investor and other stakeholder hesitation.[31]

A recent government policy paper (National Treasury, 2019) has argued that a firmer policy approach will be required to address the vicious circle of low investment, low growth, and sharply rising unemployment that has afflicted the country in the past decade. Half-hearted measures will not do, and only those targeted at economic transformation should be entertained. They include the reform of the power sector, notably that of the parastatal, Eskom, which has been talked about for decades, with limited results. In the absence of power, South Africa will not be able to grow its industrial sector nor improve its competitiveness. Additionally, several barriers to entry have persisted, caused by red tape, cost of credit, and distorted patterns of ownership. Moreover, given the need to create employment, more attention must be paid to the promotion of labor-intensive technologies in the country, including in rural areas.

The paper also argues that industrial policies must be accompanied by a good deal of realism and flexibility. While the current priorities are employment and BEE, they must be implemented in tandem with changes in domestic and external economic environments and the need to mitigate currency risk and preserve export competitiveness. It concludes that promoting exports and harnessing growth opportunities in all regions of South Africa must be cardinal features of the economic policy approach of the future.

Conclusion. South Africa's attempts at building a capable and developmental state to match its potential and ensure that its socioeconomic progress is sustained have been inherently difficult but with progress in some areas (Black and Gerwel, 2014). Despite the broadly re-distributive incidence of its taxation and expenditure programs, however, the country's history of racial suppression, exclusion, and discrimination continues to manifest in extraordinarily high levels of income and wealth inequality and relatively low-human capital development. Many households are excluded from the structures of the formal economy and continue to eke out a marginal existence in the informal sector. The official unemployment rate remains persistently high with the highest prevalence of unemployment being among the country's young people.

The South African authorities have straddled between radical and liberal policy approaches, which has led to a credibility gap with both investors and the population. South Korea faced similar challenges in the past, but ultimately chose the path of social inclusion, which meant investing in human capital and boosting the skills of its youth, and of course the generation of employment, while pursuing market-conforming policies of a mostly capitalist genre. It was able to do this by defining a mutually beneficial social compact (an alliance for development) between the government and business. A similar pact is yet to emerge in South Africa, partly owing to existing ownership patterns, with the state seeing its stakes in business as a means of leveling corporate power.

The South African case study suggests that despite modernity, abundance of resources, and regional political clout, the legacy of Apartheid, i.e. its internal contradictions and exclusive policies, continues to impose an effective cap on what the country can achieve in the short to medium term in terms of structural transformation and growth. The pursuit of a "capable and developmental state" is an attempt at reaching a grand bargain between a small and sophisticated first world economy and large and deprived peasant and informal urban economies, where the majority of the population derives livelihood. South Africa's path to a developmental state might differ significantly from the model described earlier—it certainly will not be conducted at the breakneck speed of the East Asian economic experience—but ultimately it is ideas, not structures, that will determine outcomes.

3.7 Zambia

Copper Riches, Poor Peasants. At independence in 1964, Zambia was richer in per capita terms than most Sub-Saharan African countries, thanks to its large and profitable copper industry and small, but rapidly growing industrial sector (UNCTAD, 2006). The Zambia Consolidated Copper Mines (ZCCM) was created in 1982 from the amalgamation of several mining companies that the state had nationalized in the early 1970s and became the largest business concern in the country and the region, listed among the 500 richest companies in the world by the Fortune Magazine of the US.

Zambia's first president, Kenneth Kaunda, promoted an ambitious development agenda based on his philosophy of Humanism which had a socialist orientation but also contained several developmental state attributes.[32] The government created a National Commission for Development Planning (NCDP) after independence to coordinate all development planning and investment activities. It invested in social and physical infrastructure, notably education, that included the creation of the University of Zambia. Copper mining aside, Zambian society, with a population of 3.5 million at independence in 1964, was still relatively poor, dependent on peasant agriculture and characterized by low levels of educational attainment (Seers, 1964).

Although Zambia's per capita income was roughly equal to that of South Korea (in PPP terms), in the early 1960s, the two countries' income steams had diverged markedly by 2018, with Zambia's per capita income at U$3,750, a tenth of that of South Korea. Moreover, Zambia's battle against poverty, underlined half a century previously in UNIP's election manifesto, mentioned above, had been lackluster. Some 57.5% of Zambia's population lived on less than U$2 a day in 2015, and infant mortality was 67 per 1,000 live births. Defined by that metric, poverty had been entirely eliminated in South Korea, while infant mortality was 4 per 1,000 livebirths. In 2016, the doctor-patient ratio for Zambia was 1.6 doctors to 10,000 patients compared to 22.3 doctors to 10,000 patients for South Korea. The latter showed that South Korea's emphasis on human development and shared growth not only had paid off considerably but also its success was not beyond reach given the start conditions (Mbah and Wasum, 2019; Zambia Team, 2017).

In the first decade of independence (1964–1974), Zambia's economic growth was above 5%, thanks to good copper prices and prolonged good rains that increased maize production and ameliorated food inflation (Figure 3.6). Subsequent decades were characterized interchangeably by "too much state intervention or too little market" (Zambia Team, 2017). Inspired by a socialist-type national planning ethos, the government sought to determine, in fine detail, what was produced in all sectors of the economy and by what means. It controlled farmgate prices for maize farmers, set food subsidies, especially for maize, the national staple, as well as public sector wages. The government then created a department focused on price controls, while the ministry of agriculture adjusted prices regularly for fertilizer and related farm inputs.

With time, the lack of incentives for private sector participation, and the copper-dependent economy's limited bearing capacity for the fiscal burden, meant that the government's planning and control systems were condemned to become pro forma and irrelevant (Jepson and Henderson, 2016; Rakner, 2003). The control regime and food subsidy system soon led to price distortions and rent-seeking activities, which spilled into the macroeconomy. The copper-led prosperity ended in the 1980s, however, while attempts to diversify into agriculture and manufacturing failed. Zambia changed rapidly from a country with good development prospects to a crisis-ridden economy, with mounting external debt and deepening poverty (Bigsten and Kayizzi-Mugerwa, 2000; Gulhati, 1989).

Returning to Growth. By the end of the 1990s, political patronage and corruption within the public sector had become widespread, while discipline within the parastatals, including the utilities sector, had dissipated, with serious fiscal implications. Notably, ZCCM, the copper conglomerate, the country's biggest foreign exchange earner, and also loss maker, was considered by the government, in modern parlance, to be "too big to fail." The state underwrote its debts to keep it solvent and to avoid the political fallout that a confrontation with the still feisty Mine Workers Union of Zambia (MUZ) would entail. ZCCM was ultimately unbundled and its assets sold, although the process was circuitous and economically and politically destabilizing for the country (Craig, 2001; Fraser and Lungu, 2006).

Hence, 30 years after independence, a coherent and vision-driven development strategy had yet to take root in Zambia. In retrospect, and in contrast with South Korea, the government lacked the bureaucratic capacity to drive key policies. The hope that such capacity would materialize with time proved to be as illusionary as did the notion that the demand for high-level bureaucratic skills within government would beget its own supply without concerted training

(Seshamani, 2014, Shafer, 1990). Following external shocks and economic decline, Zambia turned to the IMF and the World Bank for support in the 1990s. The decade entailed economic liberalization, including letting the markets determine resource allocation, the prices of goods and services, and the exchange rate, and reducing the size of the public sector. Although the reforms helped remove some of the egregious economic distortions created by the previous control regime, public institutions remained unenthusiastic and weak.

In retrospect, the donor-supported SAPs of the 1980s and 1990s, while bringing some economic respite, generated lackluster growth (Figure 3.6). Their socio-economic outcomes, notably with respect to social service provision and poverty reduction, were also quite indifferent. Matters briefly came to a head when, reacting to the paucity of reform results, the government sought to abandon all external policy advice and accompanying technical impositions and attempted to put in place a national program that would help generate "growth from own resources" and lead to self-reliance. The hasty effort, which alluded to a simpler era when the Zambian authorities enjoyed a degree of policy autonomy, and sought to escalate the role of agriculture in the economy as a diversification strategy, was quickly abandoned, however (Kayizzi-Mugerwa, 1990; Andersson and Kayizzi-Mugerwa, 1993).

In December 2006, Zambia launched its Vision 2030 with the theme "Prosperous Middle-Income Country by 2030" (Box 3.6). It sought to promote inclusion and shared values: gender-responsive sustainable growth, democracy, respect for human rights; good traditional and family values; a positive attitude to work; and peaceful coexistence and public–private partnerships. Within the longer-term vision, the government crafted five-year development programs and budget statements to meet its objectives (Republic of Zambia, 2000a, 2006b, 2011, 2017). Zambia's 7th National Development, under Vision 2030, seeks to reposition Zambia explicitly as a developmental state (Box 3.6).

Box 3.6: Repositioning Zambia as a developmental state

The theme of the Seventh National Development Program (2017–2021) was to "reposition Zambia as a developmental state." The plan specifically points to South Korea as a country whose development experience is worth emulating. It notes that "South Korea was able to achieve economic development by putting in place a developmental vision and strong state structures, which were effectively and efficiently applied to perform developmental roles." The repositioning of Zambia would entail the following:

(i) Putting emphasis on expanding economic opportunities and efficient use of resources to address poverty i.e. imperatives of economic growth must be balanced with those of social development.

(ii) Using state-owned institutions to spur growth and development.
(iii) Eliminating patronage, inefficiency, malfeasance, and other inhibitors of good service delivery and promoting meritocracy throughout the civil service.
(iv) Making a commitment to build a developmental state that has the support of the population.
(v)   Creating an environment that attracts private sector involvement in projects geared at socio-economic upliftment.

Source: Compiled from Zambia's Vision 2030
(Republic of Zambia, 2006a).

Zambia, like most other African countries, has put much effort in achieving macroeconomic stability in 2000s, although countervailing pressures have been considerable: unbudgeted fuel and electricity subsidies, significant expenditure overruns in the maize sub-sector in response to political commitments (input subsidies and boosting food reserves), incomplete infrastructure projects, particularly in road construction, sharp increases in public sector wages, and election-related expenditures. In 2012, the Bank of Zambia adopted full-fledged inflation targeting as the main monetary policy tool, helping to keep inflation at around 10% since then, compared to an average of 20% between 1995 and 2011. While raising policy rates has helped to stabilize the kwacha, it also raised the cost of borrowing for businesses, especially small-scale and medium-sized ones at the lower end of the distribution.

The period 2000–2015 marked the longest era of sustained growth in Zambia (Figure 3.6). GDP per capita reached US$1,800 in 2013, returning the country

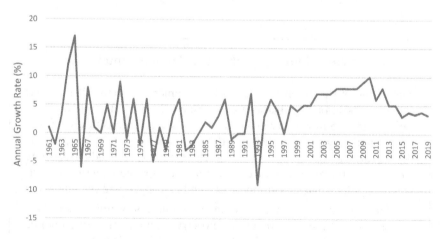

Figure 3.6 Zambia: GDP Growth, 1961–2019 (%)
Source: World Bank (various issues).

to (low) middle income status, a position it had reached for the first time in the late-1960s. Prolonged good performance of the copper sector was a key driver, with the sharp increase in copper prices that started in 2004/2005 on the back of strong demand from Asia, and particularly China, having a significant cumulative impact. There was an unprecedented increase in FDI to the copper mining sector in the 2000s, with new mines coming on stream—notably, Lumwana and Luanshya-Muliashi. The question in the minds of the authorities was whether this rapid increase in mining investment and its spillovers to other sectors of the economy would be enough to propel the economy onto the path of sustained growth and diversification (International Council on Mining and Metals, 2014; Kragelund, 2017; Republic of Zambia, various years).

Fatal Attraction to International Markets. On returning to middle-income status, Zambia became ineligible for concessionary financing, while it could go to the markets on its own. In 2012, it did that, issuing a debut $750 million Eurobond, at a coupon rate of 5.625% and 10-year tenor, which was oversubscribed. Buoyed by the positive sentiment and the prestige of holding its destiny in own hands, Zambia returned to the Eurobond market twice in quick succession i.e. in 2014 for US$1 billion at 8.5% and in 2015 for US$1.25 billion at 9.0%, at tenors of 10 and 12 years, respectively. Although the markets had tightened by some 300 basis points in three years, the Zambian authorities still saw the borrowing as critical for establishing a track record of economic management and financial viability. However, although the loans were said to be principally for infrastructure, a popular justification for heavy external borrowing in many African countries today, the bulk of the loans ended up gap filling the national budget. By 2019, Zambia's external debt as a ratio of GDP was 74% (above the nominal debt distress threshold of 60% for countries with a good record of economic performance), while the ratio of foreign exchange reserves to foreign debt was 11%, one of the lowest in Africa—compared to 61% for South Africa, 33% for Cameroon, and 20% for Côte d'Ivoire.[33] Zambia's external debt was estimated at some US$11 billion in early 2020.

Earlier in 2020, and with the onset of Covid19, Zambia had the dubious distinction of having the highest dollar yields on Eurobonds for countries not in default (Bloomberg, 2020). The risk for debt distress, given equally large loans from China, had risen considerably in the first half of 2020. To resolve the debt sustainability issue, the country seems poised to return to the IMF for a program, although there is internally much rearguard action to avoid this. In any case, no such program can be agreed with the Fund when problems with external lenders remain unresolved. In May 2020, the government retained the French investment bank, Lazard, to advise it on how to handle its burgeoning debt problem. The irony is that while going to the markets was initially seen as an innocuous means of signaling increasing domestic economic management skills and confidence to the world, in the event, it instead displayed fiscal frailty in the face of structural challenges of large proportion and paucity of strategic planning (*Financial Times*, 2020; Nalishebo and Halwampa, 2015).

Notes

1 Per classification of The World Bank (various years).
2 Without this push, South Korea's level of economic development could not have been achieved in the time it took (less than 30 years) (Choong-yong, 2012).
3 See, for example, Choong-yong (2012).
4 A reference to "usable gross foreign reserves." It has been estimated that South Korea has had an average of over US$100 billion of foreign exchange reserves per year since the early 1970s. So, the decline in 1997 was quite substantial.
5 The IMF-Supported program included several structural provisions reminiscent of programs in Sub-Saharan Africa: eradication of monopolies, privatization, closure of unviable state-owned enterprises, increased foreign participation in economy, etc. Follow-up measures included, for example, letting 10 of 14 distressed commercial banks go bankrupt. There was, however, a general critique that by extending its concerns to structural, and therefore political, issues, in a relatively developed part of the world, the IMF had superseded its role—requiring a rebuttal from IMF leadership (Feldstein, 1998; Fischer, 1998).
6 Fischer noted that although the share of investment to GDP in South Korea had risen from 25% in the 1970s to 40% in the mid-1990s, the share of capital in total income had fallen from 55% to under 40 percent during the same period. He blamed this on the rising number of unproductive loans to the business sector, suggesting that "rates of investment and capital accumulation in those economies were excessive."
7 For example, the government had in 2003 to deal with the risk of a number of credit card companies going bust, eventually rescuing the largest one among them, LG Card, to prevent the potentially high fallout consequences (Fischer, 2004).
8 The Community includes Cameroon, Central African Republic, Chad, Equatorial Guinea, and Republic of Congo. It shares a central bank, Banque des États de l'Afrique Centrale (BEAC), and hence individual countries have no monetary policy and rely mainly on fiscal adjustments to reach their growth objectives. However, the absence of monetary policy levers has spared the region from the kind of inflationary pressures experienced in other parts of Africa during civil conflict. Today, ECCAS is one of the most conflict-ridden regions in Africa.
9 Cameroon became a frequent case study of the Dutch Disease impacts of commodity booms (Benjamin, Devarajan and Weiner, 1989; Sikod and Teke, 2012).
10 According to the IMF (2018), SONARA had accumulated debt to the banking system of some 0.8% of GDP by 2017.
11 Union members included Benin, Burkina Faso, Côte d'Ivoire, Guinea-Bissau, Mali, Niger, Senegal, and Togo. They share a central bank: Banque Centrale des États de l'Ouest (BCEAO).
12 However, Marxist scholar Samir Amin (1967) famously referred to Côte d'Ivoire as a "case of growth without development," dismissing its capitalist ambitions of the 1960s as lacking a concrete basis for self-sustenance, owing to the lack of a strategy and the absence of an indigenous business class.
13 During 1975–1976, Brazilian coffee trees were damaged by a killer freeze sending global prices for coffee sky high, while also boosting those of cocoa.
14 This was less than a fifth of South Korea's GDP.
15 They include the following: (1) Department of Petroleum Resources; (2) Federal Ministry of Environment, Housing and Urban Development, responsible for approving environmental impact assessment reports with respect of oil and gas projects; (3) Federal Ministry of Petroleum Resources; (4) Joint Development Authority, responsible for the supervision of petroleum activities within the Nigeria–São Tomé and Príncipe; (5) Niger Delta Development Commission to provide basic infrastructure and amenities in the Niger Delta (and mitigate some of the resistance from the local population); (6) Nigerian Content Development and Monitoring Board,

responsible for ensuring compliance with respect to local content stipulations; (7) Nigerian National Petroleum Corporation, through which the state participates in the petroleum industry, with exclusive responsibility for upstream and downstream development of oil and gas activities; (8) Nigerian National Petroleum Investment Management Services which supervises and manages government investment in the oil and gas industry; (9) Oil Mineral Producing Areas Commission to be the government's eyes and ears on the ground; (10) Petroleum Products Pricing Regulatory Agency, which regulates the rates for the transportation and distribution of petroleum products.

16 See, for example, *Financial Nigeria Magazine*, 13 September 2017.

17 See the article by Ebuka Onyeji in *Premium Times Newspaper* "Analysis: Why Nigeria's Vision 20:2020 was bound to fail," Abuja, January 19, 2020.

18 Among them are the Dangote Group, Jumia, and United Bank for Africa.

19 In recent years, power has shifted relatively smoothly among Nigerian regimes: Olusegun Obasanjo, 1999–2007; Umaru Yar'Adua, 2007–2010; Goodluck Jonathan, 2010–2015; Muhammadu Buhari, May 2015–to date.

20 The government was able to reduce non-performing assets to 3% of total gross loans by 2014, although they have risen since, reaching 17 percent in 2018 (World Bank, various issues).

21 Writing in the *Forbes Magazine*, August 25, 2017, Tim Worstall describes the dichotomy succinctly: "the basic underlying problem is that the economy is in two parts, a small and near First World industrial economy and a much larger—by the number of people, not economic size—essentially peasant economy surrounding it." However, Fedderke and Mengisteab (2016) are of the view that low growth is a temporary aberration associated with institutional challenges and that the economy will return to the better performance of the 2000s.

22 Thus, while South Africa had a GDP of US$7.58 billion in 1960, three times that of South Korea at the time, its GDP in 2019, 60 years later, having grown to US$350 billion, is only about a fifth of South Korea's GDP of some US$1.7 trillion.

23 The *Freedom Charter* stated, for example, that "All people shall have the right to live where they chose, to be decently housed, and to bring up their families in comfort and security." The ANC election manifesto, from 1994, had committed, among others, to constructing 1 million houses for the vulnerable households during its first five years in power.

24 This was the equivalent of what used to be called "counterrevolutionary diversion." Critics, pointing north of the Limpopo, were averse to anything that smacked of the Washington Consensus.

25 See also the arguments in Cawood and Minnit (1998) and North, Wallis and Weingast (2009).

26 National Treasury (2015), pp. 32–33.

27 However, Von Holdt et al. (2011) are of a different view i.e. radical measures will be required to impede social disruption, which to them is imminent.

28 Vision 2030 argues that the issue of growth and employment generation will only be tackled successfully when business and labor endorse a shared vision. The view that the government can appeal to social corporate responsibility characterizes some of the thinking behind the Broad-Based Black Economic Empowerment (BBBEE) strategy of the government but also has developmental state intonations.

29 The vision statement is expressed in verse, including the line "We are an African Country" while its motto is "our future—make it work."

30 Moody's downgrade happened in the middle of the Covid-19 crisis and virtual lockdown of South Africa. Some, among the authorities, had hoped that the crisis would help postpone the downgrade decision, but that did not happen.

31 Sitting on the fence has been a common activity in South Africa's corporate sector in recent years, as investors wait for real movement on reforms (see Henderson, 2018).

32 See, for example, Kaunda's first election manifesto entitled "When UNIP Becomes Government" (United National Independent Party, 1963).
33 With the onset of Covid19 in 2020, the comparisons do not make much sense and African countries have decided to approach lenders as a collective. See, for example, the reporting by Soto (2020).

References

Adejumbi, S. (2011) *State, Economy, and Society in Post-Military Nigeria*, Palgrave and Macmillan: New York and London.

Adeolu, A. and Oyejide, A. (2012) 'Determinants of Backward Linkages of Oil and Gas Industry in the Nigerian Economy,' *Resources Policy* 37(4):452–460.

Ahn, C. (2001) 'Financial and Corporate Sector Restructuring in South Korea: Accomplishments and Unfinished Agenda,' *The Japanese Economic Review* 52(4):452–470.

Aiyede, E. (2009) 'The Political Economy of Fiscal Federalism and the Dilemma of Constructing a Developmental State in Nigeria,' *International Political Science Review* 30(3):249–269.

Amin, S. (1967) *Développement du Capitalisme en Côte d'Ivoire,* Editions Minuit: Paris.

Amuwo, A. (2008) 'Constructing the Democratic Developmental State in Africa. A Case Study of Nigeria, 1960–2007,' *Occasional Paper*, 59, Institute for Global Dialogue: Johannesburg.

ANC (1994) *Election Manifesto*, African National Congress: Johannesburg.

Andersson, P. and Kayizzi-Mugerwa, S. (1993) 'External Shocks and the Search for Diversification in Zambia,' in M. Blomström and Lundahl, M. (eds.), *Economic Crisis in Africa: Perspectives on Policy Responses*, 134–151, Routledge: London.

Assiga-Ateba, E-M. (1998) «Les Politiques de Restructuration de l'Economie Camerounaise: Evaluation Rétrospective à Moyen-Terme», *Revue Africaine de Développement* 10(2):54–89.

Assiga-Ateba, E.M. (2006) «Propriété du Capital, Investissement et Croissance au Cameroun», *Communication à la Onzième Conférence de la Société Africaine d'Econométrie* sous l'égide de l'Institut Africain de Développement et de Planification à Dakar – Sénégal, du 04 au 07 juillet.

Assiga-Baulin, J. (1974) *La Politique Intérieure d'Houphouët-Boigny*, Eurofor: Paris.

Ayuk, B. (2012) 'The Cameroonian Banking Sector,' *Presentation*, Ministry of Finance, Republic of Cameroon: Yaoundé.

Bagchi, A. (2000) 'The Past and Future of the Developmental State,' *Journal of World Systems Research* 11(2):398–442.

Ballo, Z. and Kimou, J-C. (2015) « Gouvernance et Planification: quel rôle pour l'émergence de la Côte d'Ivoire », *Etude commanditée par le PNUD*-Côte d'Ivoire : Abidjan.

Bamou-Tankoua, L. (2002) 'Promoting Export Diversification in Cameroon: toward which products?' *AERC Research Paper,* 114, African Economic Research Consortium: Nairobi.

Bastart, H. (2014) « Constitutions et transitions démocratiques en Côte d'Ivoire de 1990 à 2012 », *Thèse,* Université Laval: Laval.

BCEAO (various issues) *Annual Report,* National Office for Côte d'Ivoire: Abidjan.

Benjamin, N.C., Devarajan, S. and Weiner, R. (1989) 'The 'Dutch' Disease in a Developing Country: Oil Reserves in Cameroon: Oil Reserves in Cameroon,' *Journal of Development Economics* 30(1):71–92.

Beresford, A. (2015) 'Power, Patronage, and Gatekeeper Politics in South Africa,' *African Affairs* 114(455):226–248.

Bigsten, A. and Kayizzi-Mugerwa, S. (2000) 'The Political Economy of Policy Failure in Zambia,' *Working Papers in Economics*, 23, Department of Economics, School of Economics and Commercial Law, University of Gothenburg: Göteborg.

Black, A. and Gerwel, H. (2014) 'Shifting the Growth Path to Achieve Employment Intensive Growth in South Africa,' *Development Southern Africa* 31(2):241–256.

Bloomberg (2020) 'Zambia Eurobonds Extend Losses as Country Flags Restructure,' https://www.bloomberg.com/news/articles/2020-03-31/zambia-seeks-advisers-for-reorganization-of-foreign-debt.

Cameroon Team (2017) « Etude Sur L'Economie du Cameroun. La Politique de Développement dans la Pratique Enseignements Tires de L'Expérience de Développement de la Corée du Sud », Report to the African Development Bank on the *Developmental State in Africa, Lessons from South Korea Project*, Université de Yaoundé II: Yaoundé.

Cawood, F. and Minnitt, R. (1998) 'A Historical Perspective on the Economics of Mineral Rights Ownership,' *The Journal of the Southern African Institute of Mining and Metallurgy* 98(7):369–370.

Central Bank of Nigeria (various issues) *Annual Report*, CBN: Abuja.

Cherry, J. (2005) "Big Deal' or Big Disappointment? The Continuing Evolution of the South Korean Developmental State,' *Pacific Review* 18(3): September.

Choong-yong, A. (2012) 'Korea: First-Five Year Development Plan,' *The Korea Times*, November 25.

Coe, D. and Kim, S-J. (eds.) (2002) *Korean Crisis and Recovery*, Seminar Volumes, International Monetary Fund: Washington, DC.

Cogneau, D. (2002) « L'économie ivoirienne, la fin du mirage », *Document de travail* » Unité de Recherche CIPRE: Abidjan.

Cogneau, D. and Mesplé-Somps, S. (1999) « *La Côte d'Ivoire peut-elle devenir un pays émergent?, Programme d'étude Afrique émergente* », Centre de développement OCDE: Paris.

Colman, D., and Okorie, A. (1993) 'The Effect of Structural Adjustment on the Nigerian Agricultural Export Sector,' *Journal of International Development* 10(3):341–355.

Congress of the People (1955) *Freedom Charter: Adopted at the Congress of the People at Kliptown, Johannesburg, on June 25 and 26, 1955*, Pacific Press Ltd: Johannesburg.

Côte d'Ivoire Team (2017) « Etude Sur L'Economie Ivoirienne. La Politique de Développement dans la Pratique Enseignements Tires de L'Expérience de Développement de la Corée du Sud », Report to the African Development Bank on the *Developmental State in Africa, Lessons from South Korea Project*, Le Centre Ivoirien de Recherches Economiques et Sociales (CIRES): Abidjan.

Craig, J. (2001) 'Putting Privatization into Practice: The Case of the Zambian Consolidated Copper Mines Limited,' *The Journal of Modern African Studies* 39(3):389–410.

den Tuinder, B. (1978) *Ivory Coast: The Challenges of Success*, Johns Hopkins University: Baltimore.

Devarajan, S. (1991) 'Comment on Paper by C. Chamley: 'Côte d'Ivoire: The Failure of Structural Adjustment,'' in V.E. Thomas et al. (eds.), *Restructuring Economies in Distress: Policy Reform and the World Bank*, 305–308, Oxford University Press: World Bank.

Diabi, Y. (2000) « L'information et le Pouvoir Politique en Côte D'ivoire entre 1960 ET 1990 », HERMES 28, Université de Cocody: UFR Information, Communication et Arts.

Dittmer, L. (2007) 'The Asian Financial Crisis and the Developmental State,' *Asian Survey* 47(6):829–833.

Fedderke, J. and Mengisteab, D. (2016) 'Estimating South Africa's Output Gap Potential Growth Rate,' *ESRA Working Paper*, 585, Economic Research Southern Africa.

Feldstein, M. (1998) 'Refocusing the IMF: Overdoing it in East Asia,' *Foreign Affairs* 77(2): March/April.

Financial Times (2020) 'Zambia Hires Lazard to Advise on $11 Debt Burden,' 28 May.

Fischer, S. (1998) 'In Defense of the IMF,' *Foreign Affairs* 77(4): July/August.

Fischer, S. (2004) 'A Development Strategy for Asian Economies: Korean Perspective,' Paper Presented at the 37th Annual Meeting of the Asian Development Bank, Jeju, Korea.

Fonjong, L. (ed.) (2019) *Natural Resources Endowment and the Fallacy of Development in Cameroon*, Langaa Research and Publishing Common Initiative Group: Bamenda/Buena, Cameroon.

Fraser, A. and Lungu, J. (2006) *For Whom the Windfalls? Winners & Losers in the Privatization of Zambia's Copper Mines,* Civil Society Trade Network of Zambia, and Catholic Centre for Justice, Development and Peace: Lusaka.

Fung, K. (2013) 'Financial Crisis and the Developmental State: A Case Study of Hong Kong,' *International Journal of Social Welfare* 23(3):321–332.

Gauthier, B. and Zeufack, A. (2010) 'Governance and Oil Revenues in Cameroon,' *OXCarre Working Papers,* 038, Oxford Centre for the Analysis of Resource-Rich Economies, University of Oxford.

Gayi, S., Nkurunziza, H. and Kasahara, S. (2007) *Retrouver une Marge d'Action: La Mobilisation des Ressources Intérieures et l'Etat Développementiste,* CNUCED: Genève.

Gboyega, A., Soreide, T., Minh, T. and Shukla, G. (2011) 'Political Economy of the Petroleum Sector in Nigeria,' *Policy Research Working Paper Series* 5779, World Bank: Washington, DC.

Gockel, R., Stokes-Prindle, C., Gugerty, M.K. and Plotnick, R. (2009) 'Political Economy of Fertiliser Policy in Cote d'Ivoire,' *Evans Policy Analysis and Research Paper*, Evans School of Public Affairs, University of Washington: Seattle.

Green, A.E. (1992) 'South Korea's Automobile Industry: Performance and Prospects,' *Asian Survey* 32(5):411–428.

Gulhati, R. (1989) *Impasse in Zambia: The Economics and Politics of Reform,* World Bank: Washington, DC.

Haddad, M., Karimjee, S., Khalifa, D. and Noumba, U. (2019) *Creating Markets in South Africa: Boosting Private Investment to Unlock South Africa's Growth Potential*, World Bank: Washington, DC.

Hayashi, S. (2010) 'The Developmental State in the Era of Globalization: Beyond the North-East Asian Model of Political Economy,' *The Pacific Review* 23(1):45–69.

Hecht, R. (1983) 'The Ivory Coast Miracle: What Benefits for Peasant Farmers?' *Journal of Modern African Studies* 21(1):25–53.

Henderson, R. (2018) 'Cash-Rich Banks Seeking Growth See Dearth of S. Africa Projects,' *Bloomberg Business*, October 26, New York.

Ikpe, E. (2017) 'The Enduring Relevance of the Developmental State Paradigm Across Space and Time: Lessons for Africa on Structural Transformation and Agriculture in Oil-Rich Contexts,' *Journal of Asian and African Studies* 53(5):764–781.

IMF (2004) *Republic of Korea: 2004 Article IV Consultation—Staff Report*, International Monetary Fund: Washington, DC.

IMF (2009) 'Cameroon: Financial System Stability Assessment – Update,' *IMF Country Report*, 09/51, International Monetary Fund: Washington DC.

IMF (2018) *Cameroon. First Review under the Extended Credit Facility*, International Monetary Fund: Washington, DC.

IMF (various years) *World Economic Outlook*, International Monetary Fund: Washington, DC.

Independent Evaluation Office of the IMF (2003) *The Role of the IMF in Recent Capital Account Crises*, International Monetary Fund: Washington DC.

Independent Evaluation Office of the IMF (2018) *The IMF's Role in Fragile States,* International Monetary Fund: Washington DC.

International Council on Mining and Metals (2014) *Annual Report*, London.

Jepson, N. and Henderson, J. (2016) 'Critical Transformations: Rethinking Zambian Development,' *SPERI Paper*, 43, Sheffield Political Economy Research Institute: The University of Sheffield.

Jeuneafrique (2015) *Côte d'Ivoire: 2011–2015, le vrai bilan*, October 23, Abidjan

Kasahara, S. (2013) 'The Asian Developmental State and the Flying Geese Paradigm,' *Discussion Papers*, 123, United Nations Conference for Trade and Development: Geneva.

Kawai, M., Newfarmer, R. and Schmukler, S. (2005) 'Financial Crises: Nine Lessons from East Asia,' *Eastern Economic Journal* 31(2):185–207.

Kayizzi-Mugerwa, S. (1990) 'Growth from Own Resources: Zambia's Fourth National Development Programme in Perspective,' *Development Policy Review* 8(1): March.

Kayizzi-Mugerwa, S. (1997) 'Indebtedness, Poverty and Policy in Côte d'Ivoire: Responses of a Formerly Rich Country,' *Memorandum*, Department of Economics, University of Gothenburg: Göteborg.

Kayizzi-Mugerwa, S. and Anyanwu, J. (2015) 'Creating Local Content for Human Development in Africa's New Natural Resource-Rich Countries,' *Flagship Report Paper Series*, 6, African Development Bank: Abidjan and Bill and Melinda Gates Foundation: Seattle.

Kearney, R. (1991) *Warrior Worker. The History and Challenge of South Korea's Economic Miracle*, Henry Holt and Company: New York.

Khemani, S. (2001) 'Fiscal Federalism and Service Delivery in Nigeria: The Role of States and Local Governments,' *Paper Prepared for the Nigerian PER Steering Committee*, Federal Government: Abuja.

Kim, D. (2009) 'Korean Experience of Overcoming Economic Crisis through ICT Development,' *UNESCAP Technical Paper*, IDD/TP-09-1, August.

Kim, J. and Kim, K. (2006) 'The Electricity Industry Reform in Korea: Lessons for Further Liberalization,' *Mimeograph,* Seoul National University: Seoul.

Kragelund, P. (2017) 'The Making of Local Content Policies in Zambia's Copper Sector: Institutional Impediments to Resource-led Development,' *Resources Policy* 51(3):57–66.

Krugman, P. (1994) 'The Myth of Asia's Miracle,' *Foreign Affairs* 73(6):62–78.

Kwon, O.Y. (1998) 'The Korean Financial Crisis: Diagnosis, Remedies and Prospects,' *Journal of the Asian Pacific Economy* 3(3):331–157.

Lee, J-W. and Rhee, C. (1999) 'Social Impacts of the Asian Crisis: Policy Challenges and Lessons,' *Human Development Occassional Paper*, HDOCPA-1999-02, United Nations Development Programme.

Leubolt, B. (2014) 'Social Policies and Redistribution in South Africa,' *Working Paper* 25, International Labor Office: Geneva and Global Labor University: Berlin.

Lim, W. (2012) '*Chaebol* and Industrial Policy in Korea,' *Asian Economic Policy Review* 7(1):69–86.

Lim, Y. (2003) 'Corporate Bankruptcy System and Economic Crises in Korea,' in S. Haggard, Lim, W. and Kim, E. (eds.), *Economic Crisis and Corporate Restructuring in Korea: Reforming the Chaebol*, 207–232, Cambridge University Press: Cambridge.

Lundahl, M. (1982) 'The Rationale of Apartheid,' *American Economic Review* 72(5):1164–1179.

Makin, A. (1999) 'Preventing the Crisis in East Asia,' *Asia Survey* 39(4):668–678.

Manson, A. (2013) 'Mining and 'Traditional Communities' in South Africa's 'Platinum Belt': Contestations over Land, Leadership and Assets in North-West Province c. 1996–2012,' *Journal of South African Studies* 39(2):409–423.

Matles, A. and Shaw, W. (1990) *South Korea. A Country Study,* Government Printing Office for the US Library of Congress: Washington, DC.

Mbah, R.E. and Wasum, D.F. (2019) 'The Mystery of Development: A Comparison of South Korea and Zambia's Development Trajectory,' *International Journal of African and Asian Studies* 59(1):31–34.

Mbome, F. (1992) « Les expériences de révisions constitutionnelle au Cameroun », *Penant: revue de droit des pays d'Afrique* 102(808):10–46.

Miran-Guyon, M. (2017) 'Côte d'Ivoire: The Return of the Elephant?' *Afrique Contemporaire* 3(263–264):11–24.

Muh, E., Amara, S. and Tabet, F. (2018) 'Sustainable Energy Policies in Cameroon: A Holistic View,' *Renewable and Sustainable Energy Reviews* 82(3):3420–3429.

Nachega, J.-C. (2001) 'A Cointegration Analysis of Broad Money Demand in Cameroon,' *IMF Working Paper* 1/26, International Monetary Fund: Washington, DC.

Nalishebo, S. and Halwampa, A. (2015) 'A Cautionary Tale of Zambia's International Sovereign Bond Issuances,' *Paper,* Zambia Institute for Policy Analysis and Research: Lusaka.

National Treasury (2015) 'South Africa's Budget Review,' National Treasury: Pretoria.

National Treasury (2019) 'Economic Transformation, Inclusive Growth and Competitiveness: Towards an Economic Strategy for South Africa,' *Memorandum*, National Treasury: Pretoria.

Ngoa, H., Atangana, H., Okah, F., Soumtang, V. (2017) 'Modernisation du Secteur Industriel au Cameroun' in H. Ngoa (ed.), *Document de Stratégie pour la Croissance et L'emploi: comment atteindre une croissance à deux chiffres au Cameroun?* Afredit: Yaoundé.

North, D., Wallis, J. and Weingast, B. (2009) *Violence and Social Orders: A Conceptual Framework for Interpreting Recorded Human History,* Cambridge University Press: Cambridge.

Ntaryike (2015) 'Cameroon's New Wells, New Gas and Rising Oil Production,' *The Africa Report*, August 4.

OECD (2000) *Economic Surveys: Korea 2000*, Organization of Economic Cooperation and Development: Paris.

Office of the United States Trade Representative (2019) 'President Trump Terminates Trade Preference Program Eligibility for Cameroon,' Statement, October 31, Washington, DC.

Ohiorhenuan, J. (1989) *Capital and the State in Nigeria,* Greenwood Press: Westport.

Okonjo-Iweala, M. and Osafo-Kwaako, P. (2007) 'Nigeria's Economic Reforms: Progress and Challenges,' *Paper,* Global Economy and Development Program, Brookings Institution: Washington, DC.

Olinga, A. (1996) « L'aménagement des droits et libertés dans la Constitution camerounaise révisée », *Revenue universelle de droits de l'homme* 8(4/7):116–126.

Ovadia, J.S. (2016) *The Petro-Developmental State in Africa: Making Oil Work in Angola, Nigeria and the Gulf of Guinea,* Hurst: London.

Oyewunmi, O. and Olujobi, O. (2016) 'Transparency in Nigeria's Oil and Gas Industry. Is Policy Re-engineering the Way Out?' *International Journal of Energy Economics and Policy* 6(3):630–636.

Plagerson, S., Patel, L., Hochfeld, T., and Ulriksen, M. (2019) 'Social Policy in South Africa: Navigating the Route to Social Development,' *World Development* 113(C):1–9.

Rakner, L. (2003) *Political and Economic Liberalization in Zambia, 1991–2001*, Nordic Africa Institute: Uppsala.

Republic of Cameroon (2009) *Vision 2035*, Yaoundé.

Republic of Cameroon (2010) *Growth and Employment Strategy. Reference Framework for Government Action over the Period 2010–2020*, Yaoundé.

Republic of Côte d'Ivoire (2009) *Strategie de Relance du Développement et de Réduction de la Pauvreté*, Abidjan.

Republic of Côte d'Ivoire (2012) *Plan National de Développement, 2012–2015*, Abidjan

Republic of Côte d'Ivoire (2015) *Etude Prospective Côte d'Ivoire 2040*, Ministry of Economic Development and Planning: Abidjan.

Republic of Côte d'Ivoire (2016) *Plan National de Développement, Cap Sur l'Emergence 2016–2022*, Abidjan

Republic of Korea (various years) *National Five-Year Development Plans*, Seoul.

Republic of Nigeria (2009) *Vision 20: 2020*, Federal Ministry of Budget and National Planning: Abuja.

Republic of South Africa (2012) *National Development Plan, 2030*, National Planning Commission: Pretoria.

Republic of South Africa (2014) 'Labour Market Dynamics in South Africa,' *Report*, Statistics South Africa Pretoria.

Republic of Zambia (2006a) *Vision 2030*, Ministry of Finance and National Planning: Lusaka.

Republic of Zambia (2006b) *Fifth National Development Plan*, Ministry of Finance and National Planning: Lusaka.

Republic of Zambia (2011) *Sixth National Development Plan*, Ministry of Finance and National Planning: Lusaka.

Republic of Zambia (2017) *Seventh National Development Plan*, Ministry of Finance and National Planning: Lusaka.

Republic of Zambia (various years) *Annual Statistical Report*, Central Statistical Office: Lusaka.

Rhee, C. and Lee, H. (2012) 'Lessons from 1997 and the 2008 Crises in Korea,' *Asian Economic Policy Review* 7(1):47–64.

Rey, H. (2013) 'Dilemma not trilemma: The Global Financial Cycle and Monetary Policy Independence,' *Paper* presented at Kansas Federal Reserve Bank Policy Symposium: Jackson Hole, Kansas.

Sanogo, V. and Moussa, R. (2017) 'Financial Reforms, Financial Development, and Economic Growth in the Ivory Coast,' *Economies, MDPI Open Access Journal* 5(1):1–23.

Sanusi, L. (2012) 'Banking Reform and Its Impact on the Nigerian Economy,' *Lecture Delivered on February 17 at an Economic Summit*, University of Warwick: Warwick, UK.

Seers, D. (1964) *Economic Survey Mission on Economic Development of Zambia*, Report of the UN/ECA/FAO, Falcon Press: Ndola.

Sen, K. and Te Velde, D. (2009) 'State Business Relations and Economic Growth in Sub-Saharan Africa,' *Journal of Development Studies* 45(8):1267–1283.

Seshamani, V. (2014) 'In Search of a Comprehensive and Rigorous Measure of Human Development and Well-being: The Social Progress Index 2014 with Special Reference to Zambia,' *Asian Journal of Social Sciences, Arts and Humanities* 2(2):1–9.

Shafer, M. (1990) 'Sectors, States and Social Forces: Korea and Zambia Confront Economic Restructuring,' *Comparative Politics* 22(2): 127–150.

Shina, H-H. and Parkb, Y. (1999) 'Financing Constraints and Internal Capital Markets: Evidence from Korean 'chaebols',' *Journal of Corporate Finance* 5(2):169–191.

Sikod, F. and Teke, J. (2012) 'Governance and Economic Growth in Cameroon,' *AERC Research Paper 250*, African Economic Research Consortium: Nairobi.

Soto, A. (2020) 'African Ministers Launch Debt Talks with Creditors,' *Bloomberg*, May 11.

South Africa Team (2015) 'The Role of Institutions in Underpinning Inclusive Economic Growth in South Africa.' Report to the African Development Bank on the *Developmental State in Africa, Lessons from South Korea Project*, Development Policy Research Unit, School of Economics, University of Cape Town: Cape Town.

South African Reserve Bank (various issues) *Annual Report*, Pretoria.

South Korea Team (2017) 'KOAFEC—Development Policy in Practice Project,' Report to the African Development Bank on the *Developmental State in Africa, Lessons from South Korea Project*, Korea Institute for International Economic Policy (KIEP): Seoul.

Steinberg, D. (2016) 'Developmental States and Undervalued Exchange Rates in the Developing World,' *Review of International Political Economy* 23(3):418–449.

Torres, E. and Zeidan, R. (2016) 'The Life-Cycle of National Development Banks: The Experience of Brazil's BNDES,' *The Quarterly Review of Economics and Finance* 62(1):97–104.

Tybout, J., Gauthier, B., Navaretti, G. & De Melo, J. (1996) « Réponse des entreprises camerounaises à la dévaluation du franc CFA », *Revue d'Economie du Développement* 96(4):5–39.

UNCTAD (2006) *Investment Policy Review, Zambia*, United Nations: New York and Geneva.

United Independence Party of Zambia (UNIP) (1963) *When UNIP Becomes Government*, Publishing Bureau: Lusaka.

Van Kessel, I. and Oomen, B. (1997) 'One Chief, One Vote': The Revival of Traditional Authorities in Post-Apartheid South Africa,' *African Affairs* 96(385):561–585.

Von Holdt, K., Langa, M., Molapo, S. Mogapi, N. and Ngubeni, K. (2011) 'The Smoke that calls: Insurgent Citizenship, Collective Violence and the Struggle for a Place in a New South Africa,' *Published Report*, Centre for the Study of Violence and Reconciliation: Johannesburg.

Wade, R. (2018) 'The Developmental State: Dead or Alive?' *Development and Change* 49(2):518–546.

Wautelet, J-M. (1990) « Cameroun, Accumulation et Développement: 1960–1990 », *Mondes en Développement* 18(69):75–85.

Woo, T.W. (2000) 'The Asian Financial Crisis: Hindsight, Insight, and Foresight,' *Journal of Southeast Asian Economies* 17(2):113–119.

Woo-Cumings, M. (ed.) (1999) *The Developmental State*, Cornell University Press: Ithaca.

World Bank (various issues) *World Development Indicators*, Washington, DC.

Zambia Team (2017) 'The Zambian Society and Economy: Development Policy in Practice in Comparison with South Korea.' Report to the African Development Bank on the *Developmental State in Africa, Lessons from South Korea Project*, Southern African Institute for Policy and Research (SAIPAR): Lusaka.

4 Governance, transparency, and avoiding elite capture

4.1 Introduction

This chapter looks at the challenges of governance, transparency, and elite capture in aspiring developmental states and at ways of preventing the political and business elites, the erstwhile promoters of the developmental state, from cutting corners when it comes to complex issues of political economy (Khan, 2012). Drawing on the concurrent experience of South Africa and its neighbors, the South Africa Team (2015) observes that if corruption, self-enrichment, and malfeasance are tolerated at the top of the bureaucracy, it does not take long before they engulf the rest of the government. The Weberian notion of the state bureaucracy as professional, "embedded but autonomous," and meritocratic, where civil servants "are committed to their tasks" and not focused on self-enrichment, is not possible in such circumstances. This is because corruption and poor governance destroy "any possibility of rule governed behavior in the lower levels of the bureaucracy, giving individual maximization free reign underneath" (Vartiainen, 1999).

Although South Korea and other East Asian countries have been indisputable champions of rapid development, researchers have pointed out that during the formative decades of the 1960s to 1980s, they were also prone to autocratic excess and hostility to social movements, including labor unions. Moreover, they tended to emphasize centralization and social conformity at the expense of spatial inclusion and individual initiative. Civil society, though largely kept at arms-length by political elites in East Asia at this time, became increasingly critical of governments' human right abuses, practice of crony capitalism, and other forms of anti-democratic and corrupt behavior (Minns, 2001; Kang, 2002a&b; You, 2005). Thus, how South Korea addressed the social and political tensions arising from rapid development, including the issues of institutional frailty, corruption, and poor governance and how it picked winners without succumbing to crony capitalism, are equally important issues to examine (Kim, 1997; Martin and Solomon, 2016; Wederman, 2013).

4.2 Inclusion, mindset change, rule of law, and democratic dividend

Mindset Change and Inclusion. In looking at governance lessons from the East Asian development experience, two strategic but interrelated elements can be identified: first, governing in the widest interest garners legitimacy among the "non-elite, excluded sectors, making compliance less demanding of state resources, which are then freed for other purposes" (Yuen, Sudo and Crone, 1992).[1] On the other hand, regimes that govern solely in the interest of a small elite, whether political, regional, or ethnic, are susceptible to corruption and malfeasance and eventually to implosion from within. Second, governing in the widest interest is not an evolutionary process and requires a deliberate mind-set change among leaders and the population. Hence, in the formative years, successful developmental states pushed conscientiously for a collective change in mindset in society, which included valuing and rewarding hard work, team-work, innovation, and productivity, and applying sanctions where required. Ultimately, the outcome depends on whether governments are able to pursue reforms that benefit the broadest number of citizens and attract popular support while resonating with the goals of the national development plans (Benczes and Szent-Iványi, 2010).

Post-World War II, it was evident that Japan needed to social engineer its way out of the economic doldrums of the war, focusing on changing the popular mindset. In the 1950s, the productivity enhancing movement, Quality Circle, was launched to get citizens to contribute to boosting productivity in their workplaces and the overall economy.[2] It became an important symbol for collective effort and inclusion in decision-making and implementation, which was copied and adapted accordingly among second-generation developmental states (South Korea Team, 2017).[3] In 1970, South Korea launched its Saemaul Udong Movement, drawing on traditional approaches to communal cooperation, to increase productivity in rural towns and villages (Douglass, 2013). In the 1980s, Singapore set up a national movement to bring about a popular mindset change, raise standards, and boost growth. While no broad-based application or adoption of the quality circle concept has been attempted in Africa, similar ideas have gained traction in education and other social services, especially in health, where the concept has proved to be quite relevant, given that tasks can be allocated to easily identifiable functional teams.[4]

As outlined in Agenda 2063, Africa's flagship development document (African Union Commission, 2014), changing the national mindset is absolutely necessary if African countries wish to transform from low-income, subsistence-type, economies, with a limited sense of self-determination, to higher-income ones, where they can begin to set their own development priorities.[5] It is only when a popular mindset change has been achieved that the new technical tools suggested above regarding the developmental state can have the desired impact on policy implementation and growth. Fostering a new mindset begins with the public sector through its recruitment and related human resource framework, procurement systems, and those for subsidies and social service provision. However, the experience of many African countries is that in the midst of economic crises, they tended to be paid fleeting attention, with "best practices" easily abandoned.

Democracy and Political Elites in Nigeria. Despite the escalation of corruption in Nigeria in recent years, democracy has been a powerful antidote in several ways. When the opposition party took power following the 2015 presidential elections, it was the first time that the incumbent party in power had been so defeated. Even more important was the gracious manner in which power was transferred. Nigeria was well on its march to full-fledged democracy. For a long time in the past, political parties had pursued the "politics of electability"—which was based on promising the electorate anything it desired, even when not politically or fiscally plausible, so long as it would pave the way to power. This bred cynicism and disdain for politicians. However, parties have become much more disciplined and issue-based and run Western-style elections campaigns, with all the trappings and expense (Nigeria Team, 2017).

Opposition parties have been credible in holding the government accountable, through parliamentary process and recourse to the media in cases of corruption, nepotism, and the like (Sowunmi et al., 2009). But while democracy has raised transparency and accountability in Nigeria to some extent, state institutions, especially those crucial to driving the development process, are still fragile, and political contestation is yet to have a real impact on the way the business of government is done, with entrenched elite groups still able to wield countervailing power, as indicated below with respect to the annual budgetary process (Box 4.1).

Box 4.1: Nigeria's budgetary process as a form of elite capture

In Nigeria, the budget process has no fixed completion point in the calendar of the National Assembly and hence is subject to political exigencies. Although a draft bill prepared by the Ministry of Finance is invariably ready by end-October of each year and is sent to the National Assembly and eventually to the Presidency for signature (by January the following year) for it to become law, before the fiscal year commences. This timetable is rarely met. Aside from the logistical and technical shortcomings associated with the budget process, often resulting in lengthy amendments, the bulk of the delay is to blame on confrontations among the political elites.

While the government might disregard opposition party criticism during the course of the year, it needs opposition collaboration at the various committee levels of the National Assembly to get the budget passed. Hence, politicians on both sides see the process as an opportunity to settle political scores, while wringing concessions out of the Federal Government. Such machinations not only delay planning and execution at the federal and state levels but also affect the investment decisions of the private sector, reflecting a lacuna in overall governance in the country.

Figure 4.1 indicates the time it took to complete the budgetary process (from presentation of budget to the National Assembly and signature by the President) between 2000 and 2013. For a total of nine fiscal years (two-thirds of the time), it took five months or more to complete the budgetary discussions. It was, however, on time (three months or less) during five fiscal years. The delays were costly not only in terms of delayed project expenditure but also in terms of government credibility and policy coherence. As the fiscal year itself begins promptly in January, a number of expenditure adjustments and delays are forced on the government, and, by implication, the states if the budget is not passed on time. Such delays indicate the difficulty that Nigeria still faces in establishing the institutional discipline that will be required to sustain its developmental state quest.

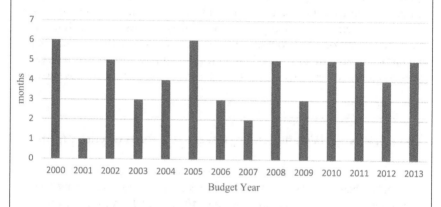

Figure 4.1 Nigerian Budget Process: Time Taken (in Months) from Budget Submission to Parliamentary Assent, 2000–2013
Source: Nigeria Team (2017), compiled from Nigeria Economic Summit Group (2013).

Rule of Law: Zambia and South Korea. The composition and performance of the judiciary is often depicted as a proxy for the effectiveness of state institutions and the capacity to protect human rights and arbitrate between political and civilian interests in the country, including those of the private sector. The speed at which business litigation is settled in a country is now a key component of the World Bank's Ease of Doing Business Index. For the judiciary to play these roles effectively requires that it be kept at arms-length from the executive, and its independence must be beyond reproach. The Zambian and South Korean examples outlined here show that judicial structures have implications for politics and vice versa and hence for long-term development outcomes.

Within the South Korean judiciary, the appointment, tenure, and dismissal process for judges is meant to build autonomy and professionalism in the institution. To defray the risk of political pressure, most appointments to constitutional offices in South Korea are fixed term and non-renewable. The chief justice is appointed by the president with the consent of the national assembly and has a six-year term limit and a 70-years age limit. Supreme Court judges, on the other hand, are appointed by the president on the recommendation of the chief justice. They serve a six-year renewable term and retire at 65. The president of the country serves for a fixed term of five years, giving the judiciary a measure of independence from him and his tenure. The lower court judges serve a term of ten years.

In contrast, Zambian politics has often come in the way of expending justice, with only a nominal separation between the judiciary and the executive. Since the system for appointing and promoting judges is run from within the presidency, it is susceptible to political patronage, with implications for credibility. In Zambia, all judicial officials have lifetime appointments (Barrie, 2009; Ndulo, 2014, 2017; Zambia Team, 2017).

Aside from institutional structures, South Korea has shown that a careful system of checks and balances helps maintain the stability of the three branches of government. For example, the executive and the legislature have a say in the appointment of judges of the Constitutional Court. Likewise, when the legislature passes a resolution of impeachment, as happened in 2017, the judiciary makes the final decision. Furthermore, the president lacks the power to dissolve the national assembly. The prime minister recommends the appointment and dismissal of cabinet ministers. The national assembly can impeach members of the executive. The tenure of the national assembly overlaps that of president and chief justice. The tenure of office for the national assembly is four years.

4.3 Corruption and the developmental state

South Korea and other East Asian economies show that corruption and poor governance are collective action problems that can only be resolved by well-coordinated institutional measures and arrangements, administered over a long period of time and with definitive goal posts in mind. Despite popular lore, South Korea was not immune to corruption and malfeasance during its development process. As noted earlier, its state agencies were sometimes biased, inefficient, and corruptible. The reason why South Korea is an interesting example is because ultimately malfeasance and the contradictory issues arising from the political economy of transition, including fiscal federalism, soft-budget constraints, state capitalism, moral hazard, and state-business relations, did not derail its plan execution strategy, and it was able to maintain policy coherence (Nee, Oper and Wong, 2007).

Recent African experience suggests that when the state is captured as has been alleged in South Africa, it is not possible to pursue economic development with the credibility exercised by the developmental states of East Asia (South Africa Team, 2015).[6] Thus, although corruption is sometimes seen as a necessary evil in resource-scarce environments, such as those of African countries, the broader experience of developing countries suggests that the cost in terms of corroding national institutions is high (Gray and Kaufmann, 1998; Wederman, 1997).

Recent decades have seen many attempts across Africa at addressing the "scourge of corruption," but on the basis of fragile institutions and little staying power. In many cases, "one-off" attempts to satiate the politics of the day (i.e. fire brigade operations) have not been successful (Carson and Prado, 2016; Doner, Ritchie and Slater, 2005). In fighting corruption in South Korea and the rest of East Asia, political skill and malleability were essential factors. An area where these features were especially required was in setting up agencies to manage the burgeoning rents, especially export-related, emanating from the control regimes of the developmental state.

For example, in South Korea, switching to an export-oriented strategy in the 1960s required literary thousands of administrative interventions, including drawing up firm lists for imposition or exemption of tariffs, import quotas, indirect taxes on intermediate goods and services, taxes on equipment, indirect taxes on exports, and domestic subsidies and other financial inducements. The export superstructure provided vast opportunities for rent-seeking and bribery. The South Korean government had embarked on this framework with its eyes open and had, in anticipation of the export push, built a vast export management system based on enhanced technical competencies, good remuneration, a high moral ethic, including "corruption proofing" based on frequent auditing, and technical controls (Kim, 2015).

Moreover, in Singapore, Taiwan, and China, extraordinary measures (zero tolerance of corruption) were used to ensure compliance, including long prison terms and even capital punishment (in the case of China). Vartiainen (1999) notes that "corruption and mediocrity are self-enforcing phenomena"—corrupt regimes tend to attract corrupt people and encourage the corruption of those who originally tried to enforce the common interest. Anti-corruption measures need to be a permanent feature of government operations, but in many African countries, as discussed ahead, they are often undertaken as emergence and "flashing out the drain" operations—repeated as often as the political economy allows.

4.4 Agencies of restraint and civil society

At the urging of the international development community, "civil society" took on the role of domestic agency of restraint during the era of structural adjustment. The argument was that civil society inclusion would bring to the table the views of other social groups, helping to liberate economic policies from the stranglehold of the bureaucrats and the urban elite. Moreover, since civil society-based organizations operate outside politics, and not for profit, they were expected to be well placed to fight malfeasance and corruption in the public service and promote human rights.

Like most ideas promoted by the international development community in Africa, without taking into account the needs of individual countries, the promotion of civil society groupings and their activities has been roundly criticized for being lopsided (mainly urban based), lacking in self-criticism i.e. they have few tools for self-monitoring and evaluation and reliance on foreign resources for sustenance i.e. "who pays the piper calls the tune" (Levy, 2007; The Economist, 2014). Still, in a situation like that of South Africa, where, for a period, key state institutions were quite compromised, civil society organization proved to be the last line of defense in terms of governance (South Africa Team, 2015).

However, Leftwich (1995) has argued that to eradicate stumbling blocks in the formative years, developmental states, such as South Korea, were forced to curtail civil society activities and agenda because addressing all its issues would have diverted the policy thrust of the developmental state.[7] The question raised by some debaters is whether a truly altruistic civil society movement, not perceived as a threat by the state nor as another avenue for the elite to extract rents (many NGOs in African countries are run by sophisticated urban professionals that are well-versed in the rules of the game), could truly emerge in the fluid political environments that characterize many African countries today (Ikelegbe, 2001; Segoun, 2018). Civicus (2019), an annual monitor of the state of civil society around the world, noted that on a classification ranging from entirely free to blocked, many African countries were not entirely free, although globally, they were not the worst performers.[8]

Anti-Corruption and Good Governance Efforts in South Korea. Fighting corruption has been, in many respects, an important task for the government of South Korea from the years before takeoff. In 1961, the new military regime promulgated a law to try individuals charged with corruption in the previous regime and thereby enhanced its anti-corruption credentials. Given the politics of the time and the importance of not diverting the energies of the private sector conglomerates that were generating exports and rapid growth, the military government decided to adopt a more diffuse approach, revisiting its anti-corruption drive in the mid-1970s to eliminate mismanagement and encourage a "values and mental revolution" (Rahman, 1986).

Despite earlier setbacks, civil society in South Korean has been able to pursue a consequential political agenda since the 1980s and to mobilize from across the country. Its ability to finance activities from membership fees and to elicit volunteers among its membership boosted its activism and independence, enabling it to raise its profile during the pro-democracy movement demonstration in Kwangju in May 1980 and to openly oppose the purging of students, teachers, and professional groups that accompanied it. The National Student Coalition for Democracy Struggle and Korean Council for Labor Welfare that were created in 1984 helped resurrect the student-labor alliances from the 1960s and 1970s that had threatened regimes and heightened the political discourse during the earlier decades of the emerging developmental state.

But, in retrospect, the epoch-making event was the coming together of civil society groups, under the leadership of a national umbrella organization, the People's Movement Coalition for Democracy and Reunification (PMCDR) in 1985. The group's composition and reach were unprecedented, encompassing urban labor, landless peasants, leading intellectuals, and Buddhist, Protestant, and Roman Catholic clergy and lay groups (Kim, 1996; Sunhyuk and Jeong, 2017). The grouping was a key segment and driver of the politics of democratic transition that took place in the second half of the 1980s and led to a new constitution (that included provisions for direct presidential elections, protection of human rights, and promotion of economic equality). As indication of both maturation and diversification, 1993 saw the creation of the Korea Federation for Environmental Movement (KFEM), with 48 regional offices and some 80,000 paying members. The movement helped put the environmental agenda high up on the development priorities of the country i.e. long before other developed countries came to similar policy emphases.

Box 4.2: South Korea and selected African countries: perceptions of corruption—more than meets the eye

Corruption is a global challenge, distorting development strategies and making it difficult to extract the full benefits of development policies. This Box presents comparative results of corruption perceptions for South Korea and sample African countries drawing on data from Transparency International. Table 4.1 shows that between 2005 and 2017, South Korea ranked between 40 and 52 (of a sample ranging from 159 to 180); South Africa between 46 and 71; Zambia between 76 and 107; Côte d'Ivoire between 103 and 152; Nigeria between 134 and 152; and Cameroon between 130 and 153. In the sample, Côte d'Ivoire has shown a steady improvement (from a low base).

Although African countries perform poorly on the transparency index, on average, there are some extremely good Sub-Saharan African performers. In the corruption perceptions survey for 2017, which covered 180 countries, Botswana ranked 34, Seychelles 36, Cape Verde 48, Rwanda 48,

Table 4.1 South Korea and African Countries: Corruption Perceptions (Index) Rankings 2005–2017

Country/ Rank	2005 (of 159)	2010 (of 178)	2013 (of 175)	2014 (of 174)	2015 (of 167)	2016 (of 176)	2017 (of 180)
South Korea	40	39	46	44	37	52	51
South Africa	46	54	72	67	61	64	71
Zambia	107	101	83	85	76	87	96
Côte d'Ivoire	152	146	136	115	107	108	103
Nigeria	152	134	144	136	136	136	148
Cameroon	137	146	144	136	130	145	153

Source: Transparency International (2018).

Namibia 53, and Mauritius 54.[9] The performance of Rwanda and Cape Verde (both ranked better than South Korea and many other African countries in 2017) shows that initial phases of rapid development need not be accompanied by high levels of corruption.

For such a large and strategic economy, Nigeria's scores have been quite low, also reflected in its low scores in the World Bank's Ease of Doing Business indices. But since the country's poorer neighbors had better scores on corruption perceptions, resources are not the issue; rather, it is organizational arrangements and politics. According to the Nigeria Team (2017), the regimes have variously been accused of embezzlement, often to the tune of billions of dollars. A survey from 2007 showed that 40.9% of Nigerian firms made informal payments to public officials (Nigeria Team, 2017). Since 2015, Nigeria has undertaken a range of reform measures, and there has been some amelioration of corruption, although, as argued above, anti-corruption must be a permanent policy quest.

Source: Nigeria Team (2017).

The engagement of civil society in the anti-corruption drive in South Korea was formalized when civil society groups presented an anti-corruption petition to the National Assembly in 2000, leading to the promulgation of the Anti-Corruption Act and creation in 2002 of the Korea Independent Commission Against Corruption (KICAC). The new institution, unlike similar ones in some African countries, was not the result of external (i.e. donor) pressure but that of domestic demands for corruption prevention and promotion of transparency. The civil society effort is credited for bringing about a greater degree of integrity and honesty in the public service of South Korea in recent decades, and also for the country's relative success in addressing poverty, as corruption skims off resources from antipoverty programs and low-income households are the most affected by such malfeasance (Brillantes, 2003; Sunhyuk, 2012). More recently (2017), the formal trial and dismissal of President Park Geun-hye on corruption charges, but without putting the work of government in jeopardy nor disrupting daily life in the country, illustrates the maturation of South Korea's political and civil institutions and its broadening liberal freedoms.

Cameroon: Cleaning the Government's Hands. In 2006, at the urging of international development agencies, who were threatening to withhold financial support if strong anti-corruption measures were not adopted by the government, as well as demands from civil society, including the Church, the Republic of Cameroon launched a program to rid the country of corruption that came to be known as *Opération Épervier*, hence, giving it a near-military profile.[10] It was embarked on some two dozen years after the ascendancy to power of President Paul Biya in 1984.

The process had started with the arrest and interrogation of several ex-ministers, businesspeople, and owners of media houses—among them CEOs of the airline, Comair, and the Port of Douala. They were brought before a purposefully constituted tribunal (*Tribunal Criminel Spécial*) for trial. Soon after, a pattern of how the government's anti-corruption effort was being conducted started to emerge. Individuals under investigation comprised mainly former members of the government turned adversaries, while their misdemeanors were conveniently from the past, despite newer corruption scandals, to ensure that the incumbent members of government were not ensnared. For example, charges were proffered on several former political leaders in 2012, under Operation Albatross, for involvement in the purchase of a presidential jet in 2004 that had failed to return from its maiden trip abroad—much to the embarrassment of the government at the time. It also was not a coincidence that the anti-corruption efforts tended to intensify during the periods leading up to or just after elections—perhaps as a wish to signal presidential alertness.

Even as *Opération Épervier* seemed to have sunk into the bureaucratic recesses of the government, it returned with a vengeance in 2018, again coinciding with the presidential elections. An ex-minister, and former "untouchable" and stalwart of the ruling party, was returned from Nigeria by Interpol to face trial for transgressions related to the privatization of the water parastatal (*Société national des eaux du Cameroun*) several years previously. While the government's anti-corruption drive was hailed in earlier years for its timeliness, given the serious concerns of the international community,[11] and with sizeable amounts of money and properties recouped, in later years, the population has been less sanguine, seeing the drive, in the absence of broader public sector reforms, as increasingly sectarian and punitive, more akin to a "war of succession" than an attempt at washing the government's hands clean (*mains propres*).

As a show of commitment, the government created several institutions to fight corruption, financial waste, and money laundering during the 2000s. They included the National Anti-Corruption Commission (NACC), the National Agency for Financial Investigation (NAFI), the Council for Budgetary and Financial Discipline, and the Supreme Audit Department (CONSUPE), the latter is a full-fledged ministerial level department. Unlike in South Korea, where the role of civil society as an anti-corruption watchdog was explicit and fully recognized by parliament, its role in Cameroon has been circumspect (Cameroon Team, 2017). Hence, the proliferation of anti-corruption institutions in the country in the past decade, not accompanied by a more active civil society to buttress accountability, has not had much impact. Corruption perceptions in Cameroon, as measured by Transparency International, have, in recent years, been rising, not falling.[12]

Côte d'Ivoire: How Corruption Disrupted Progress. The relatively efficient hierarchical and centralized structures that epitomized Côte d'Ivoire during the presidency of Houphouët-Boigny had helped contain corruption within government. The rents from the various control structures, including commodity trading, were carefully distributed among politically influential groups, while, thanks to commodity booms and the government's wish to encourage farmers by passing on a greater share to them of the good prices for coffee and cocoa, the countryside benefitted from above average income growth (Chauveneau and Dozon, 1985). Things changed drastically with the passing of the "old man" in the early 1990s, with the carefully crafted instruments for political and economic cohesion and control falling asunder (Côte d'Ivoire Team, 2017).

As noted in Chapter 3, it took two decades before Côte d'Ivoire could arrest the socio-economic decline and return to sustainable growth. In the late-2000s, the international community had identified that corruption had become entrenched in four main areas: the dispensation of justice, including the work of the police; customs and other structures related to external trade and border control; the organization and management of public procurement; and the management and equipping of the security forces, which had lost the cohesion required of a national army, with many of its units taking on functions, such as protecting trade posts at the borders, which belonged to other agencies of the government.[13]

However, general government was not performing much better, with bribes (*pots-de-vin*) demanded for the most basic of services—partly to blame on the government's tardiness in paying workers, but mostly owing to the general decline in standards and discipline in the civil service that had set in during the crisis years. The World Bank (2009) noted, for example, that 40% of normal government service recipients had paid a bribe (*cadeaux*) to receive it. By the end of the 2000s, the bulk of the population believed that bribes were necessary to grease the system. Tolerance for small-time corruption soon evolved into "grand corruption." For example, the commodity exporting parastatals accumulated vast arrears with producers, even though exports were uninterrupted. On the other hand, a potential source of revenue for the government such as the Ivorian Electricity Company was losing money, owing to fraud—with some 30% of the connections done surreptitiously. Spot checks indicated that many richer households paid a fraction of the cost of their electricity. Possession of a regionally convertible currency enabled well-connected groups to siphon large amounts of public resources out of the country. Moreover, during this time, Côte d'Ivoire was also accused of involvement in human and drug trafficking and money laundering.

The new government of President Alassane Ouattara sought to end grand corruption by strengthening public institutions, introducing reforms targeted at the business climate, and hardening sanctions for corrupt officials. The government signed the UN Convention Against Corruption in 2012, while it created a High Authority for Good Governance in 2013 to act as the national anti-corruption watchdog, and a Court of Audit to monitor public accounts, social security, and the accounts of publicly financed agencies. Moreover, the government strengthened legislation related to financial crimes, money laundering, and other forms of corruption. Although the level of corruption and fraud in the public sector, as measured by Transparency International, for example, is still high, progress has been made in the past decade. In 2015, the US recognized Côte d'Ivoire's efforts in promoting good governance, fighting corruption, and introducing anti-money laundering legislation by making it eligible to the Millennium

Challenge Corporation (MCC) compact. It was signed in 2017 and entered into force in 2019.[14]

As in other African countries, civil society participation in Côte d'Ivoire's economic and political life has been welcomed by the government, although formalized structures for engagement, as discussed in the case of South Korea, are incomplete. Before the reintroduction of multiparty democracy (in 1990), the government had discouraged the development of civil society organizations, as they seemed to distract attention from its grand plans and programs. Above all, it feared that if civil society activities eventually reached the countryside, they would interfere with the coffee-cocoa sector—the backbone of the Ivorian economy (Chauveau and Dozon, 1985). In any case, the government's Council for Economic, Social, Environment and Culture, created already in 1960, seemed, in the eyes of the government, adequate for tackling the issues of social exclusion that NGOs sought to address. However, the state-civil society interaction became moribund during the crises-ridden decades of the 1990s and 2000s. Notably, the violence that broke out in Côte d'Ivoire in 2002, leading to a temporary partition of the country, meant, at least in the eyes of the belligerents, that civil society had become partisan in both construction and intent.

Several years after the return of peace, there is still no formalized working relationship between the central government and Ivorian civil society. With so many small organizations pursuing too narrow concerns (i.e. environment, peace, women and girl children, or pastoralists) and lacking an effective umbrella organization, it has been difficult for civil society in Côte d'Ivoire to raise its national profile. Many NGOs still depend on donor support or that of local businesses to make ends meet, while a number are allied to political parties—which erodes their claim to independence. As a result, civil society, and NGOs in particular, have, despite appearances, continued to have a tenuous footing in Côte d'Ivoire. The government harbors the fear that given the latent political divisions in the country, the poorly regulated and amorphous NGO activities could distort its development agenda. Some have argued that the real fear of the government is that a strong and independent civil society could become a disruptive adversary, able to expose the festering malfeasance in the public sector. Still, at the local level and in conflict situations, civil society in Côte d'Ivoire has been instrumental for helping the country return to normalcy, reconciliation, and for the consolidation of peace in swathes of the countryside (Segou, 2018; United States Institute of Peace, 2006).

Nigeria's Efforts to Address Governance Challenges. In the past two decades, the Federal Government of Nigeria has established three agencies to fight corruption: Independent Corrupt Practices and Other Related Offences Commission (ICPC), set up in 2000; Economic and Financial Crimes Commission (EFCC), 2003; and the Bureau of Public Procurement (BPP), 2007. The institutions wield considerable powers with respect to the crimes of drug and human trafficking and money-laundering, and corruption, which are endemic in the country. Between the agencies, there have been tussles over the delineation of responsibilities, with implications for many other institutions and individuals within and outside government. The ICPC was set up as an independent commission that was not subject to the direction or control by any other person or authority in the execution of its duties. This autonomy was meant to give it leeway in performing its duties but became an obstacle when powerful groups felt pressured by its activities. The EFCC was similarly designated and faced with similar operational difficulties (Obuah, 2010). While the government is fighting corruption along several fronts and has had some success, including the termination of the 419 phone scums that proliferated in the 2000s, there have been serious issues of coordination at the federal and state levels.

Nigeria's experience in combating corruption can be summarized as follows: first, fighting corruption requires a comprehensive approach. Attempts to circumvent key institutions such as the Central Bank and the judiciary, in efforts at managing the flow of information, only breed confusion. Second, financial crimes cannot be fought effectively without access to the latest technologies, including electronic surveillance, and human resources for combating them. Third, to have impact, new approaches to fighting corruption must be accompanied by procurement reforms. Nigeria's Bureau of Public Procurement has improved the country's procurement procedures and has helped reduce incidences of gross corruption. It did this by promoting efficiency, competition (a level playing field for all), monitoring and oversight, value for money, and transparency. Notably, open competitive bidding was adopted for all public sector procurement in the country (Ezeh, 2013).

Although Nigeria's civil society played a prominent role in agitating for independence (some 60 years ago) and has also been credited for contributing to the country's return to civilian governance, following decades of military rule, and for contributing to the consolidation of peace, developing a cogent national agenda for civil society has been difficult (Bradley, 2005; Ikelegbe, 2001).[15] Even then, many researchers have argued that compared to other countries in the region, civil society in Nigeria has been "punching under its weight" for years, showing a timidity in confronting the authorities on issues of corruption, poor governance, and human rights abuses that contrasts markedly with its population's reputation for boldness and innovation (Essia and Yearoo, 2009).

The government's recent attempts at putting some legal structure on NGO operations and align their activities more closely with the national development plan and vision strategy, and hence enhance sector accountability, have been resisted by civil society. Its representatives argue that the government's plan to create an NGO Regulatory Commission and make NGO registration mandatory, is meant to void criticism of government and stifle civil society activism. Such disagreements not only illustrate the deep underlying distrust between the two sides but also indicate the complexity of the underlying political economy. Many NGOs have a clear political profile and are reluctant to be monitored by a government agency while many others, sponsored by bilateral donors and international NGOs, are equally reluctant to be interrogated or brought into the tax net of the government. Moreover, given previous disinterest in the issues of civil society, there is little assurance that the new legislation and the proposed

NGO agency will improve government–civil society interaction in the long term (Nigeria Team, 2017; Ukase and Audu, 2015).

South Africa: Challenge of Political Incumbency. The ANC has been in power in South Africa since 1994. While incumbency has a number of political advantages, if too long, it leads to a sense of entitlement and erodes good governance. The extent to which this has happened in South Africa is debatable, but it is clear that post-1994 expectations with respect to improving governance were overblown (Martin and Solomon, 2016). Table 4.2 compares scores on governance performance in South Africa with those of South Korea using data from the World Bank's World Governance Indicators[16] for the years 1996 and 2013, where scores range from 0 to 100% (South Africa Team, 2015).

Although South Africa has seen improvements in political stability, regulatory quality, and rule of law since majority rule was achieved, it has also experienced sharp declines in voice and accountability, government effectiveness, and control of corruption. The latter outcomes suggest that less than two decades after majority rule was achieved, neo-patrimonial relationships had become quite entrenched in South Africa. The next decade would witness what South Africans would call with poignant introspection "state capture." On the other hand, South Korea saw improvement in all measures of governance since 1996, with the exception of political stability—which declined from 63% to 57%.

The ANC has offered an introspective critique of corruption among its ranks. Reports presented at ANC congresses in recent years have warned against the dangers of "careerism" i.e. there is a heightened risk of exposure to corruption when a career is pursued without regard to social values.[17] Southall (2007) suggests that the push for personal enrichment that underlies the black empowerment agenda might trounce entrepreneurship and productive investment, which might obviate the goal of employment creation. More to the point, BEE could well be described as a form of rentier capitalism, where changes in ownership do not necessarily lead to investments in new plants, products, or services. In the circumstances, "black capitalism will veer down the barren path of crony

Table 4.2 South Africa and South Korea: Scores on Governance Indicators % (1996, 2013)

Indicator/Country	South Africa 1996	2013	South Korea 1996	2013
1. Voice and Accountability	73.56	65.4	65.9	68.2
2. Political Stability and Absence of Violence/ Terrorism	31.73	44.08	63	56.9
3. Government Effectiveness	79.02	66.51	73.2	82.3
4. Regulatory Quality	62.75	64.11	66.2	79.9
5. Rule of Law	50.24	57.82	68.9	78.7
6. Control of Corruption	78.54	54.55	64.9	70.3

Source: South African Team (2015) and World Bank (2018).

capitalism, encouraged by the more unscrupulous elements of established business" (Gqubule, 2004; Sindzingre and Dufy, 2014; South Africa Team, 2015).

Whilst critics tend to highlight that the threats of "spoils politics" and "crony capitalism," that tend to ensue in a situation where the political and business elites are too closely allied, are real in South Africa, the situation is not beyond remedy. They reflect a conflict within the political and legal systems, where two potential sources of neo-patrimonial relationships are embedded—the issue of black economic empowerment, which has historical justification, has, in application, benefited elected officials and business elites, and fewer of the common people than expected. On the other hand, the democratic system of South Africa, lauded globally for its innovation and resilience, still recognizes the role of (unelected) traditional leaders that continue to have a sway on important issues such as land. The relationship between democratic institutions and traditional leadership is hotly debated in the country, given the history surrounding the establishment of "homelands" in South Africa. In the search for development conforming ideas, the traditional institutions, as constituted, pose serious challenges to governance and transparency in South Africa and need to be part of the ongoing discussion on how to fashion the country as a developmental state (Ntsebeza, 2005).

South Africa: Mending Social Cleavage.[18] The role of civil society in ending the policy of apartheid and subsequently during the Truth and Reconciliation Commission (TRC) boosted its relevance as a tool for social mobilization, while ironically eroding its utility as an instrument for social intervention when the ANC-led government (i.e. the government is a coalition of political parties and civil society groups) took power. As a group, civil society in South Africa had close to 140,000 registered institutions, mostly within the urban centers, although only about 35% of them were active in 2017. The Funding Alliance Report for Civil Society in South Africa revealed that the sector employed some 1 million people and that some 40% of their financial resources came from international agencies and 25% from the government.[19]

South Africa's Bill of Rights, enshrined within the Constitution, entrenches both civil and political rights and freedoms and mandates the progressive realization of socio-economic rights, such as the rights to education, health, housing, welfare protection, food, and water. Moreover, a number of institutions were created by the South African Constitution to ensure a high level of governance and social inclusion (Box 4.3).

With active civil society involvement, the government organized a series of anti-corruption summits from 1999 onward. Weidman (2015) has noted that although the state generally welcomes civil society participation in political and economic life in South Africa, the relationship became strained as economic performance deteriorated and the government became embroiled in corruption scandals. It felt that a number of civil society groups had become too confrontational and suspected them of harboring an anti-government agenda. In 2016, the government claimed for example that some NGOs were receiving funds from abroad to sabotage its programs, especially on land. The strikes by

---

Box 4.3: South Africa's elaborate institutional framework for governance and protection of human rights

The South African Constitution established six independent state institutions:

1. Public Protector
2. South African Human Rights Commission (HRC)
3. The Commission for the Promotion and Protection of the Rights of Cultural, Religious and Linguistic Communities (the CRL Commission)
4. Commission for Gender Equity
5. The Auditor General
6. The Election Commission

Source: South Africa Team (2015).

---

university students under the social media banner #FeesMustFall, as depicted in a volume edited by Booysen (2016), was blamed on such foreign interference.

Today, South Africa's civil society is involved in several sectors and social concerns: rural outreach, education and skills development, women's empowerment and welfare, HIV/AIDS, youth affairs, environment, and political mobilization more generally. Some NGOs have specialized in social policy monitoring, thereby garnering a high level of analytical capacity as well as that for media dissemination (Weidman, 2015). Hence, despite financing and capacity concerns, civil society in South Africa is not in decline and continues to play an important role in ensuring accountable government—indeed, the recent change of government was largely thanks to actions by civil society groups in opposition to "state capture."

Zambia: Anti-Corruption and Good Governance. Zambia entered multiparty politics in the early 1990s, when legal injunctions against opposition politics were removed. Among the "hot" election topics for the opposition party, the Movement for Multiparty Democracy (MMD), which contributed to its win, was putting an end to regime corruption, caused in its view by the long political incumbency of the ruling party, UNIP. President Kaunda was accused of being overly dominant and autocratic. His wish to control the commanding heights of the economy during his quarter century in power had led to an extensive parastatal sector with nodes throughout the economy, which exceeded the supervisory capacity of the central bureaucracy. With time, such companies became fiefdoms for the elites and the political goals of ensuring that Zambians benefitted from the national assets were not realized. Moreover, external shocks and inflation steadily reduced the take home pay for civil servants in real terms, with many resorting to taking bribes to make ends meet (Chikulo, 2000).

When MMD won the presidency in 1991, and the new government ushered in unprecedented pro-market policies, reversing much of the UNIP agenda, while emphasizing the importance of reforming the public sector, seemed that the stage had been set to reduce the malfeasance that had become rampant in the country. Although a range of anti-corruption and good governance strategies and legal statutes have been enacted by successive governments in the past 30 years, there have been no breakthroughs in reducing the problem of corruption on a sustained basis.[20] The power of the executive has not diminished, while the incidence of corruption among the civil service, notably education, health, and the police has not abated under the era of multiparty democracy.

Hence, while Zambia has not been among the countries most affected by corruption in Africa, the indices of Transparency International show that it has failed to rise to the high standards that it has set for itself in recent policy documents, including the adoption of a comprehensive, coordinated, inclusive, and sustainable framework to fight corruption (Republic of Zambia, 2009). Significantly, the government has completed all requirements (2012) for being fully compliant with respect to the Extractive Industries Transparency Initiative and has also become a member of the Construction Sector Transparency Initiative. These are, however, "stroke of the pen" initiatives and it is far from evident that they will have the impact desired on the more structural aspects of malfeasance in local contracting.

The government acknowledges that corruption and poor governance entail complex cross-cutting issues which require a multifaceted approach. In the past two decades, it has created or reinvigorated several institutions with the goal of safeguarding human rights, governance, and transparency to strengthen its fight against corruption. They include the Office of the Auditor General, the Ombudsman, the Human Rights Commission, membership of the Extractive Industries Transparency Initiative, the Anti–Corruption Commission, and the Financial Intelligence Centre. Zambian history suggests that creating institutions has been easier than ensuring that they have real impact on the ground (Szeftel, 1982). While lack of resources is the most often cited reason for the limited impact on the ground, inadequate planning and hasty mid-course adjustments in spending and human resource and financial allocation have also been significant contributors. For example, many of the anti-corruption agencies listed above depend on support from the donor community to make ends meet, sometimes including staff salaries and overheads.

In one instance, that of establishing integrity committees in the public and private sectors, donor support has helped the government (through the Anti-Corruption Commission) to embark on a notable innovation for raising transparency and combating corruption in the country (Hope, 2019). The integrity committees use the same approach as that of the quality circle discussed earlier and allow members to study the situation in the organizations and to suggest solutions. Together, they increase local knowledge about the real costs of corruption, especially with respect to service delivery, the benefits of its elimination and the anti-corruption techniques required to address the problem on a sustainable basis. They have the potential of creating critical mass for anti-corruption activities among the population and public and private institutions in Zambia.

Zambia has had a much longer history of civil society activism and engagement than many other African countries, thanks partly to the labor unions on the Copperbelt.[21] Over the years, NGOs have played a significant role in promoting human rights, exposing corruption, and promoting good governance, constitutionalism, and rule of law. Notably, the critical intervention of Zambian civil society prevented President Chiluba from amending the Constitution to run for a third term of office. Recent amendments to the Constitution (Republic of Zambia, 2016) have, notably, underlined human rights and fundamental freedoms and the upholding of the principle of democracy and good governance. As in other African countries, NGOs in Zambia are still hampered by organizational issues, including the widely differing political stances of the various institutions. Like in Côte d'Ivoire, some of the NGOs are run by individuals[22] or political parties—the incumbent government is bound to see them as potentially obstructionist and not well aligned to its interests and plans. In light of this, NGOs fear that the government could use the Public Order Act and the NGO 2009 Act, which allows for government oversight of NGO activities but has not yet been implemented, to muzzle civil society activities (Haapanen and Waller, 2007).

Many local advocacy NGOs are funded by international agencies, which leaves them open to the charge that they are merely fronts for donor and foreign business interests and do not care much for those of Zambia. Moreover, stiff competition among NGOs for donor funding has seriously constrained local cooperation among them on key issues, making it difficult to establish long-lasting and effective advocacy networks (Haapanen and Waller, 2007).

Notes

1 As this is not necessarily a reference to Western style democracy, there is a question, hardly new, about who decides whether the state is governing in the broader interest.
2 Such innovations are reminiscent of Nyerere's Ujamaa. He tried to use the village and community as bases for socio-economic development in Tanzania. Göran Hydén (1980) famously argued that despite efforts from the center, Tanzanian peasants were not enthralled and remained "uncaptured."
3 See the Economist Magazine (2009) for a more recent discussion of the concept.
4 South Korea has introduced the Saemaul Udong concept in several Africa countries, including demonstration villages in the countryside under the movement's motto of "diligence, self-help and cooperation."
5 The Agenda 2063 document of the African Union underlined that development success could only be assured if there were "changed attitudes and mind-sets to rekindle and strengthen Pan-African values of self-reliance, solidarity, hard work and collective prosperity, and build on African successes, experiences, and best practices to forge the African model of development and transformation."
6 Tummala (2006) differentiates between petty corruption i.e. bribery and regime corruption with respect to India. The latter is what threatens state capture if not addressed in a timely manner.
7 This "focus on the prize view" has been criticized (South Africa Team, 2015; Asuelime, 2017). As noted in Chapter 3, South Africa advocates for a "a capable and developmental state" that has democratic credentials and fully embraces civil society.

8 The state of civil society in South Korea and South Africa had the designation "narrowed" (i.e. below completely free) while that of Côte d'Ivoire and Zambia is "obstructed" and that of Nigeria and Cameroon "repressed" i.e. the designation before "blocked," which characterizes Burundi and Algeria.

9 Others are Sao Tome and Principe (64), Senegal (66), Burkina Faso (74), and Lesotho (74).

10 *Opération Épervier* or Operation Sparrow Hawk was the codename for the French military presence in Chad during 1986–2014. The name had a certain poignance in Cameroon as much of the corruption related to the purchase of military equipment, the bulk of it from France.

11 In 1998, Transparency International had designated Cameroon as one of the most corrupt countries in the world, while the Catholic Church, which commands a strong following there, condemned corruption and its impact on the economy and people from 2000 onward. The country needed debt forgiveness from the Paris Club (US$3.5 billion was written off in 2006) and funds for the construction of the Cameroon-Chad oil pipeline (which it eventually got from the World Bank), so it chose to toe the line.

12 Muto Mulema has referred to corruption in Cameroon as a "necessary evil" (Cameroon Post, July 2, 2012).

13 See, for example, Bureau of Democracy, Human Rights and Labor (2019) of the US Department of State and World Bank (2019).

14 This compact is worth US$524.7 million.

15 Ikelegbe argues that "in plural society, civil society may become so parochial, divisive, divergent and disarticulate that it actually undermines democracy."

16 The World Governance Index measures six broad dimensions of governance:
Voice and Accountability—capturing perceptions of the extent to which a country's citizens are able to participate in selecting their government as well as freedom of expression, freedom of association, and a free media.
Political Stability and Absence of Violence/Terrorism—capturing perceptions of the likelihood of political instability and/or politically motivated violence, including terrorism.
Government Effectiveness—capturing perceptions of the quality of public services, the quality of the civil service and the degree of its independence from political pressures, the quality of policy formulation and implementation, and the credibility of the government's commitment to such policies.
Regulatory Quality—capturing perceptions of the ability of the government to formulate and implement sound policies and regulations that permit and promote private sector development.
Rule of Law—capturing perceptions of the extent to which agents have confidence in and abide by the rules of society, and in particular the quality of contract enforcement, property rights, the police, and the courts as well as the likelihood of crime and violence.
Control of Corruption—capturing perceptions of the extent to which public power is exercised for private gain, including both petty and grand forms of corruption as well as "capture" of the state by elites and private interests.

17 See Acting President Kgalema Motlanthe speech to ANC Youth League at Mangaung in December 2012, which discussed some of the challenges related to the transition from a liberalization movement to the party in power.

18 See Weidman (2015) and South Africa Team (2015) for further discussion on why South Africa's civil society has been less effective in holding the ANC governments to account during the post-1994 period.

19 The Report was authored by Inyathelo: The South African Institute for Advancement, Johannesburg, 2017.

20 They include among others the National Anti-Corruption Policy (2009); Anti-Corruption Act (2012); Prohibition and Prevention of Money Laundering Act (2001); and the Public Interest Disclosure Act (2010). Governments have also set up commissions of inquiry over the Zambia Revenue Authority, Oil Procurement, Land, etc. although with limited follow-up on recommendations.
21 However, miners were a fairly elitist group and pursued their interests (mostly wages and related benefits) in a relatively parochial fashion. It is noteworthy that the second President of Zambia, Fredrick Chiluba, was a former leader of a miners' trade union.
22 Dubbed accordingly as "Non-Governmental Individuals" or "Briefcase NGOs."

References

African Union Commission (2014) *Agenda 2063. The Africa We Want*, African Union Commission: Addis Ababa.

Asuelime, L. (2017) 'Civil Society and the South African Developmental State: An Appraisal,' *Journal of Social Development in Africa* 32(1):45–68.

Barrie, G. (2009) 'Paradise Lost: The History of Constitutionalism in Africa Post Independence,' *Journal of South African Law* 292:289–332.

Benczes, I. and Szent-Iványi, B. (2010) 'State-Society Relations in a Dynamic Framework: The Case of the Far East and Sub-Saharan Africa,' MPRA Paper 23384, University Library of Munich.

Booysen, S. (ed.) (2016) *Fees Must Fall: Student Revolt, Decolonisation and Governance in South Africa*, Wits University Press: Johannesburg.

Bradley, M.T. (2005) 'Civil Society and Democratic Progression in Post-Colonial Nigeria: The Role of Non-Governmental Organizations,' *Journal of Civil Society*, 1(1):61–74.

Brillantes, A. (2003) 'Public Sector Reform and Poverty Reduction,' in E. Pernia and Deolalikar, A. (eds.), *Poverty, Growth and Institutions in Developing Asia*, 97–136, Palgrave and Macmillan: New York.

Bureau of Democracy, Human Rights and Labor (2019) *2019 Country Reports on Human Rights: Cote d'Ivoire*, US Department of State: Washington, DC.

Cameroon Team (2017) 'Etude Sur L'Economie du Cameroun. La Politique de Développement dans la Pratique Enseignements Tires de L'Expérience de Développement de la Corée du Sud,' Report to the African Development Bank on the *Developmental State in Africa, Lessons from South Korea Project,* Université de Yaoundé II: Yaoundé.

Carson, L. and Prado, M. (2016) 'Using Institutional Multiplicity to Address Corruption as a Collective Action Problem: Lessons from the Brazilian Case,' *The Quarterly Review of Economics and Finances* 62(1):56–65.

Chauveneau, J-P. and Dozon, J-P. (1985) 'Colonisation, Économie de Plantation et Société Civile en Côte d'Ivoire,' *Cahiers ORSTORM des Sciences Humaines* 21(3):68–80.

Chikulo, B.C. (2000) 'Corruption and Accumulation in Zambia,' in K.R. Hope and Chikulo, B.C. (eds.), *Corruption and Development in Africa*, 161–182, Palgrave Macmillan: London.

Civicus (2019) *State of Civil Society*, Civicus: Johannesburg, New York and Geneva.

Côte d'Ivoire Team (2017) 'Etude Sur L'Economie Ivorienne. La Politique de Développement dans la Pratique Enseignements Tires de L'Expérience de Développement de la Corée du Sud,' Report to the African Development Bank on the *Developmental State in Africa, Lessons from South Korea Project,* Le Centre Ivoirien de Recherches Economiques et Sociales (CIRES): Abidjan.

Doner, R., Ritchie, B. and Slater, D. (2005) 'Systematic Vulnerability and the Origins of Developmental States: Northeast and Southeast Asia in Comparative Perspective,' *International Organization* 59(2):327–361.

Douglass, M. (2013) 'The Saemaul Undong: South Korea's Rural Development Miracle in Historical Perspective,' *Working Paper Series*, 197, Asia Research Institute: Singapore.

The Economist (2009) 'Idea—Quality Circle,' November 4.

The Economist (2014) 'Foreign Funding of NGOs. Donors Keep Out,' September 12.

Essia, U. and Yearoo, A. (2009) 'Strengthening Civil Society Organizations/Government Partnership in Nigeria,' *International NGO Journal* 4(9):368–374.

Ezeh, E. (2013) 'Public Procurement Reform Strategies: Achieving Effective and Sustainable Outcomes,' *Presentation*, Chartered Institute of Purchasing and Supply Pan Africa Conference: Accra.

Gqubule, D. (2004) 'Grow to empower,' *The M&G Online*: http://mg.co.za/article/2004-10-13-grow-to-empower/

Gray, C.W. and Kaufmann, D. (1998) 'Corruption and Development,' *Finance and Development* 35(1):7–10. Haapanen, T. and Waller, M. (2007) 'Civil Society in Zambia and Mozambique,' *KEPA Working Paper* 17(9).

Hope, K.R. (2019) 'Controlling Corruption Though Integrity Committees: The Case of Zambia,' *Journal of Public Integrity* 21(3): 248–262.

Ikelegbe, A. (2001) 'The Perverse Manifestation of Civil Society: Evidence from Nigeria,' *Journal of Modern African Studies* 39(1):1–24.

Kang, D. (2002a) 'Bad Loans to Good Friends: Money, Politics, and the Developmental State in South Korea,' *International Organization* 56(1):177–207.

Kang, D. (2002b) *Crony Capitalism. Corruption and Development in South Korea and the Philippines*, Cambridge University Press: Cambridge.

Khan, M. (2012) 'Governance during Social Transformation: Challenges for Africa,' *New Political Economy* 17(5):667–675.

Kim, E.M. (1997) *Big Business, Strong State: Collusion and Conflict in South Korean Development, 1960–1990*, State University of New York: Albany.

Kim, S. (1996) 'Civil Society in South Korea: From Grand Democracy Movements to Petty Interest,' *Journal of Northeast Asian Studies* 15(2):81–87.

Kim, S. (2015) 'Side by Side with the People: Korea's Experiences of Participatory Auditing,' *Learning Note* 1, Public Participation in the Budget and Audit Process, World Bank Group: Washington, DC and The Board of Audit and Inspection of the Republic of Korea: Seoul.

Leftwich, A. (1995) 'Bringing Politics Back In: Towards a Model of the Developmental State,' *Journal of Developments Studies* 31(3):400–427.

Levy, B. (2007) 'State Capacity, Accountability and Economic Development in Africa,' *Commonwealth and Comparative Politics* 45(4):499–520.

Martin, E. and Solomon, H. (2016) 'Understanding the Phenomenon of 'State Capture' in South Africa,' *Southern African Peace and Security Studies* 5(1):21–34.

Minns, J. (2001) 'Of Miracles and Models: The Rise and Decline of the Developmental State in South Korea,' *Third World Quarterly* 22(6):1025–1043.

Ndulo, M. (2014) 'Review of the Anti-Corruption Legal Framework in Zambia,' *SAIPAR Bookshelf*, Southern Africa Institute for Policy and Research: Lusaka.

Ndulo, B.M. (2017) 'Subversion of the Judiciary, Creeping Dictatorship and Arrogance of Power in Zambia,' *Lusaka Times*, November 7.

Nee, V., Oper, S. and Wong, S. (2007) 'Developmental State and Corporate Governance in China,' *Management and Organization Review* 3(1):19–53.

Nigeria Team (2017) 'Towards Developmental State in Nigeria: Lessons from Korea,' Report to the African Development Bank on the *Developmental State in Africa, Lessons from South Korea Project,* Nigerian Economic Society: Ibadan.

Nigerian Economic Summit Group (2013) 'Unpublished Proceedings of the 19th Nigerian Economic Summit,' NESG: Abuja.

Ntsebeza, L. (2005) 'Rural Governance and Citizenship in Post-Apartheid South Africa: Democracy Compromised?' in J. Daniel, Southall, R. and Lutchman, J. (eds.), *The State of the Nation: South Africa 2004–2005,* 58–85, HSRC Press: Cape Town and Michigan State University Press: Lansing.

Obuah, E. (2010) 'Combating Corruption in a 'Failed' State: the Nigerian Economic and Financial Crimes Commission (EFCC)' *Journal of Sustainable Development in Africa* 12(1):27–53.

Rahman, A. (1986) 'Legal and Administrative Measures against Bureaucratic Corruption in Asia,' in L. Carino (ed.), *Bureaucratic Corruption in Asia: Causes, Consequences and Control,* 147–152, JMC Press: Quezon City and College of Public Administration, University of the Philippines: Manilla.

Republic of Zambia (2009) *National Anti-Corruption Policy,* Government Printer: Lusaka, Zambia.

Republic of Zambia (2016) *Constitution of Zambia (Amendment),* Government Printer: Lusaka, Zambia.

Segoun, J.-M. (2018) 'Société civile, jeunesse, politisation et compétition politique en Côte d'Ivoire,' www.thinkingafrica.org.

Sindzingre, A. and Dufy, C. (2014) 'Developmental' Policies and Rent: Comparing Russia and Sub-Saharan Africa,' *Post Print,* Centre National de la Recherche Scientifique, Université Paris: Nanterre.

South Africa Team (2015) 'The Role of Institutions in Underpinning Inclusive Economic Growth in South Africa.' Report to the African Development Bank on the *Developmental State in Africa, Lessons from South Korea Project,* Development Policy Research Unit, School of Economics, University of Cape Town: Cape Town.

South Korea Team (2017) 'KOAFEC—Development Policy in Practice Project,' Report to the African Development Bank on the *Developmental State in Africa, Lessons from South Korea Project,* Korea Institute for International Economic Policy (KIEP): Seoul.

Southall, R. (2007) 'Ten Propositions about Black Economic Empowerment in South Africa,' *Review of African Political Economy* 34(111):67–84.

Sowunmi, F., Raufu, A., Oketokun, F., Salako, M. and Usifoh, O. (2009) 'The Role of Media in Curbing Corruption in Nigeria,' *Research Journal of Information Technology* 2(1):7–23.

Sunhyuk, J. (2012) 'Contentious Democracy' in South Korea: An Active Civil Society and Ineffectual Political Parties,' *Taiwan Journal of Democracy* 8(2):51–61.

Sunhyuk, J. and Jeong, J-H. (2017) 'Historical Development of Civil Society in Korea since 1987,' *Journal of International and Area Studies* 24(2):1–14.

Szeftel, M. (1982) 'Political Graft and the Spoils System in Zambia – the State as a Resource in Itself,' *Review of African Political Economy* 9(24):4–21.

Transparency International (2018) *The Corruption Perceptions Index (CPI) Scores:* www.transparency.org.

Tummala, K. (2006) 'Regime Corruption in India,' *Asian Journal of Political Science* 14(1):1–22.

Ukase, P. and Audu, B. (2015) 'The Role of Civil Society in the Fight against Corruption in Nigeria's Fourth Republic: Problems, Prospects and the Way Forward,' *European Scientific Journal* 11(2):171–195.

United States Institute of Peace (2006) *Édification d'une inclusive en Côte d'Ivoire,* USIPeace Briefing, August.

Vartiainen, J. (1999) 'The Economics of Successful State Intervention in Industrial Transformation,' in M. Woo-Cumings (ed.), *The Developmental State,* 200–234, Cornell University Press: Ithaca.

Wederman, A. (1997) 'Looters, Rent-Scrapers, and Dividend-Collectors: Corruption and Growth in Zaire, South Korea and the Philippines,' *The Journal of Developing Areas* 31(4):457–478.

Wederman, A. (2013) 'Xi Jinping's Anti-Corruption Campaign and the Third Plenum,' *Paper,* Department of Political Science, Georgia State University: Atlanta.

Weidman, M. (2015) 'The Changing Status of Civil Society in South Africa, 1994 to 2014,' *Background Paper, Southern Africa,* Hanns Seidel Foundation: Munich.

World Bank (2009) *Côte d'Ivoire: Economic Governance and Recovery Grant,* Washington, DC.

World Bank (2018) *World Governance Indicators,* Washington, DC.

World Bank (2019) *Côte d'Ivoire: Relever le défi de la mobilisation fiscal,* Washington, DC.

You, J. (2005) 'Embedded Autonomy or Crony Capitalism? Explaining Corruption in South Korea Relative to Taiwan and the Philippines Focusing on the Role of Land Reform and Industrial Policy,' *Paper Presented at the American Political Science Association Meeting,* Washington, DC, September 1–4.

Yuen, N., Sudo, S. and Crone, D. (1992) 'The Strategic Dimension of the 'East Asian Developmental States," *ASEAN Economic Bulletin* 9(2):199–233.

Zambia Team (2017) 'The Zambian Society and Economy: Development Policy in Practice in Comparison with South Korea.' Report to the African Development Bank on the *Developmental State in Africa, Lessons from South Korea Project,* Southern African Institute for Policy and Research (SAIPAR): Lusaka.

Part II

Implementation and impact

5 National planning, decentralization, and rural development

5.1 Introduction

This chapter focuses on the interrelated issues of national planning, decentralization, and rural development, contrasting African and South Korean experiences. As noted earlier, many African countries embarked on elaborate national planning exercises post-independence, with the goal of rapid modernization. Given that the economies were overwhelmingly agrarian and rural, the reform of agriculture was invariably the place to start. However, post-independence national development plans quickly became proforma and did not provide the institutional and economic transformation that countries longed for, as illustrated by the cases of Nigeria and Zambia, where ambition was not backed by action. (Bevan, Collier and Gunning, 1999; Du Plessis, 2006; Whitworth, 2015).

In retrospect, few African countries felt completely comfortable with the laissez faire approach and "flaring in the wind" that characterized the de facto banning of national planning during the era of structural adjustment programs in the 1980s and 1990s. The recent return to national planning indicates both a renewed faith in the role of the public sector in providing development guidance and the importance of establishing a credible long-term domestic framework on which to base private sector and other stakeholder interventions.

In South Korea, national planning provided a solid framework for the mobilization and deployment of national resources. However, it was not done in a vacuum, and governments had to address the political economy of resource redistribution. What is notable is that, despite setbacks, East Asian countries were able to reach their development goals quicker, and with a higher degree of consistence, than other countries and regions of the world (Choi, 1987; Haggard and Moon, 1990).

5.2 Planning, institutional prestige, and policy coherence

A key lesson for aspiring developmental states is how seriously South Korea and other East Asian states took national planning exercises in their formative years. They allocated sufficient financial and human resources for the exercise, making sure that nothing was left to chance. African governments that seek to steer their economies in a similar direction need to examine how to enhance the effectiveness of their national development frameworks and associated institutions. The latter will require strong and accountable government and heightened prestige of the public sector as an agency of change (South Korea Team, 2017).

Planning and Export Promotion. South Korea demonstrated that for an economic planning agency to be successful, the importance of its mission i.e. overseeing the country's economic transformation via an export-oriented development strategy had to match its prestige within government. Hence, the Economic Planning Board (EPB), established already in 1961, became one of the most important institutions in South Korea's economic management and planning during the first 30 years of the country's emergence and was given extra-ordinary powers in the public-sector constellation to draft development plans (it introduced the first national development plan in 1962) and allocate resources and credit, otherwise usually functions of the finance and budget ministries (Seunghee, 2014).

The EPB was the instrument that helped to alleviate South Korea's post-war deprivations and steer its path to developed country status. In practice, it worked like a well-oiled machine, with clear terms of reference, and a meritocratic and well-remunerated labor force, headed by a deputy Prime Minister (i.e. he was able to "pull rank" on his ministerial colleagues in the cabinet).[1] Crucially, its meetings were sometimes attended and chaired by the President, hence amplifying its mission. As the premier planner, the EPB facilitated the change toward export promotion and ensured overall policy coherence i.e. controlled crucial junctures in policy processes to bring secondary ministries into a common policy framework and protect the country's export edge (Kim, 1991).

Its objectives were more focused than those of other government agencies i.e. to deliberate and execute investment priorities for economic development, coordinate conflicting views among ministries, and oversee price stability and external economic policies. It would do this by setting up short- to long-term economic development plans, administering annual government budget allocations, and devising ways to attract foreign capital (Han, 2014)

It should be noted that while the EPB was preeminent, it was by no means the only institution involved in the construction of the developmental state. Part of its success derived from its ability to work effectively with other agencies of the government—Office of the President, Ministry of Finance, Ministry of Labor, Ministry of Trade and Industry, and the Bank of Korea. In many African countries, the ministries of labor (often lumped together with gender and youth issues) are among the lowest ranking in the pecking order, even though the labor portfolio is among the most important ministries in developed countries. Furthermore, while the trade and commerce ministries were extremely strategic during South Korea's emergence, especially in relation to licensing, they featured rarely in the broader strategy formulation of the African countries, which often, as argued earlier, took on more diffuse goals i.e. national integration.

It is important to point out that the South Korean government did not promote the interests of exporting companies out of a sense of altruism. It saw them as key to the implementation of its export-oriented development plan and growth strategy. Aside from the EPB, mentioned earlier, another crucial institution in this regard was the Enlarged Meeting for Export Promotion (EMEP) which grew out of the Export Promotion Committee established in 1962. As an indication of its convening power, the EMEP had, by 1976, a total of 172 participants, including the president, 18 ministers, 18 vice ministers, 5 scholars attached to government-run and private research centers, 39 representatives of industry-trade-export associations, and 11 businessmen representing the corporate sector (Rhee, Ross-Larson and Pursell, 1984). Chaired by the president, decisions at the meeting had significant impact on the economy. Through the EMEP, the president was able to send clear messages, once a month, to his ministers, captains of industry, and other stakeholders about what he wanted to see happening on the export front (Choi, 1987).

The Issue of Replication. The question that researchers and policymakers have posed frequently, as we saw in Chapter 2, is whether an agency like the EPB could be replicated in the more heterogeneous socio-economic circumstances of African countries today (Nigeria Team, 2017).

In Côte d'Ivoire, the *Bureau National d'Etude Techniques et de Développement* had similarities to the EPB, especially its coordination of technical studies, their financing, and works supervision within government. On the other hand, the Republic of Rwanda, from a low base, post-civil war, and genocide, some 30 years ago, has been resuscitated in recent decades by a thoroughness in planning and implementation that resembles that of the EPB—especially the interest accorded the process by the country's president (South Korea Team, 2017). The possibility of the emergence of similarly well-focused and successful planning experiences on the continent in coming decades cannot be excluded (Gumede, 2009).

Many African governments have recently created well-funded agencies ("authorities"), with wage and hiring policies separated from those of the traditional civil service, to enable them handle specialized tasks, such as tax collection, road construction, and for running electricity and water and sewerage utilities. Vaguely patterned on East Asia's institutional experience, the goal is to keep political interference at a minimum, while raising efficiency in service delivery. Interagency rivalry and duplication of responsibilities have blurred the policy agenda, while the enhanced remuneration packages for staff in the specialized agencies have caused disgruntlement in the rest of the civil service. Typically, each ministry has created an authority or agency where its staff can operate under much better terms of service and get better pay—hence defeating the original idea of a smaller and more effective public sector.[2]

Still, African experience has shown that setting up a powerful agency like the EPB is fraught with political difficulties. In the past decade, anxious African governments wishing to speed up the implementation of their development plans have found ways of augmenting the system by establishing "presidential delivery units" within the executive.[3] These have, however, taken away some of the impetus of the national planning agencies and threaten a return to the lethargy of the past.

The factors cited for the relative success of the EPB and its plans, in contrast to the African cases, deserve reiteration. First, the EPB was staffed by talented and technically trained bureaucrats and had a substantial budget of its own. Second, it received direct support from the president of the country and acted to all intents and purposes as an extension of the presidency. This patronage protected it from partisan interference. On its own, presidential patronage does not necessarily explain why the EPB worked so well, since similar units around African leadership have failed to deliver in the past. So, the third reason must be that it was able to deliver in spite of the complex political economy and hence endeared itself to the government and population. The government sustained the EPB and the national planning frameworks for as long as they were useful tools. For a rapidly developing and increasingly market-oriented economy, the usefulness of the EPB as an institution for policy implementation and monitoring ended, as did its tenure.

Focused Plan versus Smorgasbord of Initiatives and Targets. In comparison to the compartmentalized and proactive planning approach pursued in South Korea and other East Asian economies, those of many African countries seem like a smorgasbord of vaguely defined initiatives and targets, with no likelihood of being met during the plan period. This is illustrated by Cameroon's six national development plans covering 1960–1991 (Table 5.1). The first, second, and third national development plans focused on boosting social and economic infrastructure, reducing spatial inequalities, through rural and agriculture development, and laying the ground for industrial development. The instruments included promoting the cooperative system and creation of village communities to enhance productivity, targeting investment to industry, energy, mining, and, crucially, undertaking land reform.

The targets of the fourth, fifth, and sixth plans were similarly quite expansive in scope. They included the realization of national unity, pursuit of centrally driven development, the diversification of production techniques in the economy, and provision of social services, notably health, education, water, and electricity. As oil production increased from the late-1970s, and the economy started feeling the impacts of the Dutch Disease in earnest, the plans also emphasized the benefits of economic diversification. It is difficult to say that Cameroonian national planning helped the country meet a given set of objectives, hence allowing it to move on to a new level on the development trajectory. Indeed, given the themes of the six plans, the challenges seem circular in nature.

Table 5.1 Cameroon: Themes and Outcomes from Six National Development Plans, 1960–1991

Plan and Period	Key Themes and Goals	Comments on Outcomes
First Plan 1960–1965	• Double per capita income • Construct economic and social structures • Extend the cooperative system • Create village communities • Reduce regional disparities.	Like national development plans from neighboring countries (i.e. Nigeria and Cote d'Ivoire) rapid growth was projected. It was lower than expected, but higher than in other African countries. Regional disparities continued.

Plan and Period	Key Themes and Goals	Comments on Outcomes
Second Plan 1966–1971	• Double per capita income in 20 years • Reduce regional disparities • Modify infrastructure to better link to agriculture and industry • Undertake land reform • Creation of a ministry for agriculture.	Impressive infrastructure investment during second plan and linkage of the countryside to urban centers. Land reform did not go anywhere—while conflicts over land increased. Hopes of rapid increases in per capita incomes not realized.
Third Plan 1971–1976	• Targeted investment to industry, energy and mining • Infrastructure investment	Some success in establishing an import-substituting industrial base. But largely dependent on state subsidies. Public sector investment choices largely driven by domestic politics.
Fourth Plan 1976–1981	• Realization of national unity • Centrally driven development • GDP per capita of 5% per annum.	The oil discovery lowered the resource constraint and the fourth national development plan became more or less moribund, as the government found other expenditure vehicles.
Fifth Plan 1981–1986	• Achievement of endogenously driven development • Health, potable water, and electricity for all by 2000 • Universal (free) primary education for children less than 14-years old. • Curricula development and introduction of continuous education • Diversification of production techniques in the economy • Boosting income per inhabitant by no less than 4% per annum	The fifth plan was quite goal-oriented and indicated an ambition to address long-standing structural and economic challenges. Universal education at the primary level was introduced. The hopes of extending electricity and potable water to all households were not met, nor were those of diversifying the economy.
Sixth Plan 1986–1991	• Self-sustaining and balanced development • Democracy and social justice • National integration	Following a quarter century of planning, the sixth national development sought to return to basics i.e. investing in growth sectors and revisiting the rural-urban gaps. However, the government was also very much aware that little would be achieved if the regional conflicts persisted.

Source: Cameroon Team (2017), Touna-Mama (2008), and Kimengsi and Gwan (2017).

Transition to Developed Country. South Korea, although considered the quintessential developmental state today, experienced serious socioeconomic problems during its emergence, including military coups, corruption, and serious political disruptions. What are important as lessons for Africa's aspiring developmental states is how it overcame them and was able to forge ahead with confidence. As indicated in the literature overview, it is also often claimed that South Korea was dealt a good hand by geopolitics, including proximity to Japan and being on the side of the US during the Korean war of the 1950s and the subsequent Cold War. These advantages did not prevent the country from the external shocks caused by sharp increases in oil prices in the 1970s and early 1980s and the Asian Financial Crisis of the late-1990s and early 2000s.

The two shock periods revealed that despite its development strides, South Korea had inherent structural vulnerabilities that needed to be addressed. The shocks had dented the country's growth performance and sharply limited its options. It resisted the temptation of reverting to insularity on both occasions choosing flexibility in the face of external challenges. For example, in the second half on the 1980s, the government took full advantage of the "three lows"— low-energy prices, low-international interest rates, and low value of the won, compared to the yen, to engineer an unprecedented export boom. Likewise, as argued in Chapter 3, South Korea showed much policy perception and strategic resilience in confronting the effects of the Asian Financial Crisis of the late-1990s (Côte d'Ivoire Team, 2017; South Korea Team, 2017).

For South Korea, the Asian Financial Crisis had revealed that the control regime, as practiced thus far, no longer was tenable and that akin to other OECD member states it had to resort to more market-based instruments to run the economy. The government embarked on the privatizations of key parts of the economy, notably the financial sector, while also gradually opening it up to foreign participation. With most of its power for delegating the economy removed, and the formal economic planning of the past abandoned, the remaining functions of the EPB were takeover by the Ministry of Finance, which hence took on the name Ministry of Finance and Strategy. In contrast to previous emphases, the state now wished to boost the small and medium-size enterprises, more appreciative of their dynamic impacts on employment and welfare.

With the introduction of multiparty democracy at home in the second half of the 1980s, membership of the WTO, at its creation in 1995, and accession to OECD membership in 1996, South Korea's engagement with the world changed, with implications for the policy approach at home. Previously, the country's engagement with the world had been based on how best to promote its export-driven industrial sectors and hence promote domestic welfare. But now, the global institutions were becoming agencies of restraint at home.[4] South Korea had graduated and could not expect any form of concessional treatment from the global community.

National Development Plans: Not Works of Fiction. When Africa's national development plans were first launched in the 1960s, the independence decade, they were meant as serious expressions of intent, backed up by credible investment and financing plans. They had not yet become the "works of fiction" that stakeholders would call them in the decades ahead.

In 1964, Ghana's President, Kwame Nkrumah, launched one of the better integrated national development plans in Africa at the time. It was focused on transforming Ghana from dependence on peasant agriculture to a "mixed economy with socialist and cooperative goals" (Government of Ghana, 1964). The Plan pushed for a strong link between agriculture and industry and highlighted the importance of a cheap and sustainable source of electric power for industrial development. The Plan's Volta River Project was projected to increase domestic power generation capacity fivefold, while also providing irrigation.

In the view of the South Korea Team (2017), Ghana's first post-independence national development plan was best positioned to have developmental impact but was cut short by Nkrumah's removal from power in 1966. It could also be said that the plan failed because while it was technically sound, it was perceived by stakeholders as a one-man show and not a nationalist project. Hence, it expired with the exit of its champion. On the other hand, although the implementation of Côte d'Ivoire's initial national development plans under Félix Houphouët-Boigny was successful, the system came under serious stress when he died in late-1993. Solid planning did not return in earnest to Côte d'Ivoire until the 2010s (Côte d'Ivoire Team, 2017; Republic of Côte d'Ivoire, 2012, 2015).[5]

The question then regards what needs to be done to ensure that the policy and development thrust of national development plans is sustained over the longer term. The Nigeria Team (2017) argues that this focus on the long term, even when dealing with shorter-term political concerns and the exigencies of regime change, is the distinguishing feature of the South Korean experience—but also one which is hardest to replicate as it combines patience, tenacity, and focus on detail, without losing sight of the bigger picture and ultimate goal.

Fit for Purpose: Taking Advantage of Context. While the authors of the six case studies have argued that being original, committed, and hardworking were major factors behind South Korea's success, the degree of preparedness to fully take advantage of all available opportunities mattered a whole lot as well. The lesson here is that it is important for aspiring developmental states to actively look for market openings and niches for future growth, keeping in mind the much-changed global context (Box 5.1).

In that context, one could pose the question whether a country like South Africa is taking full advantage of its fairly sophisticated economy on the one hand and potential for reducing the cost of doing business by adopting a low-wage production strategy, on the other. South Africa's overall strategy could be developed around a similar emphasis, as that of South Korea in the 1960s, on employing as many low- to medium-skilled workers as possible, and not waiting for high-skilled workers to become available for higher value-added niches of the industrial sector as that takes time. Likewise, South Africa's energy shortage and logistical challenges provide domestic opportunities for solar power, infrastructure development, and for deploying the country's formidable engineering capacities for job creation. In other words, policies must be "fit for purpose."

One approach used in East Asia and India that is worth emulating by African countries is that of hiring the best minds available, including from the Diaspora, to undertake the analysis and the R&D required for developing future economic strategies. At the moment, this approach is fairly underutilized by African governments, preferring to hire international consultancy firms to do analyses for national branding and/or national vision strategy.

Box 5.1: Conditions under which the state's plans become effective—lessons for African countries[6]

Competent institutions. The creation of a meritocratic civil service was imperative for the success of the developmental states of East Asia. However, it should be borne in mind that the question is not simply adopting an approach that worked well in some far-off country without reference to local context and needs (Ohno, 2011). In South Africa, for example, where skills are concentrated among certain groups, some form of affirmative action may be required.

Mindset change. To emulate the successful developmental states will require a collective mindset change. South Korea's approach has been described as planned capitalism, based on profit-making, while African governments continue to pursue elements of the old socialist approach, where commercial viability was not that important.

Stakeholder pragmatism. Africa's social partners—government, business, and trade unions—will have to be more pragmatic, versus ideologically rigid, in assessing the policy prescriptions on the table, and in discussions with government. The latter should be aware that to secure buy-in for its economic reforms will require the creation of "growth coalitions" between the government's own bureaucracy and business, organized labor, and civil society.

Prudent policies. Prudent economic policies must be the backbone of the economic transformation being sought by African governments. Although many countries are well endowed in natural resources—fertile land, minerals, and forestry and associated business prospects—sustainable growth and development will require doing things differently.

Eschew cronyism and reward hard work. Recruitment to the civil service must ensure that critical public functions are staffed and managed by individuals recruited on the basis of merit and not that of political or family connections. Successful developmental states engendered a mind-set that appreciated and rewarded hard work no matter the ideology and ethnic orientation of the individual.

Develop a shared vision. In policy documents, African governments like to project a shared vision of economic transformation and prosperity.

In practice, this is often only skin deep, with little evidence of a "whole of government" approach to ensuring that individual households have a fair chance of improving their incomes and livelihoods. A shared vision is crucial for developing the bureaucratic structures, public–private interactions, and civil society participation that are needed for sturdy long-term development (Schneider, 1999).

Setting aside factionalism and ideology. Finally, the question which remains open is whether Africa's ruling political and business elites can muster the required political will to set aside ideology, patronage, and narrow political interests to pursue the combination of strategies which East Asian developmental states followed to make their countries prosperous.

Encourage private sector competition. Developmental states encouraged their private sectors to position themselves competitively at home and abroad. This was often measured by ability to export to the West.

Source: South Africa Team (2015) and South Korea Team (2017).

5.3 Lessons from decentralization in the developmental state

Centralized and Hierarchical to Decentralized and Accessible. It can be argued that the "developmental state," at least from the example of South Korea, is an inherently centralizing idea—starting with centralized planning agencies (with regional bureaus reporting to the center) planning the industrialization process, the large industrial entities (chaebols) that agree output targets and employment policies with the government, and the private universities that nevertheless follow the research and capacity enhancing measures laid down by the central government.

The reality, even in South Korea, was much more complex. Already, in 1949, in recognition of the future role of the local authorities as pillars of stability at the local level, the government had issued a Local Government Act (the Local Autonomy Law) to devolve central government functions to local authorities. In the event, implementation of the Law was interrupted by the Korean war in the early 1950s, while, in a bid to secure centralized government control over the whole economy, the military regime that seized power in 1961, suspended the Law.

The demand for local autonomy did not go away, however, increasing even as the South Korean economy entered its high-growth phase in 1970s and 1980s. The demands eventually led to the revision of the 1949 Law, local elections in 1991, and full local autonomy by 1995. The heads of local governments were democratically elected thereafter, and the autonomous regional and local governments that resulted became real counterweights to policies from the center. This introduced another aspect to policymaking not witnessed previously—the wishes of local populations could potentially supersede the dictates of the central bureaucracy.

Democracy-Surrogate Properties of Decentralization. Ultimately, the political objective of decentralization was to promote local democracy and provide local populations the means to subject local leaders to scrutiny, especially in the provision of social services, something which was not possible during the military regime (Moon, 2003). With the solidification of democracy in South Korea during the 2000s, decentralization became its most important expression. It has boosted regional development and helped foster balanced development between rural and urban areas—hence alleviating the traditional tensions between center and periphery.

By 2000, three levels of government were in place in South Korea: (i) Central, (ii) Middle (comprising Provinces and Metropolitan Cities), and (iii) Lower Level Government (comprising Cities, Counties, and Districts). Each of these levels has executive and legislative bodies of their own. The heads of local government and councilors are elected through direct elections, although civil servants are appointed by the central government. However, decentralization is both politically fractious and costly in terms of budget outlays to finance the new institutional structures. It is plausible to argue that the decentralization process in South Korea would not have proceeded as smoothly as it did, from the mid-1990s onward, in the absence of good economic performance.

A traditional argument for the promotion of decentralization in many African countries, as noted in the case of South Korea above, is that it allows local residents to monitor the performance of their leaders, especially with respect to service delivery. This promotes the growth of political and bureaucratic structures that are crucial for sustaining local-level democracy, with local dwellers' ability to vote in new leaders as the key disciplinary device (Collins and Green, 1994). In practice, two issues have impeded local democracy from flourishing in African countries (Golola, 2003): first, unlike in the case of South Korea above, not enough consideration is given to the financial implications of decentralization ex ante. Typically, local leaders have few sources of revenue (i.e. lack powers of direct taxation, though many compensate with ad hoc measures, including in-kind options) and remain beholden to the center for current and capital expenditures; second, and related to the first point, local politics could be captured by local-center alliances, hence disenfranchising local voters.

The experience of many African countries indicates that if the devolution and fiscal federalism required for effective service delivery and accountability are to be realized, fiscal devolution must happen alongside local capacity enhancement and political decentralization. Here, the adage "no taxation without representation" would be appropriate as the autonomous entities collecting taxes and fees would need to account to the local population. Ultimately, the local development plan would derive from local level development needs rather than bureaucratic dictum from the center—and therein lies the tension i.e. parochial needs versus national level imperatives.

Even in the fairly socially homogeneous country like South Korea, the convergence of local needs to those of the center took time and involved much political rancor. In the more conflict-prone African societies, a convergence of local and national aspirations might be more difficult to attain. It was probably with this tension in mind that the Cameroonian Constitution (already in its first article) declares that the Republic of Cameroon is a "decentralized unitary state."[7] It continues to underline that any actions at the decentralized level that would threaten the unity of the state would be contrary to the provisions of the Constitution.

In South Korea, fiscal devolution was attained through a careful assignment of the taxes to be collected at the local level—i.e. property taxes, land taxes, and commercial business taxes (Kim and Kim, 2015). Thus, although the local entities continued to depend on transfers from the center to pay the bulk of their salaries, they nevertheless enjoyed a level of autonomy. The share of the central government's subsidy to local authorities' budgets fell steadily, reaching 21.8% in 2013 from close to 60% in 2000. As part of the decentralization, but also spatial inclusion strategy, the South Korean government established a Local Finance Equalization Scheme to assist local governments with a weak revenue base. This is done through various subsidies and the sharing of local taxes and surcharges notably on liquor and communication.

South African Exceptionalism? South Africa, like South Korea above, pursued decentralization as a means of reinforcing its democratic project. The former also saw decentralization as a key means of keeping the country, composed of disparate regions and populations, together. In recent years, the pendulum has been swinging toward greater centralization as financing difficulties are testing fiscal federalism to the limit (Calitz and Essop, 2012; Powell, 2012). As per constitutional requirement, there is a plethora of administrative areas requiring counterparts at the national, province, and local levels i.e. procurement, education, social grants, and housing. The administrative demands of these quite complex coordination issues quickly exceeded local capabilities. It became clear that in the absence of improvements in local capacities, there would be limited improvement in service delivery.

Recent assessments have shown that while decentralization as a political decision was attractive, it was not allotted the financial and human resources needed to make it a success (Alm and Martinez-Vasquez, 2015). Hence, in many rural areas, decentralization is failing to raise social service delivery standards partly for lack of the policy and management structures required i.e. local capacities for making and executing fiscal policies, notably local tax collection authority (Bhorat and van der Westhuizen, 2012; Gumede, Byamukama and Dakora, 2019). The unsettled decentralization agenda implies that achieving the goals of poverty and inequality reduction and expansion of local democracy and service delivery, on which it was premised, will be delayed.

In education, for example, responsibilities for financing and curricula development were retained at the center for fear of the uneven impact that capacity differences would have on education provision, especially in rural areas (McLennan, 2003). In approaching decentralization in South Africa, therefore, there might be a case for differentiated gradualism that allows enough time for the development of the capacities required at the local level, notably in the provinces at a remove from the big cities. This also suggests the need for policy experiments in the search for what works best in the different economic and policy environments of the country, as rigid standardization is the enemy of decentralization (Koma, 2010; Siddle and Koelble, 2017; Turok, 2010).

The presence of strong traditional leaders in South Africa, also common in the other African case study countries, has added another layer of complexity to the devolution issue—a problem that did not exist in South Korea to any large extent. Traditional rulers exercise their power through cultural mores and moral suasion. Although unelected, few people could gainsay the strong followership, prestige, and even political power that such leaders command in South Africa. Sithole (2005) has argued that they represent a form of democracy that simultaneously craves national and cultural identity. A, perhaps, more critical reason for the authorities' fear of traditional leaders is the possibility that in a moment of national crisis, the latter could well turn popular sentiment against them. However, in terms of land reform, a mainstay of the developmental state, the South Africa Team (2015) notes that traditional leaders have been an obstacle. The land currently under traditional ownership has seen a lower rate of redistribution than other ownership types, with traditional leaders ably resisting the political decisions reached by elected leaders at the center (Daniels et al., 2013).

Decentralization's Unfunded Mandates. While decentralization was attempted in South Korea and South Africa from a position of relative financial strength, at least in the sense that the countries had resources to sustain the effort, many countries in Africa embarked on the process under pressure from the lending agencies and the donor community and without well-laid out funding strategies. The impact of decentralization on Dimbokro, a formerly prosperous cocoa producing region of Côte d'Ivoire is insightful (Koffi, Tere and Mel, 2013). From being one of the richest cocoa-producing areas of the country, including hosting an independence-day parade, it fell to hard times in 2000s, when the government embarked on decentralization in 2003, leaving the commodity exporting area in the hands of a small administrative outpost. The policy was an attempt at reducing public expenditure overall, though government opponents alleged that it was meant to reduce its exposure to "less strategic regions" of the country i.e. those where opposition parties drew the bulk of their support (Yaya, 2009). Ironically, decentralization, embarked on during the height of Côte d'Ivoire's political problems became the equivalent of killing the goose that lay the golden eggs i.e. coffee and cocoa production collapsed in the absence of a strong link to the center.

Zambia's decentralization, in step with the leadership's rural sympathies, was embarked on quite early and was deliberate and sustained. However, it also produced quite modest outcomes. Seeking to start from the bottom of the pyramid, the government passed the Village Registration and Development Act in 1979, which created the village productivity committee (VPC). Its responsibilities included assembling the administrative and development needs of the village and passing them on to the next level. This did not happen because the flow of information and the responses from above were not tied to any coherent incentive structure i.e. failing to demonstrate responsibility meant nothing. A major hindrance was the politicization of local level activities as the influence of the central government over local affairs increased.

When political party competition was reintroduced in Zambia in 1990, legislation was crafted to de-link local government structures from political party structures. This did to guarantee the autonomy of local governments. For lack of resources, they continued to be beholden to the center. In 2002, the government adopted a new decentralization policy (Republic of Zambia, 2002) which created four levels of governance: national, provincial, district, and sub-district, with the district as the fulcrum.

In an unprecedented move to match the new thinking in the country, where the concentration of power at the center was blamed for the country's economic and political ills, the bulk of service provision was shifted to the district level: disaster management; community development; primary healthcare; primary and basic education; water and sanitation; rehabilitation, maintenance, and construction of feeder roads; mobilization of local resources; management and conservation of natural and wildlife resources; provision and maintenance of public amenities; land allocation and utilization; trade and business licensing; by-laws; community police service; community prisons service; and youths and juvenile delinquency services.

The government had, once again, overestimated the pace at which capacities at the local level would be created to manage the devolved functions, some of which were quite technical. It had also not given much thought to the fiscal and decision-making processes that were required to sustain it. In 2013, the government revised the decentralization policy from 2002 with a view to retaining control over the bulk of the functions that it had ceded to the lower levels, but with only modest impact on flow and quality of services at the local levels.

Twice Removed: Decentralization in Nigeria. Nigeria provides another variation on decentralization and development. Here, the demand for decentralization mainly revolved around the issues of economic empowerment, self-determination, and control of natural resources. Nigeria's experience shows that decentralization is not an effective way of sanitizing lower levels of government from the political and financial stresses at the federal level. Notably, rent-seeking activities at the center tend to reach the local levels as well, notably through the encashment and expenditure of oil revenue. In recent years, the emergence of democracy and broadening of political contestation in Nigeria have made it possible for the population, through elections, to exercise credible threats to leaders at all levels of government, notably the local level (Aiyede, 2009; Jimoh, 2003) (Box 5.2).

Box 5.2: In search of coherence at the state level in Nigeria: cases of Lagos, Kaduna, and Cross River

Nigeria has 36 states, with a total of 774 local government areas, and a Federal Capital Territory, Abuja. Many states in Nigeria have sought to pursue the developmental state model in their own right, especially attracted by its insistence on focused planning, efficient delivery of services, and good governance. This Box provides an overview of how three, quite different, Nigerian states defined and sought to implement developmental state type policies on their own volition.

Lagos State to the south west of Nigeria is mostly an urban economy evolving around the former capital of the country, with a population of some 16 million and contributing a fifth (US$80.4 billion) of Nigerian GDP in 2016. The state's economy is more diversified than the rest of the country with manufacturing at 30%, transport and services at 28%, and construction at 20%. It also has a large informal sector. Lagos State is reputed for its ambitious development agenda (i.e. Lagos State Vision, 2020 and Lagos State Development Plan, 2012–2025) and ability to attract private investment on the strength of its own ratings with the agencies. In recent decades, and in spite of its reputation for being an unruly place, it has registered a number of achievements, including effective administration, the construction of an extensive transport infrastructure, a well-developed financial market, and an expanding film industry (Nollywood). The State has raised the standard of its healthcare and introduced measures to protect the environment, address decades of inadequate water and sanitation and sewage service provision, and introduce a more efficient urban mass transit system. To finance its interventions, the state government has put in place an effective mechanism for resource mobilization, including tax enforcement. This has been accompanied by a framework for transparency and accountability based on the use of ICT and statistics for planning, implementation and monitoring, and evaluation. However, Lagos State's relations with the federal government have fluctuated depending on the political parties at the helm in both places, and corruption has not been exorcised.

Cross River State in the south east of the country is one of the oldest states in Nigeria, created already in 1967. But unlike the more urbanized Lagos State, it has not diversified state revenues anywhere to the same extent and depends to a considerable level on resources from its share of the oil account from the central government. Its natural resources remain largely unexploited for lack of a conducive environment for private investment; oil production has dwindled in recent years. In 2019, the state government unveiled a Bakassi Deep Sea project, which many inhabitants see as a potential regional game changer. It will enhance the state's potential as a gateway to the hinterland, including the western parts of Cameroon. Given its long river (Oyono), the state has great hydropower generation potential, which can sustain a sizeable industrial sector. The state university, Cross River State University of Technology, established in 2002 from the amalgamation of smaller institutions, has potential to raise the state's human resource profile, although much more needs to be done to bring it to the standard of other universities in the region and country. In the stiff competition for investment and high-caliber human resources, Cross River State must rise above the average Nigerian state and profile itself more aggressively to succeed.

Kaduna State is centrally located in Nigeria, adjacent to the Federal Capital Territory. Proximity to the capital has not necessarily been a blessing, as it implies a competitive disadvantage over civil servants and technical staff. With a population of about 12 million in 2019, and despite its renowned institutions and universities, Kaduna has traditionally not had a well-streamlined planning machinery. It has depended partly on technical assistance from the donor community to raise the quality of its services and address a high-poverty incidence. Like Cross River, it too depends overly on revenue from the government for financing its activities, including infrastructure extension and education and health services. In recent years, the state's proactive governor has adopted several strategies, including American-type "townhall meetings" to discuss key policy issues affecting his constituency directly with the population. An important recent initiative is the Kaduna State Infrastructure Plan (2018–2050) targeting power supply and transportation, with the goal of "making Kaduna great again." The state aims to use its strategic location on Nigeria's urban corridor (Abuja-Kaduna-Zaria-Kano) to enhance its position as an innovation and ICT hub.

Source: Nigeria Team (2017).

5.4 Agriculture and rural development

In rapidly urbanizing environments, African countries have continued to emphasize agriculture and rural development. As a result, recent decades have witnessed a contradiction between, on the one hand, the traditional public support to peasant agriculture and rural development in a bid to reduce poverty, slow-down rural–urban migration, and promote spatial inclusion and, on the other, the pursuit of modern agriculture, through market-based production and infrastructure development, as a basis for industrialization. The two emphases have had quite different policy implications, but need to converge, for the dynamic aspects of agricultural production and rural development to be exploited for industrialization and structural transformation (Fambon et al., 2014). South Korea confronted similar tensions between the policy of industrialization and rural development in the formative years. Following the Korean war, agriculture played an important role in securing rural livelihoods, including supplying food to urban dwellers and inputs to the budding industrial sector in the 1960s and 1970s (Looney, 2012).

Agriculture and Land Reform in an Aspiring Developmental State. South Korea had become one of the poorest countries in the world after the Korea war. Food shortages were chronic, while the population had increased dramatically following the repatriation of overseas residents and the exodus from North Korea. Working with the United Nations Korean Reconstruction Agency (UNKRA), the United States and other donors helped augment the still fragile food production with food imports. Subsequently, "increasing agricultural productivity" became a major feature of South Korea's first Five-Year Development Plan. Although in terms of economic leadership agriculture and rural development played a secondary role to industrialization, they had a crucial complementary role in industrial policy and economic development. Besides, agricultural production provided a basis for rural mobilization and prevented the emergence of civil unrest.

The Park administration, contrary to what would have been expected of a capitalist-oriented administration, introduced a duo price system for the rice and barley market soon after gaining power in 1961. It offered high-farmgate prices to boost production incentives while lowering the price for consumers through the provision of subsidies to sellers, covering the differences through loans extended by the central bank. Subsequently, the development of high-yielding rice varieties became one of the enduring achievements of the Korean Green Revolution, while also boosting domestic research capacity. However, with the rapid development in incomes, the dietary patterns of the population changed swiftly as well, with demonstration effects from imported consumption habits. Consequently, food self-sufficiency, which was the spur to Korea's agricultural revolution, lost some of its policy appeal.

Land tenure reform in South Korea led to a more equal distribution of land ownership in rural areas and the emergence of an indigenous group of landowners, with capital to invest. Four factors ameliorated the process of land reform in South Korea (Cho and Park, 2013; Douglass, 2013; Kim, 2013; Park, 2009). First, redistributing land formerly owned by Japanese settlers was not controversial, being part of the post-WWII settlement. Second, post-WWII, land transactions, and law enforcement costs had become prohibitive, and many landlords chose to voluntarily sell land even before the land reform of the 1950s had begun (Jeon and Kim, 2000). Third, the need for land reform was explicitly stated in the Constitution, bringing it to the center of economic and political life of the country. Fourth, the National Assembly, although faction-ridden, was relatively autonomous and able to take tough decisions on land when required.

In terms of impact, the land reform fundamentally transformed the rural social structure in South Korea. Hong (2013) equates it to a large landlord-centered modernization project, which ultimately transferred capital tied up in agriculture to industry amidst the frailty caused by the Korean War and accompanying hyperinflation. In the process, a small group of former landlords became urban entrepreneurs, thereby forming the groundwork and nucleus for the form of capitalism that came to characterize the country. Notably, the founders of the chaebols that formed South Korea's industrial backbone emerged from their ranks. Ultimately, land reform led to greater equality among rural communities, with the self-cultivated farmland increasing from around 35% at the end of WWII to 96% in 1951. The process of land reform took more than 10 years, with 97.3% of compensation for landlords being completed by the end of 1961.

Although the benefits of land reform were delayed by the Korea war, in the event, the reform promoted nation building and created a strong basis for democratization in the rural areas and augured well for the decentralization that would be embarked on in the decades ahead. The government used the land re-distribution process to implement pro-poor initiatives, notably poor farmers only paying half of the price for the allocated land. In retrospect, South Korea's land reform was undertaken at relatively little political and financial cost i.e. there was little direct opposition from the rural elite groups. It helped to transform the countryside from a traditional base for conservative resistance to reforms to one that would support the modernization project of the Park government, thanks to the incentive-compatible initiatives and pro-poor actions that the latter had undertaken (Kim, 2013).

Reforestation and the Power of Collective Action. In 2015, forestlands in South Korea covered some 6.4 million hectares, about 65% of its total land area. During the Japanese occupation in the first half of the 20th century and the Korean War (1950–53), the country experienced severe deforestation. Both food and energy demand had led to the conversion of vast patches of forest-lands to agricultural use, while forests were also exploited for fuel, illegal trade in timber, and shifting cultivation (Lee, 2013). In turn, forest degradation aggravated landslides, soil erosion, and floods during monsoons, while moun-tain soil swept through rice paddies and destroyed harvests. The government's National Greening Program rolled out in the 1970s and 1980s, including the mobilization of civil society, eventually led to forest recovery in South Korea (Box 5.3).

Box 5.3 South Korea's new village movement

In 1970, South Korea launched the Saemaul Udong movement, i.e. the New Village Movement (NVM), with the goal of combining the best in modern and traditional approaches to development i.e. technical diligence, self-help, and cooperation. Furthermore, the Third National Development Plan, 1972–1976, underlined the importance of rural infrastructure and reforestation for improving the lives of rural dwellers. NVM projects in-cluded village road expansion, construction of feeder roads, bridges, water reservoirs, irrigation channels, warehouses, and utilities, notably electric-ity. Reforestation was initiated at the central level and passed down the bureaucratic chain of command until it reached the villages.

In terms of financing or contributions in kind, NVM projects expected villagers to contribute their fair share, which nevertheless placed a sub-stantial burden on the poorer households. It is estimated that during the 1970s, villagers contributed two-thirds of the rural infrastructure project cost through direct cash payments and/or material and direct labor con-tributions (Park, 2009). Nevertheless, the NVM campaigns resulted in widespread improvement in the quality of life in the rural areas especially in terms of rural infrastructure and forest recovery.

South Korea Team (2017) and Zambia Team (2017)

Nigeria: Travails of an Oil-rich Country's Agriculture. In the 1960s, Nigeria was a net producer and exporter of agricultural commodities—cocoa, groundnuts, palm oil, and cotton. At this time, the goal of the government was to extract as much surplus as possible from agriculture i.e. the farmer, in favor of manufacturing, through the control of farmgate prices and the exchange rate. Nevertheless, the relatively good macroeconomic environment of the 1960s meant that the government could adjust farmgate prices on a regular basis to sustain agricultural production and stem rural–urban migration.

During the oil revenue boom of the 1970s, the government established the Nigerian Agricultural and Cooperative Bank, removing taxes on agricultural exports and compelling commercial banks to extend at least 6% of their loans to agriculture (later raised to 12%). It launched Operation Feed the Nation (1976), ostensibly to eradicate hunger, although rising oil revenues would go toward food imports and not production (Olayemi, 1998). From the 1980s onward, the government embarked on an integrated rural development approach to agricultural development, with several agencies created for the purpose i.e. the River Basin Development Authorities, the Directorate of Food, Roads and Rural Infrastructure (meant to help ease farmer access to markets), the National Agricultural Land Development Agency (NALDA), the Operation Feed the Nation, and the Green Revolution Program. However, the parallel adoption of structural adjustment policies in the second half of the 1980s complicated the policy framework for agriculture as the goal of the reforms was to enhance the sector's market response and reduce public sector involvement.

In 2011, the government launched the National Agricultural Investment Plan (NAIP), 2011–2014, crafted as a private sector-led strategy, linked to the entire agricultural value chain, notably crops, livestock, and fisheries. It would be financed by the federal and state governments and the private sector through PPPs. Besides, Presidential initiatives targeted at commodities with export potential such as cassava and rice were also launched by the governments. An innovative fertilizer delivery strategy that has been lauded for its targeting efficacy and impact was launched during this time (Cross River State Planning Commission, various years; Kaduna State Government, 2014; Olayemi, 1998; Olakojo and Folawewo, 2013).

During the 2010s, there have been improvements in Nigerian agricultural performance, thanks to real price increases for produce, greater availability of improved technology, efficient dissemination of information by the agricultural departments to farmers, and increased capacity for value-addition across crops and other agricultural output. On the other hand, a number of downstream impediments continue to have a negative effect on agriculture, including political instability, and related risks to investment, incomplete markets for farm inputs and produce, and the generally non-supportive macroeconomic policies, including exchange rate overvaluation.

In comparison to South Korea, Nigeria's agricultural policies have lacked the coherence and link to the overall national development that would generate sustainable development and lay the basis for industrialization. The proliferation of institutions associated to agriculture, in the face of ineffective policy coordination and implementation, has made it difficult to mobilize farmers. Each new institution requires a counterpart at the local level, while financing and human resource challenges, along the policy formulation and implementation chains, are formidable, with weak feedback loops to the center.

5.5 Conclusion

African countries returned to development planning in large numbers from the late-1990s onward, as their economic growth numbers rose markedly, fiscal space expanded, and the examples of the developmental states of East Asia allured by their rapid development and relative policy autonomy. The chapter has argued that in South Korea national development planning was pursued as a package, not a set of discreet activities, with well-specified accountability structures for implementation, including enough attention paid to financial mobilization, performance monitoring, and impact assessment. In Africa's renewed attempt at national development planning, in an admittedly much changed global environment, a similarly rigorous and comprehensive approach will be required if the development results are to be different from the past.

Notes

1 It was the most prestigious among a number of elite agencies created by the government to meet specific policy objectives: Korea Labor Welfare Corporation, Agricultural Products Marketing Corporation, Korea Promotion Corporation, Industrial Sites and Resources Development Corporation, Agricultural Development Corporation, Korea Overseas Development Corporation, Office for National Tax Administration, and Enlarged Meeting for Export Promotion, and research agencies: Korean Institute of Science and Technology, Korean Advanced Institute of Science and Technology, Korea Nuclear Fuel Development Institute, Korean Atomic Energy Research Institute.
2 As part of its reform of the public sector, with a view to eliminating the duplication of functions, the Ugandan Government embarked on a comprehensive program to restructure its ministerial and agency composition. The associated study (Republic of Uganda, 2017) had recommended the return of most agencies and authorities to their "mother" ministries. Typically, ministries such as agriculture have several semi-independent agencies under them, initially setup as project implementation units but which had morphed, thanks to donor money, into powerful agencies, with equally powerful constituencies. The difference being that after the project ends, they are sustained by the government's central budget. Given the intricate political economy that led to their creation in the first place, the reversal has proven difficult.
3 In the past decade, several African governments have created "delivery units" in the offices of the President or Prime Minister (Kenya, Ghana, Tanzania, Uganda etc.), which have taken some of the oxygen from the revived national planning agencies. The new delivery units were patterned on PM Tony Blair's Delivery Unit that he set up at 10 Downing Street i.e. with a more focused and time-bound delivery mandate for unravelling structurally significant policy bottlenecks, such as those related to the National Health Service. Tanzania's Presidential Delivery Unit, dubbed pointedly, "Big Results Now" was praised for making universal primary education more

impactful, through the use of policy experiments. In Uganda, the Prime Minister's Delivery Unit chose, oddly enough, to focus on boosting coffee production and exports, with the military helping with the distribution of seedlings.

4 For example, the OECD listed South Korea as the lowest spender on welfare among its members, about 10% of GDP compared to an average of 20%—especially highlighting the plight of the old people in the country. This has led to policy changes (Korea Herald, 2015).

5 Likewise, in Tanzania and Uganda (Hickey, 2013) the continuity of development plans and strategies was challenged when the leaders that had championed them left the scene.

6 The notes were initially focused on South Africa but have clearly much broader relevance.

7 See Republic of Cameroon (2008).

References

Aiyede, E. (2009) 'The Political Economy of Fiscal Federalism and the Dilemma of Constructing a Developmental State in Nigeria,' *International Political Science Review* 30(3):249–269.

Alm, J. and Martinez-Vasquez, J. (2015) 'Re-designing Equalization Transfers: An Application to South Africa's Provincial Equitable Share,' *Journal of Developing Areas* 49(1):1–22.

Bevan, D., Collier, P. and Gunning, J. (1999) *The Political Economy of Poverty, Equity and Growth: Indonesia and Nigeria,* Oxford University Press: Oxford.

Bhorat, H. and van der Westhuizen, C. (2012) 'Poverty, Inequality and the Nature of Economic Growth in South Africa,' *Working Paper* 12/151, Development Policy Research Unit, University of Cape Town: Cape Town.

Calitz, E. and Essop, H. (2012) 'Fiscal Centralisation in a Federal State: The South African Case,' *Stellenbosch Economic Working Papers* 10/12, Bureau for Economic Research, Stellenbosch University: Stellenbosch.

Cameroon Team (2017) «Etude Sur L'Economie du Cameroun. La Politique de Développement dans la Pratique Enseignements Tires de L'Expérience de Développement de la Corée du Sud» Report to the African Development Bank on the *Developmental State in Africa, Lessons from South Korea Project,* Université de Yaoundé II: Yaoundé.

Cho, S. and Park, T. (2013) 'Suggestions for New Perspectives on the Land Reforms in South Korea,' *Seoul Journal of Korean Studies* 26(1):1–26.

Choi, B. (1987) 'The Structure of the Economic Policy-Making Institutions in Korea and the Strategic Role of the Economic Planning Board (EPB)' *Korean Journal of Policy Studies* 2:1–25.

Collins, C. and Green, A. (1994) 'Decentralization and Primary Healthcare: Some Negative Implications in Developing Countries,' *International Journal of Health Services* 24(3):459–475

Côte d'Ivoire Team (2017) «Etude Sur L'Economie Ivorienne. La Politique de Développement dans la Pratique Enseignements Tires de L'Expérience de Développement de la Corée du Sud» Report to the African Development Bank on the *Developmental State in Africa, Lessons from South Korea Project,* Le Centre Ivoirien de Recherches Economiques et Sociales (CIRES) : Abidjan.

Cross River State Planning Commission (various years) *Socio-Economic Development Survey Report,* Government of Cross River State: Calabar.

Daniels, R. et al. (2013) 'Rural Livelihoods in South Africa,' Southern Africa Labour and Development Research Unit, University of Cape Town: Cape Town.

Douglass, M. (2013) *The Saemaul Undong: South Korea's Rural Development Miracle in Historical Perspective,* Working Paper Series, 197, Asia Research Institute: Singapore.

Du Plessis, S. (2006) 'Institutions and Institutional Change in Zambia,' *Stellenbosch Economic Working Papers* 16/06, Bureau for Economic Research, University of Stellenbosch: Stellenbosch.

Fambon, S., McKay, A., Timnou, J.-P., Kouakepi, O. and Dzossa, A. (2014) 'Growth, Poverty and Inequality: The Case of Cameroon,' *WIDER Working Paper Series* 154, UNU-WIDER: Helsinki.

Golola, M.L. (2003) 'Decentralization, Local Bureaucracies and Service Delivery in Uganda,' in S. Kayizzi-Mugerwa *Reforming Africa's Institutions: Ownership, Incentives and Capabilities,* United Nations University Press: Tokyo and New York.

Government of Ghana (1964) *Seven-Year Development Plan,* Government Printer: Accra.

Gumede, N., Byamukama, J., and Dakora, E. (2019) 'Contemporary Perspectives on Fiscal Decentralization and New Local Government in South Africa,' School of Economics and Management Science, Sol Plaatje University: Kimberley.

Gumede, W. (2009) 'Comparative Development Planning,' *Development Bank of South Africa Series* 8, Development Planning Division, Development Bank of South Africa: Midrand.

Haggard, S., and Moon, C.I. 1990. 'Institutions and Economic Policy: Theory and a Korean Case Study.' *World Politics* 42(2):210–237.

Han, S. (2014) 'Operation of the economic planning board in the era of high economic growth in Korea,' *Knowledge Sharing Program: KSP Modularization.* Korea Development Institute School of Public Policy and Management: Seoul.

Hickey, S. (2013) 'Beyond the Poverty Agenda? Insights from the New Politics of Development in Uganda,' *World Development* 43(C):194–206.

Hong, S. (2013) 'Land Reform and Large Landlords in South Koreas Modernization Project,' *Seoul Journal of Korean Studies,* 26(1):23–45.

Jeon, Y., and Kim, Y. (2000) 'Land Reform, Income Redistribution, and Agricultural Production in Korea,' *Economic Development and Cultural Change* 48(2):253–268.

Jimoh, A. (2003) 'Fiscal Federalism: The Nigerian Experience,' *Paper Presented at the Ad-Hoc Expert Group Meeting on Policy and Growth in Africa,* United Nations Economic Commission for Africa (UNECA): Addis Ababa.

Kaduna State Government (2014) *Kaduna State Development Plan,* Ministry of Economic Planning, Kaduna State: Kaduna.

Kim, K. (1991) 'The Korean Miracle (1962–1980) Revisited: Myths and Realities in Strategy and Development,' *Working Paper,* 166, The Kellogg Institute for International Studies, Notre Dame University: South Bend.

Kim, N. and Kim, J. (2015) 'Top Incomes in Korea, 1933–2010, Evidence from Income Tax Statistics,' *Hitotsubashi Journal of Economics* 56 (1):1–19.

Kim, S. (2013) 'South Korea's Land Reform and Democracy,' *Seoul Journal of Korean Studies* 26(1):27–74.

Kimengsi, J. and Gwan, S. (2017) 'Reflections on Decentralization, Community Empowerment, and Sustainable Development in Cameroon,' *International Journal of Emerging Trends in Social Sciences* 1(2):53–60.

Koffi, A., J. Tere and Mel, T. (2013) «Decentralisation et crise economique en Côte d'Ivoire: Cas du Conseil General de Dimbokro», *European Scientific Journal* 9(25):85–109.

Koma, S. (2010) 'The State of Local Government in South Africa. Issues, Trends and Options,' *Journal of Public Administration* 45(1.1):111–120.

Korea Herald (2015) 'Korea ranks lowest in OECD for welfare spending,' February 5: www.koreaherald.com/view.php?ud=20150205001282.

Lee, K-J. (2013) 'Successful Reforestation in South Korea: Strong Leadership of Ex-President Park Chung-Hee,' CreateSpace Independent Publishing Platform: Charleston.

Looney, K. (2012) *The Rural Developmental State: Modernization Campaigns and Peasant Politics in China, Taiwan and South Korea,* Doctoral Dissertation: Harvard University.

McLennan, A. (2003) 'Decentralisation and Its Impact on Service Delivery in Education in post-Apartheid South Africa,' in G. Mhone and Edigheji, O. (eds.), *Governance in the New South Africa: The Challenges of Globalisation,* 182–214, University of Cape Town Press: Landsdowne.

Moon, S. (2003) 'Carving Out Space: Civil Society and the Women's Movement in South Korea,' *Journal of Asian Studies* 61(2):473–500.

Nigeria Team (2017) 'Towards Developmental State in Nigeria: Lessons from Korea,' Report to the African Development Bank on the *Developmental State in Africa, Lessons from South Korea Project,* Nigerian Economic Society: Ibadan.

Ohno, K. (2011) 'Learning from Best Practices in East Asia: Policy Procedure and Organization for Executing Industrial Strategies,' *Paper Presented at SOAS International Workshop on Aid and Development in Asia and Africa,* School of Oriental and African Studies: London.

Olakojo, S. and Folawewo, A. (2013) 'Institutions and Growth Drag: Evidence from Major Crude Oil Producing African Economies,' *Nigerian Journal of Economic and Social Studies* 55(3):25–47.

Olayemi, J. (1998) 'Agricultural Development Strategy: Institutional Framework and Support,' *Paper Presented at the Workshop on Policy Issues and Planning in the Agricultural Sector,* National Center for Economic Management and Administration (NCEMA): Ibadan

Park, S. (2009) 'Analysis of Saemaul Undong: A Korean Rural Development Programme in the 1970s,' *Asia-Pacific Development Journal* 16(2):113–140.

Powell, D. (2012) 'Imperfect transition – local government reform in South Africa 1994–2012,' in S. Booysen (ed.), *Local Elections in South Africa: Parties, People, Politics,* Sun Press: Bloemfontein.

Republic of Cameroon (2008) *The Constitution of the Republic of Cameroon,* National Assembly: Yaounde.

Republic of Côte d'Ivoire (2012) *Plan National de Développement, 2012–2015,* Ministry of Economic Development and Planning: Abidjan

Republic of Côte d'Ivoire (2015) *Etude Prospective Côte d'Ivoire 2040,* Ministry of Economic Development and Planning: Abidjan.

Republic of Uganda (2017) *Report on Comprehensive Review and Restructuring of Government Ministries,* Ministry of Public Service: Kampala.

Republic of Zambia (2002) *National Decentralisation Policy,* Government Printer: Lusaka.

Rhee, Y., Ross-Larson, B. and Pursell, G. (1984) *Korea's Competitive Edge. Managing the Entry into the World Economy,* World Bank: Washington, DC.

Schneider, B. (1999) 'The *Desarrollista* State in Brazil and Mexico,' in M. Woo-Cumings (ed.), *The Developmental State,* 276–305, Cornell University Press, Ithaca.

Siddle, A. and Koelble, T. (2017) 'Local Government in South Africa: Can the Objectives of the Developmental State be Achieved through the Current Model of Decentralized Government? *Research Reports*, Swedish International Centre for Local Democracy: Visby.

Sithole, M. (2005) 'The Secular Basis of Traditional Leadership in KwaZulu-Natal,' *Alternation: Interdisciplinary Journal for the Study of the Arts and Humanities in Southern Africa* 12(2):102–122.

Seunghee, H. (2014) *Operation of the Economic Planning Board in the Era of High Economic Growth in Korea*, Ministry of Strategy and Finance: Seoul.

South Africa Team (2015) 'The Role of Institutions in Underpinning Inclusive Economic Growth in South Africa.' Report to the African Development Bank on the *Developmental State in Africa, Lessons from South Korea Project*, Development Policy Research Unit, School of Economics, University of Cape Town: Cape Town.

South Korea Team (2017) 'KOAFEC—Development Policy in Practice Project,' Report to the African Development Bank on the *Developmental State in Africa, Lessons from South Korea Project*, Korea Institute for International Economic Policy (KIEP): Seoul.

Touna-Mama, A. (2008) *L'économie camerounaise: pour un nouveau départ*, Africaine d'édition: Yaoundé.

Turok, I. (2010) 'Towards a Developmental State? Provincial Economic Policy in South Africa,' *Development Southern Africa*, 27(4):497–515.

Yaya, K. (2009) *La dimension sociale du développement durable en cote d'ivoire:le role de la croissance et des depenses sociales*, Cellule d'Analyse de Politiques Economiques du CIRES: Abidjan.

Whitworth, A. (2015) 'Explaining Zambian Poverty: A History of (Non-Agriculture) Economic Policy Since Independence,' *Journal of International Development Studies* 27(7):953–986.

Zambia Team (2017) 'The Zambian Society and Economy: Development Policy in Practice in Comparison with South Korea.' Report to the African Development Bank on the *Developmental State in Africa, Lessons from South Korea Project*, Southern African Institute for Policy and Research (SAIPAR): Lusaka.

6 Service delivery, employment, and poverty reduction

6.1 Introduction

This chapter compares the experience of South Korea and the African cases in the areas of social service delivery, employment creation, and poverty reduction. While, as discussed earlier, rapid industrialization is the *raison d'être* of the developmental state, its technical competence and credibility can only be inferred by the population from its capacity to deliver social services, create jobs, and reduce poverty. The chapter proceeds as follows: the next section discusses two views of the state's role in service provision, provider or enabler, followed by a comparative discussion of education and health service provision in South Korea and the African case studies, including how they mediated between the needs of their rural and urban constituencies. This is followed by a discussion of labor market policies in South Korea and the five African case studies. The last section looks at poverty and inequality reduction issues and government responses.

6.2 Service provider versus enabler

In South Korea, the private sector provides the bulk of health and education services (including tertiary level education and training), with the public sector's role largely confined to providing enabling and regulatory frameworks. In the African country study cases, the reverse was usually true in the post-independence decades, with governments having a near-monopoly on health and education service provision, aside from institutions led by religious bodies. The provision of social services in the private realm was often scoffed at as profiteering, while private sector competition with state institutions for professional staff was resented (MacLean, 2011). It is only in recent decades, with economic liberalization, that African countries have opened up their education and health sectors to private interests.

It is important to underline that for both South Korea and the African case study countries, start conditions, including colonial legacy, were imperative. South Korea used Japan as a model in setting up its regulatory systems in the social sectors, while the administrative and financing structures of its National Health Insurance (NHI) scheme were crafted along the lines of the former colonial power (Lee, 2003). On the other hand, in designing education and health policies and strategies for employment creation and poverty reduction, the new African states sought to distance themselves perceptibly from their colonial legacies. They subscribed to a socialist ethos, giving preference to the maintenance of national unity, bridging the rural–urban divide, including with respect to access to services, poverty reduction, and maintaining their independence (Grimm, 2005; Nigeria Team, 2017; South Africa Team, 2015). Notably, post-independence, African countries saw higher education more as a means for boosting public sector competences in service delivery than as a strategic resource for enhancing the competitiveness of the private sector. Likewise, health services were targeted at lowering the disease burden, and poverty, and not necessarily for boosting rural and urban human capital and productivity (Cameroon, 2017; Cote d'Ivoire Team, 2017; Zambia Team, 2017).

South Korea, on the other hand, saw the social service provision, job creation, and poverty reduction targets as part of its accountability mechanism vis-à-vis

---

Box 6.1: Meritocratic civil service: Zambia versus South Korea

In Zambia, following independence in 1964, the government appointed Zambians to the senior positions left by expatriates in the civil service, even where a risk of professional erosion existed, taking care to share the posts equitably among individuals from regions of the country. The leadership argued that political independence and national cohesion were greater concerns for the country than short-term gains in public performance. With time and job creation pressures, however, political patronage and associated networks came to determine recruitment into the civil service, eroded its independence from the executive, and negatively affected service delivery. Today, the civil service is mapped to the Office of the President, while appointments, promotions, and retirements are done by the Civil Service Commission.

In South Korea, the civil service was modeled on the experience garnered from Japanese colonial administration and the post-World War II influence of the United States military. The principle of subservience to the politicians was upheld, while at the same time the civil service maintained institutional independence i.e. it was not politicized in the manner that came to characterize those in African countries. Top civil servants in South Korea retained their positions during changes of government and, in return, were restricted from soliciting on behalf of political parties and could not engage in political activity, including standing for public office. The quest for meritocracy has been a key feature, with a ranking system for public servants and dedicated exams for entry into government service. The public service has seen regular reforms in the past 60 years, including the introduction of information technology to promote effectiveness and efficiency.

Source: Zambia Team (2017) and Yang and Torneo (2016).

implementation of its national development plans, and, so, monitored them vigorously. This was not the result of a heightened sense of altruism but rather that of a strong belief that a healthy, skilled, and motivated workforce was good for competitiveness and economic development. Hence, as argued by many studies, capacity building for industrialization became a natural and consequential driver of all the government's efforts in human development and the improvement of social welfare (Bae, 2007; Lee, 1997, 2008; Yi, 2011). Notably, free universal primary education was declared in the 1960s for all school age children, at a time of constrained public resources, but with a view to raising literacy and, thus, potential for employability among the population.

6.3 Education: policy, goals, and outcomes

Introduction. In African countries, education is probably one of the factors most closely linked to economic development and social progress—emphasized in all post-independence policy documents. However, while the demand for education in South Korea was determined by industrial requirements and the targets of its national development plans, in the case of many African countries, the determinants were quite different. Africa's post-independence leaders, many of whom had struggled to get some of their own education, saw its provision as the principal means for reducing poverty, ignorance, and disease and for forging national unity (Dryden-Peterson and Mulimbi, 2017; OECD, 2008).

However, Africa's education systems must move more toward the approach of South Korea i.e. making education a basis and engine of economic development if their development ambitions are to be achieved. African youth typically score poorly on global standard tests and the push for science, engineering, and mathematics by countries' ministries of education have not taken root. The development of the skills required to push the developmental state agenda is constrained, even for relatively affluent South Africa (Bhorat, Goga and Stanwix, 2014).

The approaches to education that countries adopted in Africa and East Asia differed for the following reasons: first, while the South Korea population is homogeneous, with a common language, most African countries are composed of hundreds of ethnicities each with its own unique language and cultural mores. Ironically, maintaining the language of the colonial master—mostly, Arabic, English, and French, but also Spanish and Portuguese—was in most cases the principal means of preserving some unity, at least in terms of intercommunal communication. Second, the colonial legacy was also important. South Korea inherited a stronger tradition in science, technology, engineering, and mathematics, while that acquired in technical areas by the bulk of African countries from their colonial rulers was generally indifferent.

The Concept of Education for Economic Development. The South Korean government realized quite early in the 1960s that if its development ambitions were to be realized it was important to link the country's development plans to an appropriate skills base and, hence, human capital development was placed under the direct supervision of the Economic Planning Board (Kim, 2008). From the launch of South Korea's first national development plan in the early 1960s,

"Education for Economic Development" became an intrinsic part of the country's development strategy (Table 6.1).

The process was by no means static and educational policies changed with the requirements of industrial development at each stage of the country's economic transformation. Hence, the production of skills shifted to meet the government's

Table 6.1 South Korea: Linking Phases of Economic Development to Human Capital and Education Needs

Period/Phase	Social and Economic Environment and Challenges	Public Response to the Human Capital and Education Needs
Socio-political restitution/war/ reconstruction (1945–1960)	The Korean society was upended by WWII, independence from Japan, and the Korean civil war. Post-war effort focused on food sufficiency, land reform, socio-political stability, and the push for import-substituting industrialization (ISI).	• State recognized the need to raise basic education (literacy and numeracy) as a basis for economic development and poverty reduction. • Universal primary education launched (by the end of 1950s about 80% of the population could read and write)
Take-off (1960s–1970s)	The South Korean economy enjoyed rapid growth and rising welfare. First half of period focused on light, but labor-intensive, manufacturing for export-with electronics standing out. In second half of period (post-1973 oil crisis), country embarks on heavy industry (chemicals, shipping)—spearheaded by chaebols	• Expansion of secondary education • Establishment of Technical and vocational schools • Firm-level technical training by firms subsidized by government
Maturation in the age of globalization (mid-1980s–1990s)	Technology, knowledge, and ICT-intensive production of goods and services. Positioning for more competitive global environment.	• Higher education expanded with emphasis on technical and science subjects • Specialized agencies for R&D are setup, with links to chaebols and local universities
First world affluence and tribulation (mid-1990–present)	Member of the OECD and WTO. Hit by and emerges from Asian Financial Crisis. Promotes Knowledge-Based Economy and "hard" science. Becomes aid donor in the age of aid pessimism.	• Higher education is popularized. • Emphasis on lifelong education and enhancement of human resources • Support to hardcore scientific research

Source: Adopted from Lee (2008) and South Korea Team (2017).

targets for the industrial sector (Kim and Lee, 2006; Lee, 1997). For instance, when heavy industry (e.g. shipbuilding and chemical industries) bloomed in the 1970s, there was a high demand for metal workers, scientists, and engineers. A vocational training law was enacted in 1967, providing training in craft skills for the expanding manufacturing industries and technicians for the heavy engineering and chemical industries. Notably, the government subsidized companies that had training programs for their workers (Bae et al., 2011).

Enrolment across the different levels of education in South Korea increased over the years as a result of the policy of national capacity building (Kang, 1990; Kang et al., 2005). Secondary school enrolment doubled in 30 years from less than 40% enrolment rate in 1970 to over 80% in 2000. In 2004, at over 60% of the age group, the country's university enrolment was the highest among OECD countries (Joonghae et al., 2006).

With respect to boosting technical capacities for industrialization in South Korea, a look at the offerings at the secondary level is instructive. There were at least four types of secondary school training programs targets at well-defined industrial segments:

- Mechanical technical high-school-trained precision workers for the machinery and defense industry.
- Experimental technical high-school-trained skilled workers for the electronics, chemical, construction, and railroad industries.
- Specialized technical high-school-trained technicians that met special manpower requirements and that would be subjected to certification and suitable for overseas deployment, given the country's exports of machinery.
- General technical high school targeted general and local engineering needs.

Education for Nation Building. In the 1960s and 1970s, the notion of "nation building" had broader meaning in Africa than that of economic development, and there were many reasons why it pervaded the continental approach to education. For example, at the time of independence in the early 1960s, few African countries had a university in place. In Zambia, few adults had completed up to four years of primary education, while a majority were illiterate. In all, the country had barely a hundred university graduates (Seers, 1964). In contrast, basic literacy in South Korea, then at roughly the same level of economic development as many African countries, was close to 80% in 1960.

Many universities were established in the 1960s in Africa to meet the demand for well-trained civil servants, but also as a sign of independence i.e. the Federal University of Yaoundé, 1962; University of Zambia, 1964; and Université National de Côte d'Ivoire (now Université Félix Houphouët-Boigny), 1964. South African universities were much older and some enjoyed standards comparable to those in Europe. The policy of Apartheid meant that, at least up to the 1990s, non-whites received an inferior education, popularly derided as Bantu education for its unimaginative construction and the relatively limited resources expended. In Cameroon, on the other hand, the two colonial legacies (French and British) hindered the evolution of a uniform education curriculum—notably, the country's first leaders received their education in France.

Nigeria's problem was different, however. Although it has more universities today than its neighbors, including renowned ones such as the University of Ibadan, established already in 1948, and the University of Nigeria, Nsukka, established in 1960, there was an in-country regional bias which continued up to the 2000s. For example, by 2010, the country had only 24 public universities in a country of 36 states and a population of over 150 million. The bulk of the universities was concentrated in the south of the country. This led to a federal-level crash program to create universities in the new states. It was a bold political stroke for nation building, especially as it was seen by the population as the brainchild of a southern politician promoting a policy that mostly benefitted non-southern states. In retrospect, the quality of education delivery was a secondary consideration, while the eventual impact of the new universities on economic transformation was an issue for the future (Box 6.2).

Boosting Skills and Technical Capacities. A key distinguishing feature of South Korea's policy with respect to boosting domestic skills and technical capabilities was the effort put into ensuring that all actors, public and private, were

---

Box 6.2: Expanding state universities in Nigeria

At the beginning of his first full term of office in 2010, President Goodluck Jonathan sought to augment the number of universities in Nigeria, noting that although the country had 36 states, it had only 24 federal universities, most of them based in the south of the country. The government thus committed to implementing a "one federal university per state" policy. Besides, increasing the number of secondary school leavers entering universities, the policy became a key component of Nigeria's transformation agenda, for which good tertiary education is a prerequisite.

Within a year of presenting the new policy, the Federal Government had established nine federal universities, one each, in the states of Jigawa, Katsina, Gombe, Kogi, Nasarawa, Ebonyi, Bayelsa, Ekiti, and Taraba, bringing the national total to 33. In 2012, a Police Academy was established in Kano State and, a year later, three federal universities were set up in Yobe, Kebbi, and Zamfara states. The creation of 13 tertiary institutions in the space of three years, not previously included in the national development plan, would have budgetary implications, including postponement of other capital expenditures. The government's aggressive policy on extending tertiary education to all states, especially to the north of the country, elicited much positive commentary from across Nigeria's political spectrum, although some saw the policy as wrongly timed, given the country's fiscal challenges.

Source: Nigeria Team (2017).

pulling in the same direction. The thinking was that all stakeholders would benefit from the technology and managerial advances that would result. As noted, the South Korean government promoted the private provision of secondary and tertiary education (although primary education was exclusively provided by the state), while retaining regulatory responsibilities, with an eye on boosting technical capacities overall, as a form of a public good (Kim, 2001; Kim, Chung and Kim, 2012). When specific skills and training were required, but not available locally, the government stepped in, creating new institutions (Oh, 2013), but also sending students for further studies abroad (Table 6.1).

It is plausible to argue that without state involvement in advanced technology research in steel, chemicals, and electronics, the country's progress would have been much slower and less remarkable. This is an important lesson for African countries, as no private entrepreneur will want to fund basic research initiatives whose findings risk falling in the hands of competitors i.e. the way business people see it, since the production of public goods cannot not finance the bottom line, it is best left to the government.

The institutions created by South Korea included the Korea Institute for Industry and Science (KIST), established already in 1966, and the Korean Advanced Institute for Science and Technology (KAIST) established in 1971. Additionally, there were three other agencies of note: the Korea Institute of Machinery and Metals (KIMM), Electronics and Telecommunications Research Institute (ETRI), and the Korea Atomic Energy Commission. In pursuit of the public good nature of the research, all the above institutions worked closely with universities and the private industry to enhance the country's technological capabilities. Some of the effort was put into adopting and assimilating technologies from elsewhere, notably the United States and Japan.

Learning from Implementation Adversity. While South Korea and East Asian countries are sometimes popularly portrayed as indefatigable policy designers and implementers, their most useful lessons of experiences for aspiring developmental states is how they dealt with policy failure and resulting popular discontent.

Although now looked at as a major success, South Korea's efforts to expand elementary school enrolment in the 1950s led to an unprecedented increase in the demand for secondary education in the 1960s, in a situation of severe resource constraints. Much like the situation faced by African governments several decades later, there were not enough secondary schools or teachers in South Korea to accommodate all the new students.

Meanwhile, the government had introduced secondary school-level entrance examinations to moderate the inflow, which, however, triggered competition for the available places and a boom in private tutoring (Kang, 1990)—again a familiar experience from African countries. To mitigate this, the government abolished entrance examinations for middle and high schools in 1969 and 1974, respectively (Bae et al., 2011). However, this then led to larger class sizes, with parents complaining about a serious diminution in quality, which had to be resolved through expansion in school infrastructure and staffing, and hence larger basic education budget outlays.

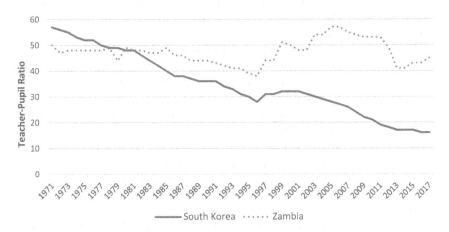

Figure 6.1 Zambia and South Korea: Primary School Teacher-Pupil Ratios, 1971–2017
Source: Zambia Team (2017) and World Bank (2020a).

With respect to teacher–pupil ratios, a comparison between Zambia and South Korea is illustrative (Figure 6.1). The teacher–pupil ratio in primary school is a good proxy of the resources being expended at the school level and for the quality of the classroom experience. Figure 6.1 indicates that while the teacher–pupil ratios in both South Korea and Zambia were high in the early 1970s, some 50-60 pupils per teacher, they had declined sharply for South Korea by the late-1990s, while those for Zambia remained high, even though education budgets had increased between 1985 and 1995 (Zambia Team, 2017). In terms of policy, what is worth noting is that in South Korea, the boom in the demand for primary education was not allowed to fester and that resources were found to resolve it in timely fashion.

The high-teacher–pupil ratios in Zambia, and in other African countries, including South Africa's poorer provinces, are caused by sharp increases in the demand for education, in responding to the introduction of universal primary education, and much slower supply of education facilities and teachers, owing to inadequate planning, monitoring, and follow-up and severe budgetary pressures. But even in cases where teachers were available, governments often failed to provide incentives for their relocation to remoter parts of countries. In Uganda, where such incentives are referred to pointedly as "facilitation," teachers prefer to teach in schools around the capital, Kampala, and/or other sizeable cities, where they or their spouses can indulge in income-generating activities, including providing extra lessons for paying students—a practice which is frowned upon by the government but which has proven impervious to public pressure.[1]

Challenges of the Expansion of Tertiary Education. Tertiary education has been a growth industry in many African countries since the 1990s, following the liberalization of the sector. The courses and training programs of the old and new institutions are still not well linked to national manpower needs nor to the countries' emphasis on economic transformation. The new private universities have invariably focused on the arts and the humanities, which are cheaper to setup and run, and eschew the costlier laboratory-driven sciences and engineering courses.

Thus, while expanding access to higher education has irrevocably changed the landscape, the mushrooming of tertiary institutions has escalated the certification syndrome at the expense of practical industry-relevant experience. There are relatively few technical (non-degree) training institutions established by the private sector as the potential student pool is not affluent enough to afford the fees. Moreover, the competition between private and public universities and other tertiary institutions, including over instructors, has weakened rather than strengthened education quality, while regulation and quality controls have become hazardous with the increasing numbers of institutions. In African universities, career guidance is fragile, with decisions largely left to the student or his/her family and subject to the family's ability to pay.

The African Economic Outlook (AEO) 2020 of the African Development Bank has noted a dichotomy between the policy pronouncements that promote the hard sciences, and the choices that the universities and their students (and parents) are making. The AEO has estimated that, in 2018, some 30% of African undergraduates were enrolled in business administration and law, about 12.5% in social sciences, 12% in education, 11% in arts and humanities, and about 6.5% in natural sciences, mathematics, and statistics. Only about 5% were taking courses in ICT. Clearly, governments have not been able to assert themselves on the issues of course delivery and choice, partly owing to the complex political economy of higher education and partly because primary and secondary schools are not necessarily geared to promoting the pursuit of STEM-based courses at higher levels. In many African countries, pass rates for mathematics and sciences at the conclusion of primary school are low.[2]

Although most South Korean tertiary institutions are privately run, the state has managed to enforce its priorities through certification, regulation, and co-financing programs. Moreover, the state plays an active guidance role in the decisions that students make with respect to their university studies, whether in private or public universities. As a result, a substantial proportion of students in its universities and colleges is registered in technical and science subjects, closely related to the country's pursuit of industrial development, while those in social sciences and education are also tied to specific professional categories i.e. the government has ensured that there is no allowance for "floaters." This relatively autocratic (i.e. not a liberal arts style) approach to education provision differs markedly from that of the US, which South Korea has otherwise sought to emulate in several areas.

Financing Education. Financing models for education in Africa have invariably fallen short owing to scarcity of resources. The African case study examples show that their ambitious education plans and projections were rarely accompanied by concrete financing plans, while governments had few means of ring-fencing education expenditure during periods of revenue turbulence. Attempts at establishing stabilization funds for the education sector, though novel, did not take off. Since large portions of the education budgets were from donor agencies, they suffered accordingly when funds were delayed or when governments failed to meet the conditionalities attached to the loans.[3] The introduction of user fees contradicted the post-independence stance that had seen education as a right for all, to be paid for by the state.

Thus, although Cote d'Ivoire had given the education sector top priority from the early 1960s, allocating it up to 40% of the total budget by the early 1970s, education budgets were halved in the 1980s and 1990s, as coffee and cocoa prices fell. The ambitious plans for the refurbishment of education infrastructure, especially in the countryside, were scaled back. Similarly, in the face of external shocks, education expenditure in Cameroon moderated in the second half of the 2000s, rising briefly in 2009 and 2010, with higher oil revenues. With the exception of this budget bump, the statements of intent following the introduction of universal primary education in the 1990s were not accompanied by real improvements in budgetary outlays (Figure 6.2)

In the face of external shocks, the government of Zambia abolished its elaborate education subsidies in 1984, introducing "user fees" across the education system. The argument was that education, especially at the tertiary level, generated long-term private benefits for users, hence fees were justified (Kaluba, 1986). The argument would be scaled back with the introduction of free primary education in 2002, which saw the number of children going to primary school in Zambia rising from 4.4 million in 2004 to 8.3 million in 2008 but with only modest increases in budget shares for education.

Two distinguishing features of the South Korea model were the relatively high level of involvement of the private sector in tertiary level education, where up to 80% of the institutions are privately owned and the relative stability of education budgets and investments. Also, significant, tertiary level education expenses were predominantly met by households. The South Korean government introduced the concept of parental contribution to education (excepting the compulsory six years of primary education and three of junior secondary, which were added later) early during the post-WWII years. The state took advantage of the demand for education to introduce a range of fees in the education system. In return, it

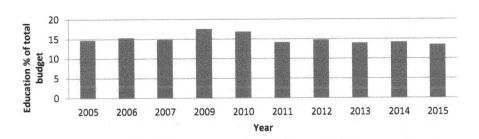

Figure 6.2 Cameroon: Share of Education Expenditure in Total Budget 2005–2015
Source: Cameroon Team (2017).

ensured households a good standard of education through an effective system of quality control, which included the direct participation of parent groups. While direct household contributions resolved the financing problem to a large extent, it also meant that the well-to-do families would get ahead of the queue for higher education—thereby putting in motion the inequalities that would surface with a vengeance decades later.

Paying for Education. In the past, the predominant argument in many African countries, including the case study countries, was that free university education was the key means of lifting the children of peasants, and hence their households, out of poverty i.e. that it was an egalitarian policy measure on the part of government. Imposing fees for education at any level was therefore contentious: stakeholders argued that since African economies were essentially driven by the produce of peasants (i.e. cocoa and coffee), charging fees would be a form of double taxation. This stance would not stand in the face of perennial external shocks and the severe revenue shortfalls that resulted.

By the 1990s, the bulk of African governments had abandoned the subsidization of education at the tertiary levels, making the charging of fees less contentious across tertiary institutions and helping state-owned institutions of higher learning to mitigate perennial budgetary shortfalls.[4] Some countries have introduced education loan schemes, while others "bond" university graduates for a number of years to work within the public sector. None of the options is entirely satisfactory, but it is difficult to envisage a future scenario where countries will revert to wholly free university education.

However, according to Mamdani (2008), in his case study of Uganda's Makerere University, the liberalization of education at the tertiary levels, partly as a response to the conditionalities imposed by the donor community, has done more harm than good. It has diluted the university experience, with rapid expansions in intake, focusing on commercially oriented courses (i.e. secretarial studies, tourism, and real estate economics) and consultancy assignments from the government and the donor community, to augment the salaries of staff. Mamdani sees the dilemma of the state-funded university as lying in how to free itself from the perennial demands for "relevance" from the authorities and other stakeholders that pay for its activities in order to revert its focus on research and student instruction.[5]

6.4 Healthcare services: structure and delivery

Background and Challenges. South Korea's experience in healthcare provision presents two innovations that are illustrative: first, as in the case of education, the private sector offers the bulk of healthcare services. Second, all households are covered by an NHI scheme. While the two seem to fit neatly within South Korea's well-designed approach to public policy, putting it together required a considerable amount of political commitment. It also called for appropriate legislation. Moreover, for the system to work, there was a need for meticulous attention to personnel recruitment, data collection, and compliance. The latter rested on heightened transparency and capacity to punish errant behavior. Kim and Kang (2016) have argued that the relatively rapid improvement in the results achieved in healthcare delivery could be ascribed partly to the country's Confucian heritage: centralization and hierarchy, emphasis on group harmony, and submission to a higher authority. Although this suggests that replication might be difficult, Japanese experience (and that of the rest of East Asia) has shown that the more productive aspects of cultural mores can be copied with relative ease.

In contrast, African governments sought to provide free healthcare, mainly in hopes of redressing the colonial legacy. Rapidly expanding populations, and increases in epidemics, notably HIV/AIDS, in recent decades, and stagnant or declining budgets, put African healthcare systems in jeopardy after the 1980s. A credibility problem arose for governments when they failed to deliver the services promised over a succession of national development plans.

In Zambia in the 1960s, for example, the plan was to establish a system where "everyone has access to curative and preventive health services" within a radius of 15 kilometers of the main settlements (Republic of Zambia, 1964). The government was counting on copper revenue and support from the donor community to achieve this. These ambitious goals were not realized, while the government ran its hospitals as exercises in crisis management.

Although the level of human resources in Africa's health sectors had improved substantially by the 2000s, thanks to training at local universities,[6] poor remuneration, long working hours, lack of equipment, and absence of work-life balance lowered morale across the board. For example, during 1980–2000, the Ivorian public health sector was faced by a serious scarcity of medical workers, especially nurses, as remuneration worsened. During the years of economic chaos, many doctors fled government hospitals to the private sector, while others left for greener pastures abroad, those that stayed behind relied on moonlighting to boost incomes.

Health Financing: Toward National Health Insurance. Systems for financing health in Africa have varied markedly over the years. In 1964, Zambia had inherited a fee-paying system for curative health services. The new government introduced free care in public institutions and regulated the private institutions that existed at the time. But even after the liberalization of the economy in the 1990s, the public sector still comprises up to 80% of the healthcare system in the country. It is financed by the state through the general budget and support from donors. The government had rolled out a national healthcare insurance scheme by 2018, although its viability is threatened by the structure and feasibility of the financing modalities.

On the other hand, Nigeria has demonstrated that in a large country, NHI schemes might not work in the absence of a critical mass of allied institutions at the federal and state levels, including for training. It is crucial to garner domestic enthusiasm for the scheme by encouraging discussion on the issues of policy, financing and implementation, and establishing communication channels for popularizing the expected benefits for participants (Box 6.3).

In Cameroon, as in many other African countries, healthcare is financed by the government, the private sector, and foreign aid—this diversification is not always for the best as it subjects health financing to external financing variability. Thus, although plans for launching an NHI have been discussed in policy forums, they are still rudimentary, with ongoing political conflicts putting them on hold.

In Cote d'Ivoire, the government introduced the universal healthcare insurance in 2014 to enable treatment of upward of 85% of the population, including rural dwellers and the self-employed in the informal sector (Dagan, 2018). The government hopes that when completely rolled out and functional, the system will provide healthcare to everyone at lower cost than today. Although the system had started in earnest by 2018, it is still too early to make a definitive statement on its performance (Box 6.3).

The South African government envisages the creation of an elaborate health insurance system with the ambition of providing citizens "access to quality affordable care based on their health needs and irrespective of their economic status" (van den Heever, 2019). In South Africa's less prosperous provinces, poverty levels are comparable to those of less affluent African countries, while its maternal mortality rate at 221 per 100,000 live births (Republic of South Africa, 2019) was higher than that of Mauritius (155) but much lower than that of Botswana (360).[7] The NHI system will help the country address its burden of disease and, for a middle-income country, low-health indicators.

In South Korea, the private sector provides 90% of healthcare services, within the country's NHI system (Chun et al., 2009). The government nevertheless plays a comprehensive role through policy formulation, regulation, and provision of healthcare infrastructure financing. It also subsidizes the cost of medical insurance for the poorer households. The NHI system recognizes both Western medicine and traditional Korean medicine, which allows patients a broad choice of treatment options. To control costs, the state regulates the operating costs of the hospitals and those of the physicians (South Korea Team, 2017).

What is laudable about South Korea's NHI experience is that the government did not wait for the country to become rich before introducing the scheme and that it allowed for a process of learning by doing. The Medical Insurance Law was introduced in 1963, and it took some 14 years before the insurance became operational in 1977. Initially, the government made it mandatory for all firms with 500 or more employees to provide medical insurance to their workers, with the cut-off point lowered in subsequent iterations. By 2000, the country had achieved universal medical insurance coverage, which incorporated self-employed workers as well as employees in agricultural households. This gradual approach helped the social partners to make appropriate adjustments, while also enabling the development of a framework for the costing of the interventions (Box 6.3).

Lessons of Experience and Conclusions on Healthcare Provision. Although the disease burden in the African country case studies and South Korea was roughly similar 60 years ago, the divergence between the two was rapid

Box 6.3: National health insurance schemes: Easier said than done and lessons from South Korea

Several African countries have taken the quantum leap toward universal health coverage by establishing NHI vehicles of various levels of complexity. Although the architecture is different, the goals and aspirations set out in Zambia's National Health Insurance Act No.2 of 2018 are shared by many other African countries attempting to create NHI schemes of their own i.e. universality, social solidarity, affordability, efficiency, effectiveness, and accountability. In practice, many of the latter have proven to be contradictory: Zambia's health insurance aims to cover all Zambians regardless of social or employment status, but so far, solidarity and affordability are proving elusive.

In Nigeria, attempts at establishing an NHI were already made in 1962, though they received little political support. An NHI scheme was formally launched by the Federal Government in 2006, with three potential segments: formal, informal, and vulnerable. Although, by 2013, almost all Federal employees were drafted in the scheme, with an additional two million others from the private sector, it is not yet a game changer. A shortcoming is that apart from Federal employees, the government has not made it mandatory.

In Cote d'Ivoire, the NHI scheme, launched in 2014, has two components, a contributory general scheme (Régime général de base) and a non-contributory medical assistance scheme (Régime d'assistance médicale), the latter being for low-income households and those living in extreme poverty. Beside individual contributions, the general contributory scheme also relies on income from investments. The non-contributory scheme is financed by the government, donations from agencies, and other financing, including taxes on regional produce. To start off the insurance scheme, the government committed some 20 billion CFA to the NHI Fund.

In South Africa, the implementation of an NHI was part of the Ten-Point Plan for the health sector agreed by the governing ANC at its Polokwane conference at the end of 2007.[8] The plan also called for a social compact for better health outcomes—including quality improvement, better infrastructure, human resource development, reviews of the drug policy, and strengthened research and development. However, having been inaugurated in January 2015, following a pilot phase in 2014, the health insurance scheme was not rolled out fully until 2018. At an average contribution of about 30 rand per month (about US$2), the presumption is that the financing burden will be borne by the government. There are fears that, if not well-managed, the system might be weighed down by too large claims, while also falling victim to fraud.

South Korea encountered many of the issues mentioned above, and there are many lessons to learn from how the challenges were resolved. Starting in 1977 with industrial workers, the national insurance system had reached the whole country in 1989. The government quickly identified three areas for action and pursued them rigorously: administration, coverage, and mobilization of resources. First, the administrative structure comprised medical insurance societies that covered various groups or regions, enabling the system to cover the whole country by accretion. Second, on the grounds of logistics and affordability, the country avoided a big bang approach and started its health insurance scheme by drawing in industrial workers in large corporations, only gradually extending to other groups, including the self-employed. Third, in terms of financing, the employer and employee paid 50% each of the premium, while the government provided subsidies to the medical insurance societies to ameliorate their administrative costs.

In South Korea, the decentralization of the health insurance scheme through formation of medical insurance societies was not universally acclaimed, however. Part of the labor movement saw it as egalitarian and evincing social solidarity, while the other detested the implicit financial burden that the industrial workers would assume in such a framework, arguing that only a fraction of the self-employed paid taxes. Although the system had performed well in the decade after full rollout, the regional financial crisis of 1997 meant that the NHI began to run a deficit, which was not closed until 2002.

Among the lessons are the following: South Korea runs an efficient but relatively expensive NHI system because it relies quite heavily on private sector provision of healthcare. Absent a countervailing amount of public provision, regulatory and enabling infrastructures frameworks are not enough to counter the power of individual private actors on the healthcare market (private medical care consumes about 90% of total healthcare resources) in determining the nature and cost of interventions. Such a system also encourages unnecessary specialization (80% of South Korea doctors are specialists compared to only 50 percent or lower in the West), use of high-tech, even for basic ailments, and treatments undertaken in relatively costlier commercial environments.

Sources Cote d'Ivoire Team (2017), Nigeria Team (2017),
South Africa Team (2015), Zambia Team (2017),
Lee (2003), and Kwon (2009).

and unrelenting. Total life expectancy at birth for South Koreas increased from 53 years (55.5 for women) in 1960 to 82.8 years (85.8 for women) in 2018. In many African countries, life expectancy, having started at around 40 years sixty years ago, and rising to 55 years in the mid-1980s, fell to below 40 years, in the following decades, owing to HIV/AIDS, malaria, and malnutrition. However, life expectancy in Zambia, for example, has risen recently to above 60 years.

Designing effective financing modalities for delivering healthcare continues to be a big challenge in many African countries. The default position for many of them would be to eschew direct charges for medical care for fear, as in the case of education, of the social and political implications. This has been somewhat ironical, as many of the state-run hospitals lack competent staff and drugs, and the negative implications of their poor service delivery are felt every day. These problems are amplified in the remoter and often rural districts of countries because professional medical staff do not find it economically attractive to locate there. Given generally low wages in the system, many health workers prefer to remain in the bigger cities, which provide access to larger healthcare infrastructure, better career opportunities, and possibilities for moonlighting.

As an example, South Korea is both good and challenging for African countries. Good because it managed to overcome poor healthcare and to build resilient systems, including the provision of universal health insurance throughout the country in a relatively short period of time. The government pursued a determined but gradual process, which allowed the reaching of domestic consensus on health delivery modalities despite stiff opposition from several domestic quarters. Besides, the country has a dedicated Ombudsman who addresses the issues arising from the provision of community and client service in healthcare, administers patient rights, and manages the resolution of complaints.

On the other hand, South Korea is also a difficult example to follow because it did not settle for small adjustments in status quo but sought to reach global standards in as a short a period as possible. The latter required the harnessing of energies across the whole political and economic spectrum, including the civil service. South Korea succeeded because the government was able to show the population that progress was being made—this was not in abstract terms and could be seen in terms of improvements in service delivery. It helped create a virtuous cycle between reform and results. Although on current evidence emulating South Korea's NHI process would be challenging for many African countries, there are many aspects related to its implementation and the requisite institution building that would be useful to bear in mind as African governments seek to craft their own approaches to universal healthcare provision.

6.5 Labor markets and employment creation

Job creation is central to the developmental state model—also the main channel through which social inclusion or shared growth can be garnered. In East Asia, job creation was premised on the rapid development of export-oriented industrialization, which in turn called for export markets, competitiveness, and market-conforming interventions on the labor market. However, from the start, the situation of the African country case studies was different from that of South Korea and its neighbors.

First, while African governments also emphasized industrialization, it was principally based on import substitution and hence on government interventions in domestic markets, notably for foreign exchange. Domestic and regional markets were, however, not big enough to sustain the nascent industrial sectors, let alone encourage their expansion. They were condemned to remain as enclaves within mostly agrarian economies, creating little employment. Second, agriculture and the urban informal sectors became the main sources of livelihood for households in the post-independence era, but a poor basis for the countries' hopes of modern job creation and economic transformation.

Labor Market Policy Tradeoffs. In the early 1960s, the South Korean authorities saw conditions on the labor market as posing two main challenges: (i) how to create mass employment while at the same time raising the quality of labor supply, through training and on-the-job programs, and human development initiatives, more generally; and (ii) how to encourage expansion into higher value and more technical niches of the economy i.e. heavy and chemical industries, without adverse impact on lower level value chains and external competitiveness i.e. without raising wage pressures. The two challenges partly arose from the rapid changes in the economy, as rapid rural–urban migration came under way in the 1960s and 1970s, thanks to industrialization, and the middle class began to expand rapidly.

Better qualified and, therefore, more productive, and competitive workers were required—hence the emphasis on the creation of vocational and technical schools—but demands for labor rights were also increasing within the expanding labor movement. The early introduction of demand-driven TVET and employment information systems helped the economy meet its huge demand for skilled workers and to reduce structural unemployment caused by rapid urbanization. This more supportive role of labor policies is certainly required in African countries if hopes of accelerated economic growth are to be achieved (Epstein, 2008).

South Korea drafted a raft of laws in the early 1960s to protect livelihoods, compensate for injuries, and introduce health insurance (as indicated above). For the new military administration, generating rapid economic growth was what mattered most. It argued that the improvement of the welfare of the workers would follow naturally. The manner in which the government approached labor relations at home was, thus, quite mechanistic. In the event, the regime's policies proved to be unduly draconian, intent on quashing labor and associated social movements, and with unfathomable political consequences in the years ahead. Amendments to existing acts restricted unionization and strikes, allowed for the continuation of a low-wage structure and conditions to sustain competitiveness i.e. the autonomy of labor unions was effectively rescinded. This, in retrospect, was the social cost of the developmental state model à la South Korea.

Tenuous Link: Labor Market Policies and Employment Data. African countries need more effective labor market information systems that can provide the data required for growth forecasts, national social service commitments, and the conduct and assessment of welfare policies. In African countries, urban informal sectors and peasant agriculture are still among the largest employers, although there is a dearth of detailed data on them in statistical surveys. Moreover, with such little knowledge on how the large and "uncaptured" sectors of the economies react to centrally delegated labor market policies, it is difficult for the authorities to assess what structural changes are required to reach policy targets, as happened in South Korea. Hoping to achieve major policy breakthroughs in the absence of such crucial data on how large population segments are responding is wishful thinking.

In Search of Economic Transformation in Côte d'Ivoire. In the 1960s, Côte d'Ivoire's initial approach was to emphasize agriculture and try to keep the young people in the countryside. However, the wage gaps soon drove them into urban areas—not into industrial jobs, as the import-substituting manufacturing was not expanding, but into the informal sector, supplying goods, and services to the expanding middle class.

The urban migration led to a labor deficit in the cocoa and coffee-growing areas of the country, threatening the inflow of foreign exchange on which the country's import-substitution was premised. Côte d'Ivoire then opened up to migrants from the neighboring countries to close the labor shortage in agriculture and maintain commodity production at a high level. In later years, immigrant demands for better living conditions, including land ownership and firmer property rights, caused much political friction and contributed to civil unrest.

With the return of peace in 2010s, the country has emphasized economic transformation, with the authorities undertaking unprecedented investments in infrastructure to reduce the costs of doing business, increase employment, and boost social inclusion. The policy of "return to agriculture" is now recognized for what it always was, a misconception that, in the face of irrevocable evidence otherwise, government could turn the tide of history (Shepherd, 2017).

South Africa: Captured Labor Market or Simply Unresponsive?[9] South Africa has a huge unemployment problem, with some analysts suggesting that the causes are nuanced and not simply to blame on past policy failures (Von Holdt et. al., 2011). For example, Seekings and Nattrass (2005) suggest that owing to the role that trade unions played in bringing about the new political dispensation in the country, unionized workers have become insiders that are able to mobilize effectively and secure beneficial policies for their members, including lower tax rates and higher wages. On the other hand, the unemployed, jobseekers, and the rural poor are outsiders, unable to transform their electoral strength into secure pro-poor reforms. Dawes (2011) has referred to this dichotomy as the "great carve up" i.e. of the benefits that the government and big business proffer those active on the labor market through the interventions of organized labor (Plagerson et al., 2019; South Africa Team, 2015).

The argument continues that the road ahead will require something of a grand bargain allowing labor market reforms to encourage the creation of labor-intensive firms and sectors, the elimination of practices that have a negative impact on employment creation, and the introduction of changes that enable the unemployed and jobseekers with low skills to participate more meaningfully in the labor market. The introduction of public works programs or a basic income grant would help mitigate the helplessness that pervades informal urban and rural livelihoods today (Black and Gerwel, 2014; Webster, 2013; Wittenberg, 2014). The bargain would also call on big business to create more low-skill jobs.[10]

Trade unions have characterized this insider–outsider narrative as misinformed and a poor understanding of the solidarity that exits between the organized working class, the unemployed, and rural dwellers in the economy, not least owing to the country's high-dependency rate, which is 3.9 per worker (Republic of South Africa, 2011b). In this scenario, well-remunerated organized workers are good for social stability and the economy.

Conclusion on Labor Markets. Although in the glamour of relative success, the tribulations of the past are a receding memory, the South Korean case shows that the government clearly suppressed workers' rights in the formative years for the "greater good" of rapid economic growth and enhanced welfare. The question is whether the policy implication should be that it is sometimes necessary to trample on workers' rights in the interest of the promised affluence ahead. The danger of course is that by definition the future is unknown, while injustice happens in the present.

Labor market policy lessons from South Korea are far from straightforward and suggest a context that might be difficult to replicate elsewhere. Not surprising, given the history of the country, the labor movement was split between a liberal and conservative tendency, with quite radical differences in approach to several issues, notably the design of social welfare benefits and how the costs would be shared among the working population. The governments of South Korea showed an uncanny ability to impose their will when it mattered i.e. suppressing some of the more radical demands of the labor movement, while maintaining a low-wage regime overall for the sake of growth. Thus, ultimately, the question is not so much about crushing workers' rights, but that of finding a national consensus for how best to generate growth and create employment in a rapidly changing economic and political environment, without eroding political stability. This is why many aspiring developmental states seek to qualify their perception of the process in some way i.e. "capable and developmental state" à la South Africa or "democratic developmental state" à la Ethiopia to avoid the authoritarian epithet.

6.6 Poverty reduction and social welfare

Introduction. The perhaps most attractive aspect of the South Korean model for aspiring developmental states in Africa is how the country managed to reduce poverty and boost social welfare in such a short period of time (Ha, 1989), while avoiding social explosion—at least not reaching the levels of social disfunction that have so frequently disrupted African social engineering attempts. In retrospect, poverty was not addressed as an isolated challenge or affliction, but as part of a broader development strategy i.e. the same strategy as that vis-à-vis education and health.

On the other hand, the Asian financial crisis of 1997–1998 showed that even South Korea, the preeminent developmental state, had socio-economic vulnerabilities, with the aged population coming under considerable distress, and was forced to undertake structural adjustment policies under an IMF program (Lee and Rhee, 1999). Estimates of inequality showed an increase during the crisis years (from a Gini of 33 in 1996 to 37 in 1998). Notably, the National Basic Livelihood System Act was reviewed in 2000, emphasizing the protection of the vulnerable groups—including the provision of meals and grants to low-income households.

Poverty and Inequality. Although African poverty and inequality are inter-twined, the case studies indicate wide disparities caused by structural rigidities and inadequate growth. The Gini coefficients for the African case study countries (indicating the year when estimated) were as follows: Nigeria, 39.0 (2018); Cameroon, 39.5 (2018); Cote d'Ivoire, 41.5 (2015); South Africa, 65.0 (2015); Zambia, 49.5 (2018) (World Bank, 2020b).[11] Compared to Algeria's Gini coefficient of 27.6 in 2011, Ethiopia's 35 in 2015, and Mauritius' 36.7 in 2017, the case study countries had much higher rates of inequality than comprador African economies. While Nigeria and Cameroon's much lower rates reflected the still agrarian nature of the economies, and, despite oil exports, above-average growth rates in agriculture in the decade before the Gini estimates, that of Cote d'Ivoire reflects an improvement from much higher levels of inequality experienced during, and as a result of, the civil conflicts.

South Africa's inequality stands out, for reasons already discussed, and will continue to weigh down on its growth prospects. The government has never-theless tried to address poverty and inequality using a variety of instruments, including payment of direct grants to vulnerable groups to the tune of 3.5% of GDP. There have been substantial increases in public expenditure on social security, education, health, electricity, and sanitation services since 1994. According to Finn, Leibbrandt and Woolard (2013), while 37% of South Africa's population was living under a multidimensional poverty line in 1993, that proportion had fallen to 8% by 2010, thanks to higher social expenditures. As a result, some 3.6 million people were lifted out of poverty i.e. above US$ 2.50 per day (PPP adjusted) by 2010. However, the expenditure outlays are huge and might not be sustained in the absence of strong underlying growth.

In Zambia, Cameroon, Cote d'Ivoire, and Nigeria, governments embarked on poverty reduction papers in the 1990s, as part of the commitment to poverty reduction under the highly indebted poor countries process. Critics have noted that there was too much focus on poverty reduction and not nearly enough on boosting growth, including by emphasizing investment promotion and private sector development (Kayizzi-Mugerwa, 2013). Several measures have been adopted since to combat poverty—including "social protection programs" and an NHI schemes, mentioned above.[12] Such efforts are inevitably urban-focused but underfunded. Non-government organizations and donors have often stepped in to close the gaps, but such relief is only short term, underlying the importance of garnering own resources for impactful and sustainable results.

Millennium Development Goals as Indicators of Progress on Social Inclusion. Table 6.2 uses a common rod in terms of the millennium develop-ment goals (MDGs) to undertake a comparative assessment of the progress that South Korea, Cote d'Ivoire, and South Africa have made in the last decade in the pursuit of improved welfare and social inclusion.[13] It shows that while South Africa and indeed Cote d'Ivoire had made some progress toward meeting the

MDGs, South Korea's performance was quite exceptional—not because it was much better endowed in terms of resources but because it focused on human development from every possible angle, taking full advantage of its homogenous population, institutional legacy, and cultural thrust.

African countries have given high priority to education provision but with vastly varying results. In Cote d'Ivoire, technical quality has failed to permeate

Table 6.2 Millennium Development Goals (MDGs): South Korea, Côte d'Ivoire, and South Africa

MDG Theme	Performance: South Korea, Côte d'Ivoire, and South Africa
MDG1: eradicate extreme poverty and hunger	*South Korea:* poverty in the country was about 50% in 1960 but the population in absolute poverty was only 2% in 2018 (although with a high incidence of poverty among the elderly i.e. aged 65+). *Côte d'Ivoire:* poverty was close to 50% in 2008. The high-growth rates since 2012 are helping to lower poverty and extreme hunger. *South Africa:* poverty reduced from 32% in 1993 to 16.5% in 2011. But high rates of unemployment and inequality persist.
MDG2: achieve universal primary education	*South Korea:* the country has historically put high priority on education, and even after World War II, the rate of school attendance was close to three-quarters of the total school-going population. Recent figures show that universal attendance has been attained. *Côte d'Ivoire:* progress has been made, but the "net rate of schooling" is 90%, while literacy among the youth (15–24 years) is only about 50%. *South Africa:* almost boasts universal enrolment, thanks to heavy recent investment, but a significant number of students drop out before completion, and quality is mediocre in rural areas.
MDG3: promote gender equality and empower women	*South Korea:* strategies for the emancipation of women are organized once in every five years. Many signs of progress, including the number of women passing the exam to join government, as well as those joining elective politics. *Côte d'Ivoire:* progress made in many areas, with a special directorate established for the promotion of women. Girl children have made progress in school, and international rankings indicate that the situation of women has improved in the past decade. *South Africa:* the country has done relatively well, but more work is required. In the sphere of political representation, women are still left behind. Moreover, many girls leave school because of "family commitments," while women generally earn less than men for equal work
MDG4: reduce child mortality	*South Korea:* child mortality has virtually ceased, thanks to many initiatives targeted at boosting family welfare and healthcare provisions. *Côte d'Ivoire:* the rate of child mortality, as high as 76 of 1,000 livebirths in 2000s, has decreased with the return of peace, thanks to programs targeted at the infant population. *South Africa:* the country has shown a decline in child mortality, although during the 1990 and 2000s, HIV/AIDS had bumped up the death rates for infants. Activist action against the disease is producing results.

MDG Theme	Performance: South Korea, Côte d'Ivoire, and South Africa
MDG5: improve maternal health	*South Korea:* almost all pregnant women have access to prenatal care, among the best in the world. The improvement since 2000, following the implementation of universal medical insurance, has been notable. *Côte d'Ivoire:* a number of programs have been introduced to lower the rates further. *South Africa.* the country has not fared well in recent years, seeing maternal death rising from 60 per 100,000 live births in 1996 to 150 as recently as 2012.
MDG6: combat HIV/AIDS, Malaria, and other diseases	*South Korea:* low levels of contraction and death from HIV/AIDS. Tuberculosis was a major problem in the past, but rates reduced over the years to low levels. The country has an informational program on the sickness as well as on malaria. *Côte d'Ivoire:* the threat is not negligible. Government set up a Council for Combating HIV/AIDS, which among others recommended free access to ARVs for all patients. Tuberculosis is still a challenge as is malaria. *South Africa:* HIV/AIDS prevalence stabilized at about 15% since the early 2000s. However, there have been extensive campaigns and improved access to care, including ARVs.
MDG7: ensure environmental sustainability	*South Korea:* has sought to integrate the MDGs in its broader development strategy, including that on the environment—and has been engaged on issues of pollution, biodiversity, and related health issues. *Côte d'Ivoire:* the forest cover has declined over the past decades, and there are few effective plans to revive it. Moreover, water resources are also under threat. *South Africa:* the country has made progress in increasing access to safe drinking water and basic sanitation from a coverage of 66% in 1990 to 81% in 2015.
MDG8: develop a global partnership for development	*South Korea:* the country is an important new donor and has tried to influence donor policies through meetings held in the country. *Côte d'Ivoire:* since the return of peace, the country gets good marks for its engagement with the donor community and its level of transparency and accountability on aid issues. *South Africa:* the government has established partnerships with private sector to boost access to information technologies among the population.

Source: Côte d'Ivoire Team (2017), South Africa Team (2015), and United Nations (2015)

through the system, and illiteracy remains a big problem despite the introduction of universal primary education. In South Africa, primary education is now accessible to all, but up to half of the students who enter the system drop out before completion (Christie and Collins, 1982; Republic of South, 2015). Still, it is instructive that the government has been sued by civil society i.e. *Minister of Basic Education v Basic Education for All*[14] for letting this situation happen under its watch. Such pleadings are uniquely South African and augur well for human rights, rule of law, and ensuring that the problems of poor service delivery are not swept under the carpet.

South Korea has shown that despite the progress made in recent decades, gender empowerment does not necessarily march hand in hand with rapid economic development and that several obstacles had to be overcome in what is at heart a tradition-bound society. South Africa, Cote d'Ivoire, and other African case studies have shown that progress on gender issues cannot happen independently of other development challenges, such as job creation and effective healthcare.

Notes

1 Universal Primary Education in Uganda has elicited much debate, reflective of the issues in other African countries. See, for example, Nishimura, Yamano, and Sasaoka (2005).
2 The harmonized test scores that combine data from major international standard achievement testing programs into common measurement units indicate that African countries have either under-invested in learning in recent years, or their education investment strategies have been ineffective. While the test core has a minimum of 300 and an advanced achievement of 625 (World Bank, 2018), scores for African countries (for 2017) were invariably in the 300s (Gabon at 454 and Senegal at 408, excepted): Cameroon, 379; Cote d'Ivoire, 373; Nigeria, 325; South Africa, 343; Zambia, 358.
3 The international community still plays a major role in funding African education, although direct involvement is less than in past decades. A new phenomenon is the massive training of Africans in East Asia, including South Korea, Malaysia, and China—training in India is much broader, having started earlier in the 20th century.
4 In the "good old days," university students in many African countries not only enjoyed free education but also received a stipend (called "boom" in East Africa) on top of free meals and lodging.
5 Mahmood Mamdani sees the poor funding of education in Africa, notably higher education, as a trap, which hinders African scholarship from reaching the global frontier through academic enquiry and research.
6 Indeed, countries, such as Rwanda, were able to recruit doctors from neighboring countries by offering lucrative pay packages.
7 The figures differ substantially by source, with UNICEF's figure for South Africa in 2018 at over 300. An overview of health sector reforms in South Africa by Schaay, Sanders and Kruger (2011) argues that the country has a quadruple burden of disease which would make the financing of a national health insurance scheme prohibitive: HIV and AIDS and TB; high-maternal mortality, infectious diseases, and undernutrition resulting in neonatal and child mortality; growing burden of chronic non-communicable diseases; and violence and injuries.
8 The full Ten-Point Program was as follows: provision of strategic leadership and creation of a social compact for better health outcomes; implementation of national health insurance; health service quality improvement; strengthen healthcare management system; improve human resource development, planning, and management; infrastructural revitalization; accelerated implementation of HIV, STD, and TB—related strategic plans; intensify health promotion programs and mass mobilization; review drug policy; strengthen research and development. See also Nelana (2010).
9 See the following reports produced by the Republic of South Africa: on youth unemployment (2011a); on human condition diagnostic (2011b) and on the flagship program "Growth, Employment and Redistribution (GEAR)."
10 See also Altman (2008), Van der Berg and Siebrits (2010), and Van der Berg and Van Broekhuizen (2012).
11 South Korean inequality was, according to Statistics Korea, 34.5 in 2018.

12 In Zambia, Government-run initiatives include the Public Welfare Assistance Scheme, the Social Cash Transfer Scheme, the Food Security Pack, the School Feeding Program, and the Urban Self–Help Program.

13 The other African case study countries also had results on MDGs but comparing these three was most insightful.

14 This case was recorded as follows: (20793/2014)[2015]ZASCA 198 (2 December 2015).

References

African Development Bank (2020) *African Development Outlook* (AEO) 2020, AfDB: Abidjan.

Altman, M. (2008) 'Revisiting South African Employment Trends in the 1990s,' *South African Journal of Economics* 76(2):126–147.

Bae, S. (2007) 'Education as the Key to National Prosperity: Korea's Experience,' *Understanding Korean Educational Policy Series*, Korean Educational Development Institute: Seoul.

Bae, S., Kim, Y., Ban, S., Huh, K., Lee, Y., Son, B., Kim, E., Na, J. and Kim, C. (2011) *Brief Understanding of Korean Educational Policy*, Korean Educational Development Institute: Seoul.

Bhorat, H., Goga, S. and Stanwix, B. (2014) 'Skills-Biased Labour Demand and the Pursuit of Inclusive Growth in South Africa,' *WIDER Working Paper* 2014/130, UNU-WIDER: Helsinki.

Black, A. and Gerwel, H. (2014) 'Shifting the Growth Path to Achieve Employment Intensive Growth in South Africa,' *Development Southern Africa* 31(2):241–256.

Cameroon Team (2017) « Etude Sur L'Economie du Cameroun. La Politique de Développement dans la Pratique Enseignements Tires de L'Expérience de Développement de la Corée du Sud », Report to the African Development Bank on the *Developmental State in Africa, Lessons from South Korea Project*, Université de Yaoundé II: Yaoundé.

Chun, C., Kim, S., Lee, J. and Lee, S. (2009) 'Republic of Korea: Health System Review,' *Health Systems in Transition* 11(7):1–184.

Christie, P. and Collins, C. (1982) 'Bantu Education: Apartheid Ideology or Labour Reproduction?' *Comparative Education* 18(1):59–75.

Côte d'Ivoire Team (2017) « Etude Sur L'Economie Ivoirienne. La Politique de Développement dans la Pratique Enseignements Tires de L'Expérience de Développement de la Corée du Sud », Report to the African Development Bank on the *Developmental State in Africa, Lessons from South Korea Project,* Le Centre Ivoirien de Recherches Economiques et Sociales (CIRES): Abidjan.

Dagan, S. (2018) 'Health System Reforms to Accelerate Universal Health Coverage in Cote d'Ivoire,' *Health Systems and Reform* 4(2):69–71.

Dawes, N. (2011) 'The Great Carve-Up,' *The Mail & Guardian Online*: http://mg.co.za/article/2011-07-22-the-great-carveup/

Dryden-Peterson, S. and Mulimbi, B. (2017) 'Pathway Toward Peace—Negotiating National Unity and Ethnic Diversity Through Education in Botswana,' *Comparative Education Review* 61(1):58–82.

Epstein, G. (2008) 'An Employment Targeting Framework for Central Bank Policy in South Africa,' *Draft Paper*, Department of Economics, University of Massachusetts: Amherst.

Finn, A., Leibbrandt, M. and Woolard, I. (2013) 'What Happened to Multidimensional Poverty in South Africa between 1993 and 2010?' *Working Paper Series*, 99, Southern African Labour and Development Research Unit, University of Cape Town: Cape Town.

Grimm, M. (2005) 'Educational Policies and Poverty Reduction in Cote d'Ivoire,' *Journal of Policy Modeling* 27(2):231–247.

Ha, S. (1989) *Korean Social Welfare History,* Park Young Sa Publishing Company: Seoul.

Joonghae, S., Aubert, J.-E., Ahn, D. and Chen, D. (2006) 'Korea as a Knowledge Economy: Evolutionary Process and Lessons Learned-Overview', *Review Document*, World Bank: Washington, DC.

Kaluba, L. (1986) 'Education in Zambia: The Problem of Access to Schooling and the Paradox of the Private School Solution,' *Comparative Education* 22(2):159–169.

Kayizzi-Mugerwa (2013) 'Banana Out of Republic?': On the Political Economy of Africa's Transformation,' *Development* 56(4):500–510.

Kang, S. (1990) *The Political Economy of Korean Education*, Hangilsa Press: Seoul.

Kang, S. G., Lee, G., Park, H. and Kim, K. (2005) *60 Year History of Education Expansion and Indices Analysis*, Korean Educational Development Institute: Seoul.

Kim, K. (2001) *Vocational Education System in Korea*, Korea Research Institute for Vocational Education and Training: Seoul.

Kim, K., Chung, M. and Kim, D. (2012) 'Successful Strategy for Training Teachers in Korean Education,' *Knowledge Sharing Program: KSP Modularization*, Korean Educational Development Institute: Seoul.

Kim, S. (2008) 'The East Asian Developmental State and Its Economic and Social Policies: The Case of Korea,' *International Review of Public Administration* 12(2):69–87.

Kim, S. and Lee, J-W. (2006) 'Changing Facets of Higher Education in Korea: Market Competition and the Role of the State,' *Higher Education* 52(3):557–587.

Kim, Y. and Kang, M. (2016) 'The Performance Management System of the Korean Healthcare Sector: Development Challenges, and Future Tasks,' *Public Performance of Management Review* 39(2): 297–315.

Kwon, S. (2009) 'Thirty Years of National Health Insurance in South Korea: Lessons for Achieving Universal Healthcare,' *Health Policy and Planning* 24(1):63–71.

Lee, J. (2003) 'Healthcare Reform in South Korea: Success or Failure?' *American Journal of Public Health* 93(1):48–51.

Lee, J-W. (1997) 'Economic Growth and Human Development in the Republic of Korea, 1945–1992,' *Human Development Report*, Occasional Paper 24, UNDP: New York

Lee, J-W. and Rhee, C. (1999)'Social Impacts of the Asian Crisis: Policy Challenges and Lessons,' *Human Development Occassional Paper*, 1999–02, United Nations Development Programme: New York.

Lee, S. (2008) 'National Development Strategy and Education Policy,' *Understanding Korean Educational Policy Series*, Korean Educational Development Institute: Seoul.

MacLean, L.M. (2011) 'The Paradox of State Retrenchment in Sub-Saharan Africa: The Micro-Level Experience of Public Service Provision,' *World Development* 39(7):1155–1165.

Mamdani, M. (2008) *Scholars in the Marketplace. The Dilemma of Neo-Liberal Reform at Makerere University, 1989–2005*, The Human Resources Research Council: Cape Town.

Nelana, B. (2010) 'The ANC Polokwane Conference and its Aftermath,' *Policy Brief 11*. Africa Institute of South Africa: Johannesburg.

Nigeria Team (2017) 'Towards Developmental State in Nigeria: Lessons from Korea,' Report to the African Development Bank on the *Developmental State in Africa, Lessons from South Korea Project*, Nigerian Economic Society: Ibadan.

Nishimura, M., Yamano, T. and Sasaoko, Y. (2005) 'Impacts of the Universal Primary Education Policy on Education Attainment and Private Cost in Rural Uganda,' Teachers College, Columbia University: New York.

OECD (2008) *Reviews of Nations Policies for Education. South Africa.* Organization for Economic Cooperation and Development: Paris.

Oh, S. (2013) 'Building an Employment Service System for Efficient Utilization of National Human Resources,' *Case Studies*, KDI School of Public Policy and Management: Seoul.

Plagerson, S., Patel, L., Hochfeld, T. and Ulriksen, M. (2019) 'Social Policy in South Africa: Navigating the Route to Social Development,' *World Development* 113(C):1–9.

Republic of South Africa (1996) 'Growth, Employment and Redistribution: A Macroeconomic Strategy,' South African Treasury: Pretoria.

Republic of South Africa (2011a) 'Confronting Youth Unemployment: Policy Options for South Africa,' *Discussion Paper*, South African Treasury: Pretoria

Republic of South Africa (2011b) 'Human Condition Diagnostic,' National Planning Commission: Pretoria.

Republic of South Africa (2015) *Report on the Annual National Assessment of 2014 Grades 1 to 6*, Department of Basic Education: Pretoria.

Republic of South Africa (2019) *National Health Insurance Bill*, Ministry of Health: Pretoria.

Republic of Zambia (1964) *First National Development Plan (FNDP)*, Government Printer: Lusaka.

Schaay, N., Sanders, D. and Kruger, V. (2011) 'Overview of Health Sector Reforms in South Africa,' *Assignment Report*, Department for International Development (DFID), London.

Seekings, J. and Nattrass, N. (2005) *Class, Race, and Inequality in South Africa*, Yale University Press: New Haven.

Seers, D. (1964) *Economic Survey Mission on Economic Development of Zambia: Report of the UN/ECA/FAO*, Falcon Press: Ndola.

Shepherd, B. (2017) 'Building Inclusivity in Côte d'Ivoire? Promoting Sustainable Growth Through Infrastructure Development,' *Research Paper*, African Programme, Chatham House, The Royal Institute of International Affairs: London.

South Africa Team (2015) 'The Role of Institutions in Underpinning Inclusive Economic Growth in South Africa.' Report to the African Development Bank on the *Developmental State in Africa, Lessons from South Korea Project*, Development Policy Research Unit, School of Economics, University of Cape Town: Cape Town.

South Korea Team (2017) 'KOAFEC—Development Policy in Practice Project,' *Report to the African Development Bank on the Developmental State in Africa, Lessons from South Korea Project*, Korea Institute for International Economic Policy (KIEP): Seoul.

United Nations (2015) *Millennium Development Goals Report 2015*, UN Secretariat: New York.

Van den Heever, A. (2019) 'Will the National Health Insurance Bill Go Far Enough to Prevent Corruption?' *Report*, Bhekisisa Center for Health Journalism: Johannesburg.

Van der Berg, S. and Siebrits, K. (2010) 'Social Assistance Reform during a Period of Fiscal Stress,' *Working Paper* 17/2010, Department of Economics, Stellenbosch University: Stellenbosch.

Van der Berg, S. and Van Broekhuizen, H. (2012) 'Graduate Unemployment in South Africa: A Much Exaggerated Problem,' *Stellenbosch Economic Working Papers* 22/12, December.

Von Holdt, K., Langa, M., Molapo, S., Mogapi, N., Ngubeni, K., Dlamini, J. and Kirsten, A. (2011) 'The Smoke That Calls: Insurgent Citizenship, Collective Violence and the Search for a Place in the New South Africa,' Centre for the Study of Violence and Reconciliation: Johannesburg.

Webster, E. (2013) 'The Promise and the Possibility: South Africa's Contested Industrial Relations Path,' *Transformation* 81/82:211.

Wittenberg, M. (2014) 'Analysis of Employment, Real Wage, and Productivity Trends in South Africa since 1994,' *Conditions of Work and Employment Series 45*, International Labor Organization: Geneva.

World Bank (2020a) *World Development Indicators*, Washington, DC.

World Bank (2020b) *Poverty and Equity Data Portal*: www.povertydata.worldbank.org

World Bank (2018) *Human Capital Index*, Washington, DC.

Yang, S. and Torneo, A. (2016) 'Government Performance Management and Evaluation in South Korea: History and Current Practices,' *Public Performance of Management Review* 39(2):279–296.

Yi, I. (2011) 'The Development of Social Service: Education and Health Policies in Korea,' *Paper Presented at the 5th Seoul ODA International Conference*, October.

Zambia Team (2017) 'The Zambian Society and Economy: Development Policy in Practice in Comparison with South Korea,' *Report to the African Development Bank on the Developmental State in Africa, Lessons from South Korea Project*, Southern African Institute for Policy and Research (SAIPAR): Lusaka.

7 Industrialization imperative

7.1 Introduction

This chapter discusses the issue of industrialization, the subject around which the developmental state debate has revolved in recent decades, which is the veritable backbone of economic transformation. The chapter discusses the interlinked subjects of enhancing export capabilities, boosting domestic contestation, as an antidote to the statist inclination to pick winners, and developing supportive infrastructure, the latter as both amenity to and input factor in production. The chapter compares the experience of the African country cases with that of South Korea, including how the latter forged mutually beneficial alliances between the government and the private sector, while taking full advantage of being located in East Asia i.e. the flying geese paradigm, access to US and Japanese markets, and the opportunities availed by the onset of globalization and emergence of associated value chains (UNCTAD, 2013).

7.2 Points of departure

The fairly obvious, but nevertheless important, lesson to draw from industrialization in South Korea and the rest of East Asia is that although market forces were important, deliberate state action in a range of structural areas was crucial in shaping industrialization i.e. creating an enabling business environment, including infrastructure services and reforming national curricula to raise technical skills and competences across the national labor force; dedicated regulatory frameworks; technical capability enhancements through R&D benefitting the whole industry; and the creation of agencies that promoted external competitiveness (export promotion), while encouraging domestic contestability among firms (Sampath, 2014).

In East Asia, governments saw the teaching of science, engineering, and mathematics and related subjects as key means of bringing countries to the global frontier in scientific research and applications and made them central features of their national education policies from the early 1960s. Improvements in healthcare, welfare services, and nutrition helped to boost human capital overall. Few developing countries have been able to pursue the above prerequisites consistently, owing to their political economy, with start conditions mattering a great deal. In many African and Latin American countries, for example, industrial policy was closely identified with efforts at import-substitution or conservation of foreign exchange. This meant that domestic markets were closed off from international competition, during a period when international trade was expanding (Hirschman, 1968; Ovadia and Wolf, 2018).

7.3 South Korea: industrial policy in practice

Characteristics of South Korea's Industrial Policy. Industrial policy was the linchpin of South Korea's development strategy since the 1960s, contributing to its rapid development and international competitiveness. The state, as noted earlier, did not shy away from strategic intervention in the market but took steps to manage incentives and allocation of resources in such a manner as not to overly distort market signals—this behavior was referred to as "market conforming" (South Korea Team, 2017). It, for example, set exchange rate and trade policies, financial policies that governed capital allocation, and undertook action that directly affected the industrial structure, infrastructure development, and the financing and deployment of technology.

In other words, pursuing export-oriented industrialization in the manner of South Korea and other East Asian countries inevitably constrained market rationality (Onis, 1991). The essence of the South Korean miracle was that the country was able to do this while paying due regard to the central precepts of a capitalist economy, including the sanctity of private property and the equilibrating role of market prices.

Also, worth noting, the government was not impervious to new information. It was not constrained by ideology and was strategic and quick in adapting its policy priorities to emerging challenges and needs, including those of the business sector. The form and nature of South Korea's industrial policy constantly changed to match the shifts at home and in the world economy. At the outset, Korea's industrial policy had two main approaches, applied in a sequential and coordinated manner to achieve notable impacts on the ground:

First, to encourage exports in already relatively well-established industries that were deemed to have comparative advantage, the government insulated export activity from the adverse consequences of policies motivated by other concerns, such as regional employment creation (Westphal, 1990). This ensured that production for export would be profitable or at least no less profitable than production for the domestic market.

Second, to actively identify and promote infant industries that were expected to achieve the competitiveness required to be successful exporters. This approach was pursued from the early 1970s, when the selective protection of industry began to play an important role in industrial policy. The government pursued non-neutral policies tilted in favor of heavy and chemical industries, as its analysis had indicated that the latter were poised to change the country's industrial structure in the medium to long term, while allowing the country to remain competitive.

For many African countries, the ability of the state to constrain or, even more strongly, subordinate the market has been the main attraction of the developmental state model. Inevitably, and despite allusions to the market-conforming potency of state intervention, the resulting production, investment, and exports profiles can be quite different from what the unadulterated market would have dictated. South Korea and other East Asian countries found their way around these hurdles by constant policy analysis and undeterred policy experimentation. This also enabled them to abandon approaches that were unviable. In other words, what aspiring African countries see today as a seamless set of steps toward rapid growth and export generation by South Korea were in many ways indeterminate approaches to development—at least in the sense that no one could have predicted in the 1960s what the outcomes would be with any degree of confidence—with the exception that they were pursued with discipline and results-orientation.

7.4 Synopses of phases of South Korea's industrialization[1]

This section describes three phases (aggressive export promotion/take-off, infant-industry protection, and gradual liberalization) of South Korea's industrial policy:

7.4.1 Phase 1: Aggressive export promotion/take-off, 1961–1973

The aggressive export-promotion phase at the beginning of South Korea's industrialization included the following main features:

(i) Design and implementation of an incentive system for channeling resources into export-oriented activities;
(ii) Adjusting the exchange rate system with a view to eradicating overvaluation (see Table 7.1) while keeping the effective exchange rate for exporters competitive;
(iii) Imposition of preferential (or zero) tariff rates on capital and intermediate inputs for production for export production and exemption from quotas typically applied to imports for other purposes than consumption;
(iv) Institution of state control of the banking system to ensure adequate credit to exporters (at subsidized rates and preferential access);
(v) Introduction of export credit insurance and guarantee schemes;
(vi) Reduction of public utility tariffs and rail rates for exporters;
(vii) Lowering of direct taxes on incomes earned from exporting as well as domestic income exemptions.

The government's aggressive export promotion led to significant growth in exports, above 20% per year, by the mid-1970s. Domestic investment and consumption were well-calibrated to meet the goal of rapid export expansion, while import-substitution ceased to be significant (Table 7.2).

Table 7.1 South Korea: Exchange Rates and Export Growth, 1960–1975

Real Exchange Rate (1965 PPP Terms) (won/$)	Average Export Growth Rate (%)	Years Included
<200	16.0	1960, 1963, 1978–1982
200–250	30.3	1961–1962, 1964, 1967–1970, 1976–1977, 1983
>250	43.5	1965–1966, 1971–1975

Source: World Bank (1987).

Table 7.2 South Korea: Sources of Growth, 1955–1975 (%)

Source of Growth	1955–1960	1960–1965	1965–1970	1970–1975
Consumption	97.6	69.9	63.4	60.5
Government consumption	5.4	4.0	9.8	8.7
Investment	–5.6	22.7	53.4	30.1
Export growth	9.6	12.8	13.9	26.2
Import substitution	1.9	1.4	–18.2	–1.6

Source: World Bank (1987).

While the high-export growth noted above was partly because South Korea was departing from a low base, given that it was sustained in the following decades suggests that the government was successful in targeting incentives to exporting firms i.e. in picking winners. Most importantly, the interventions (in the form of import quotas, to ensure that strategic sectors would have enough investment at all times) helped to put the country onto a strong growth path. The institutional structure required to calibrate the sectoral allocations and outcomes was quite elaborate and, in some respects, not easy to replicate by aspiring developmental states. Still, the main lesson here is that the risks of overreliance on the global market were not underestimated, and exporting firms were guaranteed a fair share of sales in the home market and hence a means of overcoming export troughs (Onis, 1991; Westphal, 1990).

7.4.2 *Phase 2: Heavy industry promotion, 1973–1979*

The second phase of South Korea's industrialization represented a shift from general to sector specific export promotion, focusing on heavy and chemical industries (steel, petrochemicals, shipbuilding, other chemicals, capital goods, and durable consumer goods). This phase reflected a higher degree of selectivity with respect to targeting subsidized credit (Table 7.3), assessing the level of industry protection required, adjusting regulations relating to entry, direct government involvement in industrial decision-making, and many other forms of direct control and steering of the process.

Table 7.3 South Korea: Incremental Credit Allocation by the Banking Sector (%), (1973–1979)

Sector	1973	1974	1975	1976	1977	1978	1979
Heavy industry	35.6	32.21	65.75	55.9	60.7	55.7	58.4
Light industry	54.4	67.79	34.25	44.08	39.3	44.35	41.6
Total	100	100	100	100	100	100	100

Source: World Bank (1987).

The main strategic policy thrusts during this phase were as follows:

(a) The government deliberately chose industries expected to have a high-income elasticity of demand in world markets and potential for rapid technological progress and labor productivity growth—it allowed for the emergence of "temporary monopolies;"

(b) Industrial licensing was used to limit the number of firms allowed to enter an industry. This accelerated the process of industrial concentration and realization of economies of scale, hence providing a basis for competition in international markets;

(c) The government imposed strong controls on foreign investment and proprietary technology inflows, which helped it to create the type of industrial structure at the firm level that it desired;

(d) A well-designed incentive-compatible system, based on a dual policy of subsidization and penalty, supported by strict monitoring, enabled South Korea to avoid rent-seeking behavior in the targeted industries;

(e) The government strictly controlled foreign investment and proprietary technology, with multinational corporations playing a smaller role in the Korean economy than in comparable countries at the time. Therefore, to a significant degree, export-oriented industrialization was led by nationals;

(f) With the goal of attaining technological independence, the government undertook investment in foreign licensing, while also seeking technical assistance. Moreover, it coordinated foreign technology licensing agreements, making use of national (as opposed to firm) level bargaining.

In terms of process, the government created "market agents" in the form of conglomerates such as Hyundai, Samsung, Daewoo, the so-called chaebols. The state provided generous subsidies to exporting industries, while specifying stringent performance requirements in exchange for them. It rewarded firms that met high standards, while sanctioning those whose performance was below par i.e. industrial policy-integrated subsidization as well as penalties. The discipline that emanated from this dual policy, and the government's capacity to sustain it, were the core components of South Korea's industrial policy.

In 1973, the top 50 chaebols accounted for a fifth of manufacturing employ-ment, half of exports, and about a third of South Korea's GDP, rising to 49% by 1980 (Haggard and Moon, 1990). The chaebols in effect implemented the policy thrust of the government at this time—to develop heavy and chemical industries—while it provided feedback on the quality and price competitiveness. The government's justification for its close ties with the chaebols was that the economies of scale for rapid export growth were easier to attain this way than via small and medium sized firms (Kim, 1996).[2] Although the export targets (i.e. 50% of total) set by the government for the development of the heavy and chem-ical industries had not been reached by 1980, the progress made in shifting the value-added structure of the economy toward these industries was unmatched among peer countries.

It is important to underline that the South Korean state was not infallible, and some of its industrial policy emphases were off the mark, leading to overca-pacity in some targeted sectors in an otherwise capital-starved economy, in cases crowding out the traditional export industries altogether. Supporting targeted sectors also had implications for government spending, the fiscal deficit, and ul-timately monetary growth. Inflation pressures increased, while the maintenance of a fixed nominal exchange rate meant a sharp appreciation of the won and erosion of competitiveness.

7.4.3 *Phase 3: Gradual liberalization, 1979 onward*

The third phase of Korean industrial policy, characterized by a policy shift to-ward gradual liberalization, began in 1979. The government realized that its emphasis on heavy and chemical industries has caused structural and macroeco-nomic imbalances which had to be addressed (Lee, 2016). The crowding out of traditional industries had had negative effects on the economy. These challenges had been aggravated by the second oil crisis in the 1970s and the assassination of President Park in 1979 and its aftermath. From the early 1980s, the government began to implement a policy shift toward greater industrial neutrality. This lib-eralization phase included the following approaches:

(i)   Focus on technology policy and implementation as key means for redressing the investment imbalance, increasing efficiency, and laying the groundwork for future competitiveness.

(ii)   Appreciation that the economy was complex and no longer amenable to the controls used in the past, hence, financial and import liberalization pro-grams were launched. Thanks to good performance in previous decades, economic liberalization was orderly, without the chaos witnessed in Latin America, for example.

(iii) With the goal of pushing local firms to the global competitive frontier, the government withdrew slowly from targeted domestic finance, lowered im-port barriers, and refrained from direct export promotion.[3]

Box 7.1: South Korea's structural transition: ICT and the energy challenge[4]

Transitioning to ICT. For most of the 1970s, the South Korean government's industrialization strategy focused on heavy industry and expanding physical infrastructure to reduce the cost of doing business (Kim, 1991). The next decades would mark a gradual transition to ICT. It started with a master plan for the development of the electric industry undertaken in the 1980s and culminated in the Korean Information Infrastructure plan, launched in March 1995, developed by a taskforce that included companies involved in the ICT sector, development finance institutions, as well as academic experts. It highlighted the need for the invigoration of the electronics sector, including identification of strategic areas, notably development of an advanced nationwide information infrastructure, communication network, internet access, and applications software development (Larson and Park, 2014).

The government–business partnership had earlier helped launch the Time-Division Exchange project, the largest ICT research collaboration undertaken in the country, done in partnership with local ICT companies, and coordinated by the Electronics and Telecommunications Research Institute (ETRI). Its success served as a catalyst for the rapid rise of the country's ICT industry (Lee, 2012). In championing the ICT push, the government allotted segments of the sector to leading private companies, such as Samsung and Goldstar, and assisted in partnering these companies with strategic foreign partners (Oh and Larson, 2011). A Korea Ministry of Information and Communication was established in 1994, by restructuring an earlier Ministry of Communications, but would change designation again in 2008—partly reflecting the changing perception of the ICT within the government and the country.

The Asian Development Bank (2014) noted that the bulk of investment in the ICT industry in South Korea has been from private companies, not the government. The latter mainly restricted itself to making policy, providing basic infrastructure, and market regulation. The public sector was a major beneficiary of the rapid expansion of the ICT sector—not least in terms of the positive impact on economic competitiveness and the public revenue stream—whose value had increased to US$5 billion by 1997, with over 70,000 employees.

South Korea's Energy Challenge. South Korea's growth had been much more energy-intensive than in other OECD countries.[5] Because of the high-economic growth rates, generating capacity "barely kept pace with the expansion of demand up to 1997, leading to low capability reserve margins of between 3 and 10% during the period 1990–1997" (OECD,

2000). Measured in nominal exchange rate terms, South Korea's electricity was the cheapest in the OECD, but using purchasing power parities, it is comparatively more expensive than in other OECD country cases (OECD, 2000; Junki and Kyuhyun, 2011).

In a determined industrial drive to break its dependency on oil and fossil fuel imports, South Korea had, by 1998, significantly diversified its energy mix to nuclear (42%), coal (35%),[6] gas (12%), oil (8%), and hydro-electric power (3%) (OECD, 2000). Still, in 2013, South Korea was the ninth largest consumer of petroleum in the world, using more than 2.3 million barrels of petroleum per day (US Energy Information Administration, 2014). It imported 2.5 million barrels per day, making it the world's fifth largest importer. As an illustration of strategic competency, South Korea transformed its lack of domestic oil resources into an industrial advantage by building refining capacity for imported crude for local use and export. In 2010s, it had three of the ten largest oil refineries in the world, exporting over 1.2 million barrels per day of refined oil products, such as jet fuel and gasoil (US Energy Information Administration, 2014).

Source: South Korea Team (2017).

7.5 Pathway to industrialization: capability constraints in African countries

Africa's industrialization quest is not new and has been reiterated in the bulk of Africa's national development plans since at least the early 1960s, including the continental policy flagship, Africa 2063 (African Union Commission, 2014) launched in 2013. In practice, Africa's policy approaches have varied widely, from import-substitution to laissez faire, but invariably thinly grounded, and not robust enough to resist external shocks. Compared to South Korea and other East Asian countries, many African states, including the country case studies, lacked the policy focus and the institutional coherence required to sustain the march toward industrialization and the export of manufactures (wa Gĩthĩnji and Adesida, 2011).[7]

State-Ownership as Pathway to Industrialization in Cameroon. A major differentiating feature of the role of the state in industrialization between South Korea and Cameroon is that the former was able to forge a coalition with the private sector that helped define and implement the strategy, determine the choice of priority sectors, and coordinate the process as part of the national development plan, while the latter was distracted by political developments at home. The partnership between the state and business in South Korea meant that the decisions of entrepreneurs with respect to levels of investment, production lines, and use of research results were congruent with those of the industrial sector and the macro economy.

In Cameroon, on the other hand, the state owned the bulk of the large enterprises, but exercised, until recently, a hands-off approach with regard to their management (UNIDO, 2005; Tabi and Ondoa, 2011). Instead of forming a basis on which the country's industrialization efforts could coalesce, parastatals, as constituted, proved to be the problem, not the solution (Comité Interministériel Elargi au Secteur Privé, 2006). They exhibited low productivity, did not export much, and absorbed, on average, subsidies equivalent to 2% of GDP in the late-1980s and early 1990s. The poor health of the parastatal sector contributed to the banking crisis of the 1990s in Cameroon (Assiga-Ateba, 1998, 2009).

Although the Cameroonian government had introduced a masterplan to guide industrialization in 1989, it lacked specificity in terms of priority sectors, sequencing, and financing, while the institutional structure for resource mobilization, implementation, and impact assessment was deficient (Boutat, 1991). In effect, it covered the industrial waterfront: agribusiness, textiles, wood, oil and gas, chemical industries, consumer product industries, pharmaceuticals, steel, aluminum, metal, machines, electrical appliances, electronics, maintenance industries, materials and construction, and packaging industry. It did not identify areas where the country had comparative advantage nor how it would contribute to the development of a competitive private sector. The government overestimated its institutional capacity for guiding the process and had not paid sufficient attention to the macroeconomic environment, including the viability of the many parastatals that it had set up to run the various businesses.

In discussing the constraints to industrialization in African countries in a comparative perspective, the Cameroon Team (2017) highlighted five capability constraints[8] that must be addressed (Table 7.4)—they include the domestic capacity for developing technical skills (i.e. quality, depth, and alignment of the education system); the emphasis put on research and development as well as innovation; the extent to which the country has established an attractive environment for investment, including access to finance; taking advantage of favorable external environments and building supportive partnerships; and harnessing all available technical skills, including from the Diaspora.

Zambia's Failure to Industrialize under the Copper Umbrella. For decades, Zambia's hopes for industrialization were pinned on the fortunes of its copper sector (Seidman, 1974). In the 1960s, few other Sub-Saharan African countries had such a robust platform on which to base their industrial efforts. First, the mining sector had capacities in engineering, project management, trade logistics, electricity and water supply, and human resource and financial administration that potentially would have had strong demonstration effects on the rest of the economy, if the copper sector had not been an industrial enclave. Second, the mines demanded spares, fuel, and other goods and services, including food and other consumables for mine workers, in amounts large enough to sustain sizeable manufacturing activity. Third, efforts at value addition, notably prefabricated products, copper wire, and chemical compounds, had potential to spawn downstream manufacturing companies. Fourth, copper exports generated foreign exchange, which the government planned to use to support the budding

Table 7.4 Capability Constraints to Sustainable Industrialization in African Countries

Capability Constraints	Comments
Critical manpower development	African universities are producing a large number of scientists and engineers today but their link to industrialization is more coincidental than planned. Technical and vocational schools are similarly encumbered. In South Korea and other East Asian economies, in contrast, the development of technical skills was intimately attached to the industrialization process. Countries sought to match available capacities with the needs of industries, with sufficient flexibility to adjust to changes in industrial structure.
R&D and technical innovation	In African countries, little R&D is done and few firms register patents. The role of governments in enhancing R&D and technical innovation is limited. Kim and Nelson (2000) have noted that in the absence of R&D, any talk of industrialization is incredible. In South Korea, public research agencies were given freedom to pursue R&D subject to sharing the results communally with industry i.e. as public goods. The state centralized the information on new technologies so that small and medium-sized companies could acquire them at reasonable cost.[9]
Domestic and foreign investment	South Korea did not accept invest programs and FDI that served as a death knell to its nascent domestic industry, as happened in many African countries during structural adjustment programs. The government in South Korea pursued alternative financing modules, including industrial development banks, subsidized loans, and public–private partnerships to promote what it considered strategic parts of its industrialization process.
External trade environment	At the very least, African countries must devise strategies to take advantage of growth opportunities in the global economy to increase their export of manufactures. It is important to acknowledge that the "luck" that is often mentioned with regard to East Asia's upswing, while many other regions failed to do so, can also mean that the countries there were perceptive and made the right calls.
Mobilizing frontier technical skills (including from the Diaspora)	Although paucity of technical skills is a key setback to Africa's industrialization, many Africans in the Diaspora have acquired technical skills that could be deployed to great benefit in their countries of origin, and a number of countries are waking up to this possibility. India, above all, has benefitted immensely from encouraging members of its Diaspora to return home and take part in manufacturing, research, and policymaking.

Source: Cameroon Team (2017).

import-substituting industry—as a guarantee that the economy would remain robust even after copper was exhausted.

Although copper production had helped raise per capita incomes in Zambia to among the highest in Sub-Saharan Africa, in the 1960s and part of the 1970s, the boom did not last. Besides, copper mining implied an inherent duality in the Zambian economy (advanced capital-intensive production technology, on the one hand, versus peasant agriculture, on the other) and exposure to external shocks that eroded the potential for industrialization, while highlighting the constraints (Table 7.4). For example, while copper mining had the highest concentration of technicians and engineers in the country, most of them expatriates, the training of local technical staff and engineers did not begin in earnest until after the mines were nationalized at the beginning of the 1970s. In any case, given the enclave nature of the mining industry, the sector's technical capacities took a long time to filter through to the rest of the economy—although significantly Zambia has today many more engineering service providers, spinoffs from mining, than comparable economies in Africa.

Zambia's national development plans have invariably prioritized modern job creation through industrialization. From the outset, mining companies were natural monopolies that employed capital-intensive technologies in a labor-surplus economy. Contrary to the development plans, capital-intensive production techniques permeated the rest of the modern economy, notably via the small to medium-sized firms that the government had set up in the various sectors (from food processing to fishing equipment) to spearhead industrialization. Additionally, copper miners, thanks to a strong union, became wage-setters in the economy (i.e. a labor aristocracy) with a followership that extended to the public service and the private sector—indeed, public sector unions would await the conclusions of wage negotiations on the Copperbelt before completing theirs. In other words, copper turned Zambia into a relatively high-cost industrial producer and hence less competitive than its less mineral-dependent neighbors.

The outward-oriented policy approaches that had propelled South Korea into sustainable industrialization were not paid much attention in Zambia until the 1990s. The denationalization of the mines in the 1990s enabled the authorities to rethink the potential of copper mining as a path to industrialization by focusing on value addition along the mining value chain. Subsequently, the government introduced bills in 2008 and 2015 to encourage the new mining companies to procure most of their spares and consumables from local producers and thus with potential to give a real boost to local manufacturing in a market worth some $2 billion. The situation in terms of domestic value addition has changed little, with some studies noting that the privatization of the mines has escalated transfer pricing (Readhead, 2016) while the abandoning of marginal mining prospects has ruralized many towns on the Copperbelt.

According to a value chain monitoring study by the Zambia Revenue Authority, the mining sector's supply of manufactured consumables, including spares, is almost wholly from foreign manufacturers, dominated by South African companies. In 2014, mining conglomerates spent less than US$90 million (about 5% of the total procurement) on locally manufactured goods (Zambia Revenue Authority, 2014). More recent studies have not seen much improvement in this regard (Liebenthal and Cheelo, 2018). The Chamber of Mines and the Zambian Association of Manufacturers, as key stakeholders, have argued that local firms might have a fighting chance in the evolving mining value chains if government sets up dedicated credit facilities for them, while also boosting their financial literacy. A collateral registry would be required to expedite borrowing procedures for small businesses (Kragelund, 2017).

Zambia has enjoyed robust growth in manufacturing in the past two decades, especially agro-processing, which accounts for the bulk of the activity, and cement and fabricated metals for the rest (Fessehaie et al., 2015). Graduating into sustainable job-creating industrialization has been as challenging in Zambia as in many other African countries. This is partly linked to the absence of a robust business class that is rooted in the domestic economy and hence can take or is forced to take a long-term view. When comparing East Asia and Sub-Saharan Africa, Arrighi (2002) pointed to this failure by African countries to create and sustain an indigenous entrepreneurial class. The issue can be complex, given that generations of Asian immigrants engaged in manufacturing are still not thought of locally as indigenous enough in Zambia and many other African countries (Fessehaie, Rustomjee and Kaziboni, 2016). Still, the building of a strong local content strategy might not be possible in the absence of a stronger domestic stake, as Zambia's recent disagreements with the mining conglomerates on the Copperbelt suggest (Readhead, 2016). For the country's hopes of using copper mining as a springboard to industrialization to be realized will require that the government teams up with a strong and dedicated coalition of private sector groups to pursue this goal, as happened in similar circumstances in East Asia, with national self-interest as the key driver.

7.6 Infrastructure development

Infrastructure development has seen something of renaissance in Africa in the last 20 years, closely linked to the quest for rapid industrialization. Good infrastructure has always been a prerequisite in the developmental state model, not only for reducing the cost of doing business, by lowering transport and other transactions costs, but also by opening up new markets and bringing the countryside and remoter areas of the country into the economic fold. Recent years have also seen a greater willingness by the donor community to use the funds targeted at poverty reduction and rural development to fund infrastructure in client countries—seen as key for linking rural areas to urban markets, raising rural incomes, and promoting spatial inclusion. This section looks at aspects of infrastructure development experiences from South Korea and the African country cases.

Infrastructure Development Lessons from South Korea.[10] The main lessons from South Korea's experience with infrastructure development can be summarized in five points:

First, the South Korean state eschewed informal and impromptu approaches to infrastructure development. It used a formal and orderly process, drawing on the national development plan, to execute infrastructure plans, targeted at industrialization, and more recently at supporting an ICT economy, for a long period ahead. This well-scripted approach helped to avert political pressure on infrastructure investment decisions. As South Korea, unlike African countries, is not endowed with natural resources, it did not have to deal with the infrastructure spending exuberance caused by commodity booms.

Second, good project planning and execution, and adhesion to the national development, were crucial for outcomes and the avoidance of "white elephants." Performance monitoring by the EPB, the presidency, and ministers forced bureaucrats to maintain high-performance levels.

Third, during challenging economic times, the government found innovative ways to finance infrastructure. Notably, the state established a stability fund, from fuel taxes, to finance projects. This helped alleviate the burden on the budget and prevented the costly "stop-go" infrastructure construction experiences that are common in African countries.

Fourth, public–private partnerships, when well executed, proved a crucial form of infrastructure financing, which also boosted the efficiency of service delivery in the public sector. In 1998, following the Asian Financial Crisis, government created a new law for PPPs, which introduced new infrastructure categories and created a center for private investment in infrastructure to provide technical and advisory services, including feasibility and technical studies, bid evaluations and negotiating infrastructure concessions. The law was modified in 2005 to allow for the option of Build Transfer Lease (BTL) and the expansion of private investors into social infrastructure such as education, the military, culture, and health.

Fifth, the government subjected all institutions and agencies dealing with the construction and delivery of infrastructure services to regulatory oversight and assessment, with implications for financing i.e. state actions were consequential and not proforma. In 2000, a law was passed requiring all major infrastructure projects costing more than $50 million to be evaluated within three years of completion.

Cameroon's Push for Modern Infrastructure. Cameroon's first and second national development plans (covering the period 1960–1971) had allocated the bulk of planned investment to infrastructure and rural development. In comparison to South Korea, Cameroon's push for modern infrastructure was haphazard, both in terms of planning and execution. Many of the targets were not met, for lack of financing, owing to lower than expected donor support. They were either shelved or shifted to the third national development plan. By the end of the 1980s, the supply of water and sanitation services had improved in urban areas, with some 60% of the households accessing services. In rural areas, only 45% of households had access to potable water and fewer still (27%) to modern sanitation.

Given its rich endowment of rivers, Cameroon has the third largest potential for hydropower generation in Sub-Saharan Africa, after Ethiopia and the DRC. It also has high thermal and wind power generation potential. In 2014, urban household access to electricity was close to 87%, while only a fifth of rural households had access to power. This was despite the launch in 1998 of the push for rural electrification in Cameroon, supported by the creation of a dedicated Rural Energy Fund in 2009. This illustrates that Cameroon has great potential, which is yet to be exercised in earnest.

The economic challenges elsewhere in the economy have affected the government's goals of meeting its infrastructure targets. Transport is a good example. Although Cameroon had constructed some 1,143 km of modern roads by 1980, degradation and lack of maintenance and money to extend the network meant that modern road infrastructure had declined by some 12% in 25 years, while the number of passengers had increased by over 60% and transport of merchandise by 100% during the same period. Another example of Cameroon's push for modern infrastructure falling short are the railways, which have been in poor repair for much of the 2010s, a period when the demand for rail transport, as an alternative to road transport, has been rising.

Côte d'Ivoire's Infrastructure Renaissance. More consistently than other Sub-Saharan African countries, Côte d'Ivoire embarked on a systematic extension of its socio-economic infrastructure in the 1960s and 1970s. The government demonstrated a relatively high level of coherence by building transport corridors to link the regions producing agricultural exports to the sea and the three urban economic poles: Abidjan, Bouake, and San-Pedro. The government also embarked on large regional transport and water and sanitation projects in the 1970s, which contributed to the rapid economic growth, referred to as "the Ivorian miracle."

The transition to the next stage of infrastructure development, which included the construction of rural access roads and markets, agricultural modernization, and rural electrification, on the one hand, and modernization and expansion of industrial infrastructure in the urban centers, on the other, was not realized. In spite the progress mentioned earlier, financing, largely premised on a high volume of commodity exports, was drying up. It would take another 20 years, and the coming to power of a new and ambitious administration in 2011, to return Côte d'Ivoire to economic normalcy and to embark on a new set of projects and programs for infrastructure refurbishment and expansion. As discussed in Chapter 3, Côte d'Ivoire has since gone to bond markets to borrow for its infrastructure projects, and the government believes that this time the process will be sustainable.

Nigeria: Infrastructure Challenges as Opportunity. Nigeria's infrastructure challenges, including aviation, road transport, railways, ports, and ICT, are as broad and complex as the country itself, but so are the opportunities they avail. The Federal Capital Territory, Abuja, built literarily from scratch, demonstrates that the country has both a high level of ambition and retains capacity to implement large-scale infrastructure projects, when both political and financial incentives are aligned. The Nigeria Team (2017) has argued that the notable recent infrastructure improvements in the State of Lagos, including port rehabilitation, road extensions, and power supply improvements, show that Nigeria's infrastructure deficit can be reversed by good policies and determined execution.

For the rest of Nigeria, replicating Lagos State's relative success with infrastructure service provision will continue to be a challenge. This is not entirely because the state is the most urbanized in the country, with diversified revenues, but most probably because it has created effective agencies of restraint that reduced corruption and helped boost service provision.

Access to electricity has been identified as the key constraint to doing business in Nigeria. Although the country had a total installed capacity of thermal and hydro power of some 12,000 MW in 2019, the equivalent of the electricity needs of a medium-sized European city, owing to transmission and distribution issues, only about a third of this is available, with the deficit covered by self-provisioning i.e. private generators. To begin to address the many issues affecting the power sector in Nigeria, the government launched the Electricity Power Reform Act of 2005 (Bureau of Public Enterprises, 2011).[11]

Initially, the power sector reforms seemed to have succeeded in unbundling the energy monopolies, putting the right investment framework in place, and raising the level of competition in the industry.[12] However, serious constraints remained i.e. slow bureaucratic processes at the federal and state levels, in cases involving corruption and embezzlement, have hindered the expansion of generation capacity along the lines of the national development plan. At the local and project levels, power company assets, including equipment and powerlines, have been regularly vandalized, while poor rural roads have made access to the power infrastructure for maintenance difficult and irregular.

Nigeria's fiscal federalism implies sharing a cascading structure of responsibilities for infrastructure provision with the states and local governments. The Federal Government is responsible for shipping, federal trunk roads, aviation, railways, posts, telegraphs and telephones, telecommunications, mines and minerals, and water resources that affect more than one state. The states, on the other hand, share these responsibilities with the center: electricity, industrial infrastructure, agricultural infrastructure, scientific and technological research, and universities. At the local level, the authorities are solely responsible for markets, sewage and refuse disposal, local road infrastructure, streetlighting, drains, and other public facilities, including burial grounds. To work properly, this hierarchy of responsibilities requires an elaborate coordination of plans and strategies as well as synchronization of budgets. It also presupposes that fiscal federalism, which has proven hard to get right in many countries, can actually work in Nigeria.

Still, the Nigeria Team's survey of service delivery in Lagos State, Kaduna, and Rivers State indicates that despite constrained infrastructure provision and bureaucratic inefficiency, there is a considerable scope for local initiative. Thanks to the opening up of the political space in Nigeria at all levels, where incumbents are rewarded by reelection or removed from office largely on the basis of their infrastructure service delivery record, citizens, and civil society, have more leverage on policymakers.

South Africa: Infrastructure Provision Under a New Political Dispensation. Part of South Africa's infrastructure is world class, including a network of road connections to the major cities, and modern railways, seaports, and airports as well as power stations. South Africa is an important transit country, and its railway and road infrastructure is a key gateway for the rest of the Southern African region. Issues of spatial equity have been raised in recent years, as urban-focused infrastructure has expanded, while less affluent provinces have seen fewer infrastructure projects and, even then, only a handful are linked to income generation.

From 1994, the strategy of the ruling ANC (1994, 1998, 2019) has been to reverse this legacy—mainly through sharp increases in targeted public infrastructure investment. The basic philosophy was that funding basic infrastructure would help crowd in private sector investment and stimulate growth at the lower levels of the economy. The political economy of infrastructure provision in South Africa has been complex, entailing inconsistencies and even contradictions, especially with respect to efforts aimed at boosting infrastructure access to vulnerable households and groups. A major difficulty has been how to address the issues embedded in the notion of "radical economic transformation" that politicians and citizens are equally fond of voicing, but where the way forward is still largely uncharted (Bedasso, 2014).

In 1999, the government completed the strategic framework for PPPs, and a unit was set up at the Treasury to manage all associated policy and regulatory issues.[13] Several toll roads between the major cities were constructed, thereafter, managed by the South African National Roads Agency (Sanral). PPPs have been praised for contributing to funding infrastructure construction and repairs and reducing budgetary pressure. However, tolls do not discriminate, with all income groups assessed equally. This has displeased consumers and caused considerable discomfort among politicians. Major toll roads have been boycotted by both rich and poor users alike, and there is currently no mechanism to resolve the standoff, aside from moral suasion and resorting to litigation.

Thus, although there was a presumption that the infrastructure parastatals—Eskom, Sanral, Denel, DBSA, IDC, Trans-Caledon Tunnel Authority, SAA, Transnet, Land and Agricultural Bank, South African Post Office, and SA Express Airway—would be able to finance their own activities to a large extent, through charging enough for their services or undertaking other economies, this has not been the case. Invariably, all have requested for guarantees from the government to finance activities, including current and capital expenditures, although in recent years, the big-ticket items have been those of the energy conglomerate, Eskom, and the national airline, SAA. Since guarantees are contingent liabilities, their accumulation has had serious implications for the fiscal balance and crucially for sovereign ratings. In early 2020, South Africa's bonds were rated as junk i.e. below investment grade by the rating agencies S&P, Fitch Group, and Moody's.

From the vantage point of 2020, and in the thrall of the Covid-19 crisis, it has become clear among South Africa's power brokers that, with regard to infrastructure service provision, something has got to give. Although the ruling ANC is averse to borrowing from the international development agencies, notably the IMF, as it comes with conditionalities that many individuals in government see as impositions on country sovereignty, there is broad agreement that some form of fiscal consolidation is needed. If the reforms taken in the near-term help to strengthen infrastructure performance, notably power, gains will include reducing the cost of doing business overall, exporting power to neighbors, and repairing agency ratings. A framework for regular monitoring and assessment of the performance of the infrastructure agencies will be required to undertake corrective measures in timely fashion and avoid the accumulation of malfeasance and other distortions that caused the problems in the first place.

Zambia: Extending Infrastructure Beyond the "Line of Rail." Since independence, the infrastructure challenge for Zambia's government, as elaborated in the national development plans, has been to expand road and rail services beyond the "line of rail." The success of the first national development plan was premised on the availability of domestic resources i.e. copper revenues to help roll out the planned infrastructure investment. The government had acknowledged that aid from donors would be required for a number of crucial projects, including the Kafue Hydro-Electric Scheme, construction of the University of Zambia, road construction, and the Tanzania-Zambia Railway. The latter was partly financed by the Chinese Government to shield Zambia from the effects of the trade blockade by Rhodesia and South Africa, during the heyday of the anti-apartheid struggles in the region from the 1970s to the 1990s.

As in other parts of Africa, Zambia made little headway with infrastructure development during the 1980s and 1990s—the era of structural adjustment—when large infrastructure outlays were generally frowned upon. In recent years, the government has embarked on a number of projects, including roads, and a new international airport with Chinese support and has also been able to borrow for infrastructure from the Eurobond market, amounting to US$3 billion between 2012 and 2015. Although the Eurobond coupon rate was 5.375% during the initial bond transaction, it had risen to 8.97% when the last one was completed in 2015. The sharp rise in interest rates reflected the tightening of international bond markets, but mostly the increasingly negative perception of economic prospects for Zambia (and other African borrowers).

Although access to the Eurobond market provided a rare opportunity for Zambia and other African countries to diversify sources of financing, in the event, it has also provided a broader commentary on the difficulty of financing the region's infrastructure on a sustainable basis given the amounts required and virtual absence of long tenor loans suitable for such financing. To attract financing that would not escalate total debt, the government promulgated a Public-Private Partnership Act in 2009, with a focus on infrastructure projects. It encourages the development of spurs on the main railway to remoter parts of the country, toll roads, mini-hydro power projects to supply the national grid, and irrigation projects. Unlike South Korea, where the modalities for financing infrastructure were well-linked to the budget, sustainable approaches are still being debated in Zambia.

7.7 State-business relations

Introduction. State-business relations in Africa have taken center stage in recent years, perhaps as a direct result of globalization, with most states wanting to give their national business champions a helping hand in the global marketplace.

The experience of developmental states in East Asia, and even Latin America, suggests that while collaboration between groups in society i.e. government officials, business, universities, NGOs, and specialized agencies for analysis and research, labor unions, and rural groups is crucial for driving the development process: among them the most important alliance is that between government and business (Ajakaiye and Jerome, 2015).

There are, however, two opposing views regarding what the nature of state-business relationship in African countries should be. On the one hand, sturdy state-business relations make domestic policies more predictable, reduce perceived risk, and, hence, galvanize domestic private investment and employment creation. At the beginning of rapid development in South Korea and other East Asian economies, amicable state-business relations were important in helping to defray tensions and disagreements over rapidly changing policies and regulations, ways of doing business, and taking on board new research findings.

On the other hand, there is a general fear, borne of experience, that too cozy a relationship between the state and business is bound to degenerate into malfeasance and poor governance—an experience shared by many African governments from their ownership of parastatals in past decades, as discussed above. Moreover, labor unions and other NGOs, such as those advocating for improvements in areas including gender relations, youth empowerment, and the environment, are often short-charged when state-business relations are heightened at the expense of the rights of workers and civil society, more broadly. Bugra (1994) has noted, for example, that owing to the divisive distributional implications of the outward-oriented development strategy pursued by South Korea and Japan, the governments there were, at certain junctures, forced to moderate their relations with business by also consulting closely with civil society.

State-Business Relations: Persuasion versus Coercion. In South Korea, the storied alliance between government and business resulted from a combination of coercion and inducement, contestation, and accommodation, requiring quick-footedness on the part of government, a great deal of experimentation and an underlying flexibility in setting boundaries (Haggard, 1990). The fact that the process was started by a military government made a great deal of difference. When the Korea Chamber of Commerce and Industry, comprising family-owned business groups (chaebols) showed some reticence in dealing with the new leadership, a Federation of Korean Industries (KOISRA) better aligned with the objectives of the new government (to promote sound economic policies, internationalize the Korean economy, and enhance free markets and the development of Korea) was formed in 1961. The state was not averse to alluding to threats posed by a resurgent North Korea and communism to suppress labor union demands and other left of center political expressions in the country—it introduced the Special Decree for National Security in 1971 for that purpose—and wring out what it desired from the social partners (Kwon and Yi, 2008).

A point sometimes obscured by South Korea's formidable economic success is that South Korean firms were indeed capitalist entities, and despite subsidies, were intent on making a profit and be able to stand on their own feet. In other words, the state-business alliance had to have tangible benefits for both sides—on the firm side to graduate into exporters in the medium term and/or become leaders in a given technology segment at home, and subsequently globally, while the government garnered high levels of employment, export revenue, and global reputations on the basis of institutional, technical, and scientific achievements.

As discussed earlier, the South Korean government had set up its own research agencies in the 1960s and 1970s, where the results of R&D analyses were shared across the business community as a form of public good. This centrally undertaken research, in which firms such as Samsung participated in their infancy, helped establish strong research links between government agencies, the private sector and universities, engendered scale economies and lowered R&D costs for firms. The research collaboration and pooling of costs were crucial in launching the ICT sector in subsequent years (Asian Development Bank, 2014) as noted earlier.

Attempts at Reaching Out to the Private Sector. While the government-business alliances crafted in South Korea in the 1960s have few African parallels, governments on the continent have nevertheless created several institutional vehicles and opportunities in recent years, including conferences, workshops organized by private sector foundations, as well as industrial expos, to provide opportunities for the exchanges of views between state and business. Formal structures for state-business dialog, where conclusions are converted into actionable programs tied to a timetable of execution, are quite rare. Part of the difficulty, alluded to earlier, is the lack of a critical mass of indigenous entrepreneurs in Africa that are familiar with the socio-economic layout of the countries and appreciate what is at stake.[14]

With respect to the labor market, governments have continued, perhaps out of habit, to take the side of employers in wage negotiations. As far back as the 1980s, Nigeria dismantled the tripartite wage negotiation machinery altogether, opting to set wages arbitrarily across the board. Although such approaches have been abandoned, with perhaps the exception of Tunisia, South Africa, and Kenya, serious bargaining between labor market partners in not an important topic on the political agendas of countries.[15] Encouraging discussions between labor market parties is crucial for laying a solid ground for the maturation of relations, with all three sides internalizing what is required to meet crucial national targets and needs. Above all, it helps resolve the coordination issues with respect to skills development, plant location, sources of investment, productivity, and wages that lie at the center of the quest for development.

In spite of the long delay, African governments are now putting increased emphasis on developing practically oriented research competences in their countries and are encouraging the emergence of centers of excellence, including courses specifically developed for African conditions.[16] Others, such as Morocco, Ethiopia, and Tunisia, have dramatically expanded technical education across their university systems, increasing the number of qualified engineers produced each year. Effective systems for estimating changes in future technical skill requirements must be part of the governments' strategies for supporting the industrialization process.

Elusive Reciprocity in South Africa. The idea of a social compact—involving government, labor, and business—was always central to South Africa's political construct, following the transition to democracy in the 1990s and very much in the minds of the drafters of the Freedom Charter of the 1950s (Congress of the People, 1955). The success of the ANC's first effort at pushing the economy onto a dynamic growth trajectory—the GEAR program launched in 1996 (Republic of South Africa, 1996)—was premised on this tripartite pact for development. In the event, there was little or no commitment technology to ensure the feasibility of the compact nor has there emerged a viable alternative strategy (Adelzadeh, 1996).

The issue of "radical economic transformation" has, as noted above, reputedly returned to the center of ANC discussion, although its implications in policy terms have never been clarified. It could imply continuity, but with greater focus on industrial policy or a break with the past, including rolling out redistribution measures. Hence South Africa's economic policy development has been characterized by deep levels of disagreement and polarization, which, in spite of the ambitions to the contrary, would not sustain the push for industrialization (Kaplan, 2013; Meth, 2004; North, 2010). In a recent assessment, Plagerson et al. (2019) note that the social compact between the state, labor, and capital is struggling, at best, and that new modalities are needed, including giving the mineral sector's role in the country's development a new look, if some of the older transformational aspirations are to be resuscitated. As noted in Chapter 3, it would take more than slogans to summon the will for united action by both government and business to "grow South Africa."

The South Korean and East Asian experiences suggest that policies that generated shared growth helped to boost government-business relations and vice versa. Campos and Root (2001) argue, for example, that East Asian governments were able to craft social compacts for development with the populations because they were astute at spreading "...the benefits of growth-enhancing policies widely, made the reversibility of policies costly, and consequently gave individuals and firms confidence that they would share the growth dividend." In addition, as indicated earlier, popular support was built through programs including land reform, improvements in social policy and wider access to education. More recent examinations of the South Korean experience suggest that deeper links between economic and social policy are still keen drivers of development (Yi and Mkandawire, 2014).

7.8 Financing industrialization in the developmental state

Injection of Aid in the Formative Decades. In spite of the frenetic pace at which reform measures were undertaken by the government in the 1960s, South Korea was still a poor country and needed substantial injection of foreign capital to meet its ambitious goal to kickstart rapid growth. While much of the foreign capital had come from the United States before 1962, the normalization of diplomatic relations with Japan resulted in a ten-year agreement of economic co-operation. This was a strategic move in terms of future investment and technology acquisition. The World Bank provided its first loan to the country in 1962, with the IMF following in 1965. In contrast with African countries, which were perennially dependent on donor support, South Korea's reliance on aid was already declining in the 1970s (and would cease altogether in the following decade). But perhaps most important, the aid that South Korea received did not come with the type of onerous conditionality that had deflected African countries from their chosen development paths in the 1970s and 1980s i.e. in modern parlance, it was not weaponized. It could also be argued that since South Korea evinced a high level of confidence regarding where it wanted to go, conditionality of any form would have been superfluous. But as we argued in the country overview in Chapter 3, South Korea's economic policy was not beyond blemish, and the IMF imposed some conditions for its support during the Asian Financial crisis of the late-1980s. Still, the crisis marked a prelude to a sustainable and competitive breakthrough in global markets (Rhee, Ross-Larson and Pursell, 2001).

Consolidation and Control of the Financial Sector in South Korea. In the early 1960s, the government embarked on the consolidation of the financial sector under its direct control. By 1970, it had assumed almost complete control (96.4%) of the financial assets of the country, including the Central Bank. In the process, it had created eight specialized banks: Korea Exchange Bank (1967), Korea Housing Bank (formerly Korea Housing Finance Cooperation) (1969), Citizen's National Bank (1962), Small and Medium Industry Bank (1961), National Agricultural Cooperatives Federation (an amalgamation of an agricultural bank and agricultural cooperatives) (1961), Central Federation of Fisheries Cooperatives (1962), and Export Import Bank (1976). The Korea Development Bank had been established in 1954.

Characteristic of the state-business bargain, discussed earlier, state-controlled banks catered for the financial needs of the private sector in the various branches of the economy. Notably, the Citizen's National Bank and the Small and Medium Industry Bank were created to meet the needs of the small and medium-sized entrepreneurs. The banks provided the financial umbilical cord to the developmental state, while in turn, the state paid attention to the distribution of credit and the conditionalities required to ensure that the loans had the desired impact. It is obvious, in retrospect, that the chaebols could not have assumed the commanding heights of the economy without the strategic financial support of the government. Likewise, the government could not have reached its objectives without the willingness of the chaebols and other corporations to reach a productive bargain with it, based on a positive assessment of potential outcomes (Lee, 2009, 2017; Sindzingre, 2007).

Opening up to Private Capital. In seeking to transition from the light to the heavy industry phase, South Korea introduced the "Foreign Capital Inducement Law" in 1973, allowing for direct investment and collaboration between domestic and foreign companies. It was considered a more efficient means of transferring foreign technology than purchasing licenses. The Law listed areas that were open to foreign investment (from textiles to heavy industry) while determining those that would be "nationalized" in the sense of allowing a domestic firm (i.e. chaebol) that had learnt the "rules of the game" through previous exposure to foreign competition to, with direct support from the state, in terms of subsidies and other incentives, assume prominence. According to Judet (1980), by the end of the 1970s, of the annual US$1.3 billion or so of FDI coming into South Korea, a quarter was from the US, while Japanese capital accounted for 59%. In the 1980s, South Korea witnessed a huge relocation of Japanese manufacturing to the country, along with a spike in investment.

Growing South Korean Investments Abroad. Almost counterintuitively, the government encouraged the expansion of South Korea investment abroad, even as it encouraged foreign investment at home. This was a key strategic consideration. For a country in a turbulent region and without much natural resource endowment (aside from water resources), it needed to diversify its income streams beyond East Asia. It, for example, took early shares in the Gulf Oil company, partly as a good investment, and partly as a means of guaranteeing itself supplies of oil and gas. According to Judet (1980), by the end of the 1970s, the country had invested some US$ 85 million with two-thirds in Asia, 19% in the USA and 10% in Africa.

7.9 Conclusions on industrialization

The discussion in this chapter suggests that the urge for industrialization among African economies has been just as strong as that of South Korea and the East Asian countries during the earlier phases of their development. Although African countries have drafted national development plans dutifully every five years (with gaps during the era of structural adjustment), few of them, certainly not the country case studies discussed in this volume, have been able to translate the ambitious industrialization components of their plans into dynamic projects and programs for sustainable development with anywhere near the success achieved by the East Asian economies.

The literature on the replication of the developmental state experience and evidence from the country case studies suggest that Africa's industrialization lacuna, while having several causes, is mostly to blame on pervasive domestic policy and institutional weakness. This is not to dismiss the view, which has some validity, that South Korea and the rest of East Asia had been dealt a fair hand i.e. geographical location in a region of enormous geopolitical interest to the United States, a neighborhood rivalry (i.e. flying gees) that encouraged political and economic competition, a global economy that was opening up to trade and a colonial legacy that prioritized science and technology. It should not be forgotten that Korea (in the pre-WWII world) was considered a remote and resource-scarce outpost, located near two belligerent nations (Soviet Union and Japan), whose interest to the West and the rest of the world was limited.

The issue of replication i.e. whether African countries can achieve the same type of breakneck development as South Korea and East Asia is probably overdriven, as the industrialization process, when it finally takes off in Africa, might take other forms—some have suggested for example that African countries could skip the smokestacks form of industrialization altogether, through the adoption of modern technologies. There are several endearing experiences from the developmental state practices of South Korea that many African countries could learn from when pursuing industrialization.

First, industrial policy implementation in South Korea was meticulous, based on analytical studies and those of experiences from elsewhere. Mistakes were made but then were rectified by the same careful process of analysis, monitoring, and follow-up i.e. the planning process did not become a pro forma exercise, like in many African countries.

Second, though industrialization is a broad subject, in South Korea, it was encapsulated by a simple idea: the maximization of manufactured exports.

Third, industrialization required the restructuring of the economy and the design of an implementation superstructure comprising macroeconomic incentives, labor markets, legal and regulatory institutions, analytical capacity, R&D, innovative infrastructure, and political champions.

Fourth, South Korea and East Asia showed that businesspeople can be sturdy allies for development if an appropriate and conducive environment for private sector participation is created. The government of South Korea expended considerable energy in designing incentive structures for private sector participation, and it did so not merely by appealing to heightened nationalism or sense of altruism of the business community but by demonstrating that stable and shared growth was a good business proposition.

Fifth, discipline, transparency, and a high sense of responsibility were crucial features in South Korea's industrialization drive. Given the thousands of moving parts during industrial policy implementation, linking up the facets was quite demanding. Moreover, regulatory regimes yielded opportunities for rent-seeking which had to be discouraged, sometimes with stiff sentences. This discipline in policy implementation derived not only from good training but also from favorable terms of service as well as remuneration. Robust agencies of restraint prevented the onset of "state capture."

Notes

1 Source: South Korea Team (2017), Onis (1991), Westphal (1990), and World Bank (1987).
2 It is interesting to point out that, ex ante, policy approaches were far from predetermined. The South Korea Team (2017) noted, for example, that when President Park came into office in 1961, through a military coup d'état, he was faced with two interrelated challenges: first, how to establish political legitimacy, and second, how to generate rapid economic development. With regard to the first concern, he sought to break ties with chaebols, who were seen by the public as monopolistic and corrupt, with a disproportionate political influence, and hence a potential threat to the new government (Kim, 1991; Lim, 2012). The relationship between the government and chaebols was soon restored. President Park, having reached a social pact with the chaebols, noted that to improve the living conditions of Koreans, economic development was the paramount issue.

3 Although it could be argued that South Korea could have industrialized even faster if it had maintained a free trade policy regime from the beginning, the issue is not clear-cut. Compared with other East Asian cases, it is doubtful whether South Korea would have done better in terms of growth if liberalization had come sooner.

4 Figures in this section draw on OECD (2000).

5 Three parastatals have been key in the country's power generation: the Korea Electric Power Corporation (KEPCO), the Korea Gas Corporation (KOGAS), and the Korea Hydro and Nuclear Power Company.

6 The government also compelled the state-owned Korea Electric Power Corporate (KEPCO) to use local anthracite coal at twice the price of the imported bituminous coal. The South Korean government invested heavily in new technology to use anthracite coal more effectively (OECD, 2000).

7 In South Korea, industrialization was strongly linked to the export of manufactured goods. Despite state efforts—including subsidies and direct state investments—exports of manufactures in Cameroon comprised only 4% of total exports in the 1980s.

8 See also Lee and Lee (2016), Lee and Lim (2016), and Zambia Team (2017).

9 As an example, the Pohang Iron and Steel Company, created in 1968, set up the Pohang University of Science and Technology in 1986 and Research Institute of Science and Technology in 1987. See, for example, Kim (2009) and Oh and Larson (2011).

10 This section draws on the following: Zambian Team, 2017; Côte d'Ivoire Team, 2017; Nigerian Team, 2017.

11 Among the challenges targeted are the following: limited access to infrastructure, inadequate power generation capacity, inefficient usage of available capacity, lack of capital for investment, inefficient regulation, high-technical losses and vandalism, insufficient transmission and distribution facilities, inefficient use of electricity by consumers, inappropriate industry and market structure, and unclear delineation of roles and responsibilities (Olugbenga et al., 2013).

12 The Act changed the National Electric Power Authority (NEPA) into the Power Holding Company of Nigeria (PHCN), while the bulk of electricity generation, transmission, and distribution was split among 18 successor companies (all public limited companies), incorporated into PHCN. Six companies took over the power generation aspect: Kanji, Afam, Ughelli, Geregu, Shiroro, and Sapele; the transmission company of Nigeria (TRANSCO) was put solely in charge of transmitting electricity in the country, while there are 11 distribution companies: Eko, Ikeja, Port Harcourt, Enugu, Yola, Jos, Ibadan, Kaduna, Kano, Enugu, and Benin.

13 PPPs have since spread to other sectors: health, energy, water, transport, tourism, waste, and even prisons.

14 An expression from Uganda "ebyaffe" which translates to "our things" i.e. including economic and cultural mores and sense of belonging, would be most appropriate here.

15 See, for example, Francis, Tunde, and Gbajumo-Sheriff (2011).

16 For example, Rwanda has an arrangement with Carnegie-Mellon University in the US to offer Master of engineering degree at a campus in Kigali. Students from East Africa and beyond can apply for admission.

References

Adelzadeh, A. (1996) 'From the RDP to GEAR: The Gradual Embracing of Neo-Liberalism in Economic Policy,' *Transformation* 0(31):66–95.

African Union Commission (2014) *Agenda 2063. The Africa We Want*, African Union: Addis Ababa.

Ajakaiye, O. and Jerome, A. (2015) 'Public-Private Interface for Inclusive Development in Africa,' in C. Monga and Lin, J. (eds.), *The Oxford Handbook of Africa and Economics*, Vol. 1, Oxford University Press: Oxford.

ANC (1994) *1994 Election Manifesto*, African National Congress: Johannesburg.

ANC (1998) 'The State, Property Relations and Social Transformation,' *Discussion Paper Towards the Alliance Summit*, African National Congress: Johannesburg.

ANC (2019) *2019 Election Manifesto*, African National Congress: Johannesburg.

Arrighi, G. (2002) 'The African Crisis: World Systemic and Regional Aspects,' *New Left Review* 2(15):5–36.

Asian Development Bank (2014) *A Comparative Infrastructure Development Assessment of the Republic of Korea and the Kingdom of Thailand*, ADB Publications: Manila.

Assiga-Ateba, E.-M. (1998) « Les Politiques de Restructuration de l'Economie Camerounaise: Evaluation Rétrospective à Moyen-Terme », *Revue Africaine de Développement* 10(2):54–89.

Assiga-Ateba, E.M. (2009) *Economie des Entreprises Publiques*, Presses Universitaires d'Afrique: Yaoundé.

Bedasso, B. (2014) 'Political Transition in a Small Open Economy: Retracing the Economic Trail of South Africa's Long Walk to Democracy,' *Working Paper 458*, Economic Research Southern Africa: Cape Town.

Boutat, A. (1991) *Technologies et développement au Cameroun – Le rendez-vous manqué*, L'Harmattan: Yaoundé.

Bugra, A. (1994) *State and Business in Modern Turkey: A Comparative Study*, State University of New York Press: Albany.

Bureau of Public Enterprises, (2011) 'Overview of the Nigerian Electricity Industry (Roles, Responsibilities, Structure, Expectations),' *Report*, Federal Republic of Nigeria: Abuja.

Cameroon Team (2017) « Etude Sur L'Economie du Cameroun. La Politique de Développement dans la Pratique Enseignements Tires de L'Expérience de Développement de la Corée du Sud », Report to the African Development Bank on the *Developmental State in Africa, Lessons from South Korea Project*, Université de Yaoundé II: Yaoundé.

Campos, E. and Root, H. (2001) *Key to the East Asian Miracle: Making Shared Growth Credible*, Brookings Institute Press: Washington, DC.

Comité Interministériel Elargi au Secteur Privé (2006) *Comment Relancer la Croissance Economique après le Point d'Achèvement pour faire sortir le Cameroun du sous-développement?* Actes, Palais des Congrès: Yaoundé.

Congress of the People (1955) *Freedom Charter: Adopted at the Congress of the People at Kliptown, Johannesburg, on June 25 and 26, 1955*, Pacific Press Ltd: Johannesburg.

Fessehaie, J., das Nair, R., Ncube, P. and Roberts, S. (2015) 'Growth Promotion Through Industrial Strategies: Zambia, *Working Paper*, May, International Growth Center: London.

Fessehaie, J., Rustomjee, Z. and Kaziboni, L. (2016) 'Can Mining Promote Industrialization? A Comparative Analysis of Policy Frameworks in Three Southern African Countries,' *UNU-WIDER Working Paper* 2016/83, UNU-World Institute for Development Economics Research: Helsinki.

Francis, E., Tunde, E. and Gbajumo-Sheriff, M. (2011) 'Collective Bargaining Dynamics in the Nigerian Public and Private Sectors,' *Australian Journal of Business and Management* 1(5):63–70.

Haggard, S. (1990) *Pathways from the Periphery: The Politics of Growth in the Newly Industrialized Countries*, Cornell University Press: Ithaca.

Hirschman, A. (1968) 'The Political Economy of Import-substituting Industrialization in Latin America,' *Quarterly Journal of Economics* 82(1):1–32.

Judet, P. (1980) 'Le rôle de l'Etat dans la croissance économique de la République de la Corée du Sud,' *Revue d'Économie Industrielle, Programme National Persée* 14(1):204–211.

Junki, K. and Kyuhyun, K. (2011) 'The Electricity Industry Reform in Korea: Lessons for Further Liberalization,' Graduate School of Public Administration, National University: Seoul.

Kaplan, D. (2013) 'Policy Gridlock? Comparing the Proposals Made in Three Economic Policy Documents,' *Commissioned Paper*, Centre for Development and Enterprise: Johannesburg.

Kim, D. (2009) 'Korean Experience of Overcoming Economic Crisis through ICT Development,' *UNESCAP Technical Paper*, IDD/TP-09-1, August, United Nations Economic and Social Commission for Asia and Pacific: Bangkok.

Kim, E. (1996) 'The Industrial Organization and Growth of the Korean Chaebol: Integrating Development and Organizational Theories,' in G. Hamilton (ed.), *Business Networks and Economic Development in East and South East Asia*, 272–298, University of Hong Kong Press: Hongkong.

Kim, K. (1991) 'The Korean Miracle (1962–1980) Revisited: Myths and Realities in Strategy and Development,' *Working Paper* 166, The Kellogg Institute for International Studies, Notre Dame University: South Bend.

Kim, L. and Nelson, R. (eds.) (2000) *Technology, Learning, and Innovation: Experiencing of Newly Industrializing Economies*, Cambridge University Press: Cambridge.

Kragelund, P. (2017) The Making of Local Content Policies in Zambia's Copper Sector: Institutional Impediments to Resource-led Development,' *Resources Policy* 51:57–66.

Kwon, H. and Yi, I. (2008) 'Development Strategies, Welfare Regime and Poverty Reduction in the Republic of Korea,' *Paper*, United Nations Research Institute for Social Development: Geneva.

Larson, J. and Park, J. (2014) 'From Developmental to Network State: Government Restructuring and ICT-Led Innovation in Korea' *Telecommunications Policy* 38(4):344–359.

Lee, K. (2009) 'How Can Korea Be A Role Model for Catch-Up Development? A 'Capability-Based View,' *UNU-WIDER Working Paper*, 2009/34, UNU-World Institute for Development Economics Research: Helsinki.

Lee, K. (2012) *IT Development in Korea: A Broadband Nirvana?* Routledge: London.

Lee, K. (ed.) (2016) *Economic Catch-up and Technological Leapfrogging: Path to Development and Macroeconomic Stability in Korea*, Edward Elgar Publishing: Cheltenham.

Lee, K. (2017) 'Financing Industrial Development in Korea and the Implications for Africa,' *How They Did It in Solving Policy Issues Series* 1(3) African Development Bank: Abidjan.

Lee, K. and Lee, H. (2016) 'Historical Origins and Initial Conditions for Economic Catchup,' in K. Lee (ed.), *Technological Leapfrogging: Path to Development and Macroeconomic Stability in Korea*, 15–29, Edward Elgar Publishing: Cheltenham.

Lee, K. and Lim, C. (2016) 'Catchup and Leapfrogging in Six Sectors in the 1980s and 1990s,' in K. Lee (ed.), *Technological Leapfrogging: Path to Development and Macroeconomic Stability in Korea*, 167–206, Edward Elgar Publishing: Cheltenham.

Liebenthal, R. and Cheelo, C. (2018) 'Understanding the Implications of the Boom-Bust Cycle of the Global Copper Prices for Natural Resources, Structural Change, and Industrial Development in Zambia,' *UNU-WIDER Working Paper* 2018/16, UNU-World Institute for Development Economics Research: Helsinki.

Lim, W. (2012) '*Chaebol* and Industrial Policy in Korea,' *Asian Economic Policy Review* 7(1):69–86.

Meth, C. (2004) 'Half Measures: The ANC's Unemployment and Poverty Reduction Goals,' *Working Paper, 04/089*, Development Policy Research Unit, University of Cape Town: Cape Town.

Nigeria Team (2017) 'Towards Developmental State in Nigeria: Lessons from Korea,' Report to the African Development Bank on the *Developmental State in Africa, Lessons from South Korea Project*, Nigerian Economic Society: Ibadan.

North, D. (2010) *Understanding the Process of Economic Change*, Princeton University Press: Princeton.

OECD (2000) 'Korea—Regulatory Reform in Electricity,' *Country Studies*, Organization for Economic Cooperation and Development: Paris.

Oh, M. and Larson, J.F. (2011) *Digital Development in Korea: Building an Information Society*, Routledge: London.

Olugbenga, T., Jumah, A. and Phillips, D. (2013) 'The Current and Future Challenges of the Electricity Market in Nigeria in the Face of Deregulation Process,' *African Journal of Engineering Research* 1(2):33–39.

Onis, Z. (1991) 'The Logic of the Developmental State.' *Comparative Politics* 24(1):109–126.

Ovadia, J. (2013) 'The Nigerian 'one percent' and the Management of National Oil Wealth Through Nigerian Content,' *Science and Society* 77(3):315–341.

Ovadia, J. and Wolf, C. (2018) 'Studying the Developmental State: Theory and Method in Research on Industrial Policy and State-led Development in Africa,' *Third World Quarterly* 39(1):1056–1076.

Plagerson, S., Patel, L., Hochfeld, T. and Ulriksen, M. (2019) 'Social Policy in South Africa: Navigating the Route to Social Development,' *World Development* 113(C):1–9.

Readhead, A. (2016) 'Transfer Pricing in the Mining Sector in Zambia,' *Case Study*, Natural Resource Governance Institute: New York.

Republic of South Africa (1996) *Growth, Employment and Redistribution: A Macroeconomic Strategy*, Treasury: Pretoria.

Rhee, Y. W., Ross-Larson, B. and Pursell, G. (2001) *Korea's Competitive Edge: Managing the Entry into World Markets*, Johns Hopkins University Press: Baltimore.

Sampath, P. (2014) 'Industrial Development for Africa: Trade, Technology and the Role of the State,' *African Journal of Science, Technology, Innovation and Development* 6(5):439–453.

Seidman, A. (1974) 'The Distorted Growth of Import-Substitution Industry: the Zambian Case,' *Journal of Modern African Studies* 12(4):601–631.

Sindzingre, A. (2007) 'Financing the Developmental State: Tax and Revenue Issues,' *Development Policy Review* 25(5):615–631.

Tabi, H. and Ondoa, H. (2011) 'Industrialization of the manufacturing Sector and Trade Opening in Cameroon,' *Research in World Economy* 2(1):58–68.

UNCTAD (2013) 'The Asian Developmental State and the Flying Geese Paradigm, *Discussion Papers* 213, United Nations Congress of Trade and Development: Geneva.

UNIDO (2005) *Industrial Performance and Capabilities of Cameroon: Analysis of the Industrial Sector*, United Nations Industrial Development Organization: Vienna.

US Energy Information Administration (2014) *Energy Outlook 2014*, Federal Government of the United States: Washington.

wa Gĩthĩnji, M. and Adesida, O. (2011) 'Industrialization, Exports and the Developmental State in Africa: The Case for Transformation,' *Working Paper* 2011–18, Department of Economics, University of Massachusetts: Amherst.

Westphal, L. E. (1990) 'Industrial Policy in an Export-Propelled Economy: Lessons from South Korea's Experience,' *Journal of Economic Perspectives* 4(3):41–59.

World Bank (1987) *World Development Report, 1987: Barriers to Adjustment and Growth in the World Economy, Industrialization and Foreign Trade and World Development Indicators*, World Bank: Washington, DC and Oxford University Press: Oxford.

Yi, I. and Mkandawire, T. (2014) *Learning from the South Korean Development Success*, Routledge: London, and UNRISD, Geneva.

Zambia Revenue Authority (2014) *Mineral Value Chain Monitoring Project*, ZRA: Lusaka.

8   Discussion and conclusion

8.1 Introduction

This chapter is a policy discussion and conclusion of the book focusing on the key issues of relevance and plausibility, which must be examined jointly as they are not necessarily mutually exclusive. Overall, the previous chapters have shown that South Korea and the African case studies—Cameroon, Côte d'Ivoire, Nigeria, South Africa, and Zambia—have at one time or other experienced similar development challenges, including the cultural and institutional distractions and ravages of colonial rule, the traumatic impacts of war and the insecurities of uneven reconstruction and slow recovery, wide-spread poverty, paucity of physical and human capital, poor infrastructure and spatial exclusion, aid dependence, corrosive politics and poor governance (including military dictatorships), and outright corruption. They have, in the past decades, dealt in one way or other with the impacts of globalization, positive and negative, on their trade and growth environments.

The book focuses on how this transformation was achieved in practice and the factors that contributed to South Korea's emergence as the epochal developmental state. It assesses whether the experiences of South Korea and other East Asian countries are feasible and transferable to African countries and the implications for the latter's own development strategies. The discussion in this chapter is presented in six sections: context, feasibility, and replicability of the developmental state model; South Korea's lessons as a developmental state and their implications for African countries; human capital and social inclusion; policy coherence and institutional rigor; and industrial policy, competitiveness, and growth.

8.2 Context, feasibility, and replicability of the developmental state model

First, South Korea and East Asian countries, more generally, evinced effective "catch-up" development strategies that enabled them to industrialize, exit poverty, and enter the "first world" in less than 50 years. Second, African policymakers are attracted by the prospect of autonomous policy design and self-determination and encouragement of robust savings and investment, as opposed to policy dictation from multilateral agencies and the donor community. Third, the creation of robust state institutions and a cadre of effective managers at all levels of government in East Asia (and South Korea in particular), which characterized the developmental state, seemed to validate earlier attempts by African policymakers at creating endogenous institutions to guide development. Fourth, South Korea, which is short of natural resources, encouraged the development of human capital, focusing especially on technical skill acquisition and R&D, thereby catapulting the country to the global frontier in advanced technologies, ICT, and the information revolution.

From the results end of the equation, South Korea's march from poverty to becoming the preeminent developmental state seems fairly straightforward—it derived from policy coherence, institutional rigor, and successful creation of an alliance for development between social partners (comprising mainly the state and entrepreneurs). And yet, on close inspection, the challenges it confronted were complex and politically intricate. In the 1950s, when the reconstruction of South Korea began, the country was part of a broader cultural entity split asunder by political ideology and war. South Korea had, as observed in previous chapters, a champion and protector in the United States of America—with implications for the economic policies pursued by the various regimes since the end of World War II. South Korea had thus access to the largest market in the world, while the volume of international trade was expanding exponentially under the GATT. Japanese inward investment, accompanied by technology transfers, helped set up the car and electronics industries that buttressed South Korea's export potential for the coming decades. International conditions have changed significantly since then, with implications for the new industrializers in Africa and elsewhere. However, many countries were exposed to similarly attractive global conditions, while many more had enjoyed American suzerainty in the 20th century, but few had taken advantage of them.

While it is tempting to use South Korea, and East Asia, as the measuring rods for assessing African progress, given the similarity of start conditions, notably lack of capital, one should also bear in mind that the two regions are some 14,000 kilometers apart, engrossed in completely different geopolitical environments, and with the exception of China, have limited trade and diplomatic links with Africa. South Korea, for its part, is only starting to have a presence on the continent but mutual trade is still insignificant. In one important sense, the geographical isolation of South Korea and the African case study countries helps to highlight a key conclusion of the study, which is that that neither deep poverty nor geographical location (and socio-economic adversity) can define the destiny of a country or region. With effort and determination, a former colony, once derided as a basket case, ensconced in the Asian periphery, was able to overcome poverty, institutional frailty, post-war reconstruction, and domestic political infighting and to join the group of the most affluent economies in the world, within a generation. Moreover, South Korea's transformation was driven by human capital accumulation and institutional astuteness and principally financed from domestic savings, not from natural resource endowments.

These things, are, at least on the face of it, easy to emulate by aspiring countries, in Africa and elsewhere.

8.3 South Korea's experience as a developmental state and relevance for African countries

The rapid growth of the South Korean economy in the past 60 years, perhaps with the exception of China, has known few precedents in the world economy. From the 1961 to 2020, South Korea has been ruled by 12 different administrations. Each one of them sought, as expected, to promote its own policies and projects. Despite the civil war, military coups, and political upheavals in between, the various regimes rarely diverted from the country's overarching ambition to generate rapid economic growth and achieve the status of a developed economy—collective national enhancement was the uniting factor that superseded all other considerations. Understanding how this focus on development was both reinforced and maintained for such a long time (some 30 years) would be the key to understanding the essence of the "South Korean miracle," as it was not merely defined by growth alone.

Much credit goes to the existence of an autonomous professional civil service for the coherence with which policies were implemented. This was coupled with competent political leadership and liberal market policies which derived from actual experience and, hence, subject to revision and not dogmatically driven. Furthermore, South Korea effectively used legal frameworks and kept careful records—hence the large volume of legal statutes during the last 60 years covering a host of areas—to secure the implementation of policies and subject them to monitoring and evaluation. The use of legal frameworks, instead of mere policy guidelines, deterred non-compliance as they were less vulnerable to political pressure and policy reversal. The civil services in African countries have undergone several reforms in recent decades, notably under the era of SAPs, with the goal of raising their efficiency and development impact. Invariably, public service reform in many African countries remains a work in progress—although improvements in working conditions and the professionalization of the establishments are attracting a younger set of better trained government workers. Moreover, given the difficult situations on the labor markets, government work is no longer a last resort for making a career in Africa. Still, a meritocratically recruited staff compliment to fill the civil services of Africa is still more of an aspiration than a near-term reality.

Policy pragmatism, and not ideological inclination, was the driving principle, above others, in South Korea. State intervention in South Korea was undertaken in as "market conforming" a manner as possible to reduce the uncertainties and risks related to doing business in the country and to generate information about emerging opportunities in the broader economy. The country's ideology was in essence "rapid and shared growth," other dogmas were dutifully avoided. While African governments might not be in a position to "govern" the market today, as globalization seems to have made it harder to do so, they would still need to address the fragility of their markets by strengthening policy, institutional, and regulatory frameworks. This can be done, as in the case of South Korea, through the establishment of agencies dedicated to analyzing the economy, including domestic market performance and how distortions can be eliminated to boost competitiveness and efficiency, and to raise standards.

Developmental state lessons from South Korea and their relevance:

First, the government's (initial) stance was interventionist. Given the destruction caused by the Korean War, South Korea's initial policy inclination was to intervene in as many areas of the economy as possible. It designed aggressive policies for market-intervention, created a competent and effective bureaucracy to implement them, and evinced strong political leadership and vision for economic development across all institutions of government. Two factors soon dissuaded the authorities from taking the interventionist thrust too far. First, too tight market controls were not supported by the American overlords, and second, too rigid controls risked making South Korea look like its filial neighbor to the north—where expunging liberal freedoms was the norm.

Second, with the ascent to power of President Park Chung-hee in the early 1960s, the state embarked on the establishment of an incentive-compatible alliance for development with the private sector—which in large measure excluded civil society. However, the state did not adopt the stance of a command economy and impacted private firm behavior by using available market and regulatory tools, including taxes, subsidies, and other incentives to reach desirable results. Researchers have observed, as noted earlier, that the exchange of high-quality information between the state and private firms, including from government-sponsored research institutions, and establishment of mutual confidence were necessary conditions for smooth and effective state-business relations. By creating attractive business conditions for domestic firms i.e. on the basis of charity begins at home, the country was able to attract FDI. Unlike in many African countries, foreign investment was linked closely to the needs of domestic firms. Deals that included matchups with domestic companies and were linked to technology transfers were prioritized. The full-fledged entry of foreign firms was only allowed at a later stage when domestic firms were strong enough to compete.

Third, the state undertook well-calibrated industrial, trade, financial, and other policies to meet it domestic economic goals and objectives. Many of the policies, including restrictions to foreign firm operations in the domestic market, could be described today as protectionist, although measures were undertaken to counter their negative impacts on competitiveness. Importantly, government support was contingent on firms achieving time-bound breakthroughs on the export market. To do this well, high-technical competence and a high degree of integrity were required. This was undeniably the state's attempt to pick winners, with accompanying moral hazard, however. What is significant is that for many companies, the state was ultimately able to walk away. The question for African countries is how to grow their domestic private sector in the age of globalization and how to support the business environment by encouraging "competitive collaboration," including joint R&D.

Fourth, South Korea emphasized export-oriented manufacturing and not import-substitution. It encouraged rapid investment growth into the sector and facilitated its competitiveness through carefully crafted industrial, trade, and financial policies. Agencies such as the Korean Development Bank were either created or strengthened to support the export push. State agencies and universities contributed by providing practical research on investment, employment, skills, and on the spatial impacts of the export-oriented strategy. The return of development banks in many African countries marks a renewed interest in the possibilities of government-delegated growth strategies. The notion of "picking winners" is no longer the scary topic that it was in the 1980s and 1990s, during the era of the SAPs. Working in much-changed business environments, the new development banks operate with limited financial resources and their impact on the overall domestic financial climate has been limited. They are typically inundated by applications for loans and are often forced to resort to nonmarket (i.e. political) considerations in allocating financing. This implies in turn that they have a larger share of potentially non-performing assets than commercial banks and are beholden to governments for operating capital. They are yet to become the fulcrum to lift up African manufacturing.

Fifth, South Korea pursued a capitalist approach to development. It is sometimes forgotten in the debate that South Korea has pursued an inherently capitalist approach to development since the early 1960s. The governments' attempts to "master the market" were ultimately achieved through the pursuit of "market conforming" macroeconomic policies, characterized by balanced budgets, moderate levels of inflation, and high savings and investment. There was thus a dichotomy between the more socialist-oriented pursuits of many African governments, in the 1960s and the 1970s, such as Humanism in Zambia, although they too sought to promote government-delegated development, and the capitalist and market-oriented approaches of South Korea and East Asia.

Sixth, institutional rigor has been the watchword of the South Korean state. The state established, already in the 1960s, an elite bureaucracy which was insulated from domestic politics and the demands of civil society (which was intentionally kept weak and subordinated for decades). The civil service, whose performance was the main source of legitimacy for the state, was recruited through a competitive and meritocratic screening system, with competitive state-level exams held each year for recruits. Governments in Africa have also taken steps to boost their civil services, but from a low base, with young people increasingly seeing public sector work as a potential career choice. Given the broad ethnic composition of most African countries, there have been attempts to ensure that the civil service reflects this diversity. As a result, few African countries have succeeded in insulating their civil services from the vagaries of domestic politics and the political economy of resource distribution.

Seventh, the creation of a pilot agency (the Economic Planning Bureau) was a major innovation. At its launch in the 1960s, the EPB was given enough power and resources to command the respect of all ministries and agencies. This eased inter-ministerial coordination, enabling coherence in planning, policy execution and monitoring and evaluation. Since the establishment of an agency with the powers that the EPB wielded in South Korea might be out of the question for many African countries, for both political and economic reasons, the need for an efficient and accountable unit at the center of the state structure to coordinate policy implementation and the allocation of resources is still valid. Importantly, when the EPB has served its purpose, it was merged into a ministry with planning duties and its bureaucratic prominence ended. This was a healthy demonstration of the fact that an institution should not outlive its mission.

Eighth, aside from the geopolitics mentioned above, the country had several distinguishing features: a homogeneous population, high levels of human capital formation competent bureaucracies, and until recently, fairly authoritarian governments. Additionally, the country lacks natural resources, experiences heightened insecurity, and faces the challenge of a rapidly aging population. The implication here is that South Korea is not just about fast development and has always had structure challenges to deal with at home even as it devised its growth policies. The implication for African countries is that despite challenges, they must exploit their comparative advantages to the full—they could, for example, do better at exploiting their natural resources, and geographical proximity to global markets i.e. USA, Europe, and Asia. There are no magical bullets in the developmental state story, and progress came from a relentless search for opportunities.

Ninth, South Korea saw human capital development and labor market skills development as part and parcel of its core pursuit of economic development. It has thus emphasized research and training and technical education and vocational training throughout its development process. In terms of education quality and performance, South Korea ranks in the top decile in the OECD. However, despite a number of education reforms in African countries in recent decades, including more recently, the introduction of universal primary education, quality remains a challenge across the board—especially with respect to science and technical education. For example, many infrastructure projects in Africa are still seriously constrained by lack of skilled workers, and foreign contractors are forced to import labor from their home countries—increasingly China. This has become a source of much domestic consternation, and even resentment, in African countries, while also an indicator of the capacity gaps that linger there; including the failure to link infrastructure development needs to the availability of domestic skills and employment creation.

Tenth, peace was a precondition for the evolution of the developmental state in South Korea, and East Asia, more generally. The state in South Korea did not allow the regional, political turbulence, or the domestic conflicts to disrupt its development agenda. Put differently, an ambitious coterie of South Korean bureaucrats and a firm American presence helped prevent the country from declining into chaos (it had six acting Presidents in 1960 alone), even as the existential threat posed by North Korea continued apace. Subsequently, South Korea maintained strong links with the US, while also diversifying its trade links to the Middle East, Europe, and more recently Africa. However, as in parts of the latter, the maintenance of peace was sometimes used to justify martial law and autocratic rule. This raises the question whether anti-democratic and perceptibly anti-civil society stances are required to get things moving in the earlier stages of the developmental state. The answer cannot be, as is sometimes argued by African leaders, that the color of the cat (black or white) is not important as long as it catches mice. This is because the developmental state is not just about catching mice, it is also about creating an environment that obviates the services of the cat. However, the argument requires nuance as the pressures of structural change combined with those of democratization can be formidable. African countries that aspire to become developmental states will no doubt confront these issues with time.

8.4 Policy coherence and institutional rigor

The common theme running through the previous chapters is the cardinality of policy coherence and institutional rigor for the success of the developmental state. South Korea was very much aware that an efficient bureaucracy was the key to development planning and implementation and expended all the resources required to put it in place, including the eponymous Economic Planning Bureau. As already noted, getting policy coherence and institutional rigor right was not easy, and countries wishing to replicate South Korea need to give the issue of institutional development much more attention than seems to be the case today, as there is nothing at all automatic about the emergence of strong institutions. To what extent have African governments been successful in laying the groundwork for effective bureaucracies to drive the development process?

It was noted in the chapters above that while African countries are not lacking in policies, nor indeed in institutional frameworks to implement them, the generally unsatisfactory results indicate both a lack of institutional rigor and policy coherence i.e. the strategies are not primed to engender institutional capacities nor enhance human and financial resources. Typically, the planning function in African countries is often under resourced and even an afterthought in cases: while the national plans are invariably elaborate and well-formulated, in implementation, they fall well short of the governments' ambitions and the expectations of the people—ex post, they tend to look more like works of fiction than a true basis for the countries' economic transformation. The state's commitment to the ideas of a developmental state requires that issues of planning and policy implementation be taken seriously.

8.5 Human capital and social inclusion

Underlying the creation of sustained economic growth is the importance of human capital development. Evidence from the African studies suggests that the focus on skills development has been inadequate—certainly not adequately aligned with the developmental ambitions of countries. During the era of SAPs, there was a fatal divergence of resources from the tertiary levels to make universal primary education possible. Meantime, tertiary education levels were opened up to the private sector—which expanded access, focusing on humanities rather than science and technology, while lowering quality. The certification syndrome has not enhanced the technical prowess of African countries, while current training programs are not adequately linked to the goals of the national development plans. The few exceptions, such as Rwanda, which is keen on building a technical hub in the country through collaboration with world-class universities, are too few and far between to create critical mass. In contrast, East Asian economies realized early on in their development that highly skilled workers, hired by domestic firms at modest wage rates, would provide them the ultimate comparative advantage.

Thus, in comparison to South Africa, where the policies of Apartheid had skewed skills development along racial lines, South Korea systematically (and strategically) trained its youth in tandem with the increasingly technical demands of the modernizing economy. In the process, it enjoyed a dynamic link between human capital accumulation and economic growth i.e. a healthy and educated economy was also highly productive. However, this strive for efficiency had its price. South Korea acquired a reputation for suppressing basic human rights, including labor union activities (as part of its elite bargain), at least in the earlier phases of its development. It is questionable whether this would be recommended to African countries as the price to be paid for rapid growth and structural transformation; indeed, authoritarianism was largely abandoned by South Korea following the onset of democratization in the late-1980s.

The discussion of employment and labor markets in Africa tends to focus on the formal sectors, while the informal sector is the main generator of employment. For many African economies, progress will be measured by the extent to which the livelihoods of households that depend on the informal sector (in urban areas) and peasant and off-farm activities (in rural areas) are improving. South Africa has realized this and provides monthly grants to its most vulnerable households. In South Korea, the Saemaul Udong movement was effective in mobilizing the rural dwellers for income generation and development, and environmental restoration and protection. Attempts to replicate the approach in Africa, as a form of South Korean development assistance, are yet to provide concrete signs of success.

8.6 Industrial policy, competitiveness, and growth

In the developmental state literature, how industrial policies are conceived and implemented (including how the associated political economy is handled) determine the pace at which development can be achieved. While the issue is not for African countries to copy verbatim all East Asian experiences, there are several lessons that require attention: the importance of identifying and supporting growth industries, developing requisite infrastructure to lower the cost of doing business, aligning skills training to demand, and promoting Export Processing Zones (EPZs). Several countries, notably Mauritius, Senegal, Ethiopia, and Nigeria, have embarked on EPZs with varying levels of success. The lack of a rigorous institutional framework has made replication across the region quite difficult.

Globalization, as noted above, has set limits on domestic industrial policy innovation. In early 2018, the US government threatened to exclude East African countries that had imposed discriminatory tariffs on US exports of used clothes from enjoying the duty-free provisions of its African Growth Opportunity Act (AGOA), first launched in 2000. Although the African countries argued that cheap old clothes from the US were preventing their textile industries and, by default, cotton growing and ginning, where they had comparative advantage, from taking off, the US was adamant that the rules of international trade could not be bent for the sake of social policy concerns of a handful of African countries. Some countries removed the proposed tariffs on the old clothes from the US almost immediately, while others held out, hoping that common decency, a rare commodity when it comes to trade matters, would triumph. Hence tariffs and related controls will likely not work as tools of industrial policy in the current global trade regime, and more innovative approaches, such as producing high-quality goods and services (for example) tourism cheaply i.e. internal devaluation will be required.

South Korea demonstrates that economic policy flexibility and taking a long-term view were crucial in implementing and sustaining industrial policies. For example, when South Korea had reached the end of the easier stage of the import-substitution strategy i.e. the production of consumer goods, it quickly looked for ways to upgrade its industrial structure and move up the value chain—including ensuring that the financial and human resource requirements were well aligned with the planned structural shift of the economy. Since switching to higher value production was to be done by the private sector, there was need for an elaborate sharing of analytical as well as marketing information, accompanied by support structures, including, for example, increasing access to affordable credit. Moreover, the South Korean government invested in university and related research to form a rigorous analytical basis for policy action. The authors of the case studies blamed the inability of African countries to proceed to the next level of their industrial strategies i.e. the manufacturing of industrial goods for the export market, on the lack of concrete efforts at linking the tasks at hand to the available technical and financial resources.

Appendix I

Commissioned reports on the relevance of the developmental state in Africa

Title of the report	Institution	Team members
1 KOAFEC Development Policy in Practice Project. The African Economy: Development Policy in Practice – Lessons from South Korea Development Experience, 2017 (138 pages)	Korea Institute for International Economic Policy (KIEP), Seoul, South Korea	Deok Ryong Yoon
2 Etude Sur L'Economie du Cameroun. La Politique de Développement dans la Pratique Enseignements Tires de L'Expérience de Développement de la Corée du Sud, 2017 (188 pages)	Université de Yaoundé II, Yaoundé, Cameroon	Henri Ngoa Tabi, Henri Atangana Ondoa, Patrice Ongono, Françoise Okah Effogo, Gérard-José Ebode
3 Etude Sur L'Economie Ivoirienne. La Politique de Développement dans la Pratique Enseignements Tires de L'Expérience de Développement de la Corée du Sud, 2017 (354 pages)	Le Centre Ivoirien de Recherches Economiques et Sociales (CIRES), Abidjan, Côte d'Ivoire	Assi José-Carlos Kimou, Namizata Binate, Yapo N'Dia Victor Bouaffon, Nahoua Yeo, Placide Zoungrana, Tanoh Ruphin Doua, Kodjo Pierre Innocent Kelassa, Beugré Jonathan N'Guessan
4 Toward Developmental State in Nigeria: Lessons from Korea, 2017 (517 pages)	Nigerian Economic Society (NES), Ibadan, Nigeria	Names of individual members not stated. Project Manager: Olu Ajakaiye
5 The Role of Institutions in Underpinning Inclusive Economic Growth in South Africa. Country Development Policy in Practice: Lessons from the South Korea Development Experience, 2015 (330 pages)	Development Policy Research Unit (DPRU), School of Economics, University of Cape Town, South Africa	Kenneth Kreamer, Ross Harvey, William Gumede, Ebrahim-Khalil Hassen, Steven Friedman, Brian Levy, and Anthony Altbeker

(*Continued*)

Title of the report	*Institution*	*Team members*
6 The Zambian Society and Economy: Development Policy in Practice in Comparison with South Korea, 2017 (242 pages)	Southern African Institute for Policy and Research (SAIPAR), Lusaka, Zambia	Jessica Achberger, Alex Caramento, Frank Chansa, Caesar Cheelo, Abson Chompolola, Marja Hinfelaar, Opa Kapijimpanga, John Lungu, O'Brien Kaaba, Edna Kabala-Litana, Dale Mudenda, Chrispin Mphuka, Obrian Ndhlovu, Mushiba Nyamazana, Manenga Ndulo, and Venkatesh Sheshamani*

Source: AfDB, Economics Complex.
*Professor Venkatesh Sheshamani has passed on.

Index

Note: **Bold** page numbers refer to tables; *italic* page numbers refer to figures and page numbers followed by "n" denote endnotes.